Walking
Edinburgh

Walking Edinburgh

ROBIN GAULDIE

TWENTY-FIVE ORIGINAL WALKS
IN AND AROUND EDINBURGH

PASSPORT BOOKS
NTC/Contemporary Publishing Group

This edition first published in 2000
by Passport Books, a division of
NTC/Contemporary Publishing Group, Inc.
4255 West Touhy Avenue
Lincolnwood (Chicago), Illinois 60712-1975
U.S.A.

ISBN 0-658-00365-8

Library of Congress Catalog Card Number: on file
Published in conjunction with New Holland Publishers (UK) Ltd

Commissioning Editor: Jo Hemmings
Editors: Michaella Standen
Copy Editor: Paul Barnett
Cartographer: Hardlines
Designer: Alan Marshall
Indexer: Janet Dudley

Reproduction by Pica Colour Separation Overseas (Pte) Ltd, Singapore
Printed and bound in Singapore by Kyodo Printing Co (Singapore) Pte Ltd

Photographic Acknowledgements
All photographs by the author with the exception of the following:
Crown Copyright, Reproduced by Permission of Historic Scotland: Plates 1, 34, 36; The
Edinburgh Photographic Library: Plates 20, 23; Dennis Hardley Photography: Plate 11; Life
File Photo Library/Graham Burns: Plates 13, 37, 38; Life File Photo Library/Mark
Ferguson: Plates 14, 19, 27; Life File Photo Library/Jeremy Hoare: Plate 22; Life File Photo
Library/Aubrey J. Slaughter: Plate 15; Life File Photo Library/Andrew Ward: Plates 6, 18;
David Paterson: Plate 25; Photobank/Adrian Baker: Plates 4, 33, 39; Photobank/Peter
Baker: Plates 7, 9, 16, 31; PictureBank Photo Library Ltd: Plates 10, 30; Jonathan Smith:
Plate 32; The Still Moving Picture Company/Doug Corrance: Plates 5, 8

Front cover: View across the city towards Edinburgh Castle, by
David Morrison Photography.

Contents

Introduction

Of all Britain's cities, Edinburgh offers most for walkers. It has an outstandingly rich heritage, with relics of every century of its thousand-year history. Laid out on seven hills (like Rome), it offers superb views of town and country. It has escaped many of the ravages of the Industrial Revolution, World War II and the post-war rebuilding that changed the faces of so many other towns beyond recognition. Away from the main traffic arteries, its streets are walker-friendly and many – though by no means all – of its historic and cultural sights are within easy walking distance of each other. It's almost impossible to get lost, since there are prominent landmarks like the Castle, Calton Hill and Arthur's Seat that are visible from all over the city, making it easy to find your bearings.

Edinburgh is a city of endless variety, with medieval streets – haunted by enough ghosts to make your hair stand on end – castles and palaces, elegant Georgian avenues and terraces, high culture and dusk-till-dawn nightlife. You can sample the exhibits in some of the finest museums and art galleries in Europe, then, within only a few minutes' walk, blow away the cobwebs by hiking up grassy hillsides with hardly another person in sight, wandering beside the windswept shores of the Firth of Forth or strolling along pretty waterside walkways.

Edinburgh has been in the forefront of tourism since the nineteenth century – indeed, it is one of the cities of which it can be said that here the tourist industry came of age. As a result, it has become a place that knows how to cater for visitors but has not allowed itself to be completely swamped by them. There are literally scores of visitor attractions and hundreds of pubs, bars, cafés and restaurants, yet – even at the height of the Festival season, which attracts up to half a million people annually – there are still plenty of walks that will lead you away from the crowds on Princes Street and the Royal Mile.

Nor should you ignore the scenic and historic attractions of the towns, such as Stirling, St Andrews or Linlithgow, that lie outside the city limits yet within easy reach of the capital by public transport. Many of them are well worth a day's outing by bus, by rail, by rented car or even by taxi – never forget that Scottish taxis are relatively cheap (although not as cheap in this area as in, say, Glasgow).

Within Edinburgh itself, do remember that public transport around the city is rather limited: there is no underground train or tram system, and tickets on the four competing regional bus companies are not interchangeable. You may find yourself doing quite a lot more walking in the city than you'd anticipated – for reasons other than the recreational.

Edinburgh's weather is changeable. A sunny summer day, with the temperature unlikely to climb much above 18°C (65°F), offers perfect walking weather, as can a clear and chilly winter morning – if you are warmly dressed. But even in the height of summer, wet, cool and windy weather is not unlikely. So, no matter what the month or the weather forecast, always pack a raincoat, umbrella and waterproof footwear for your holiday in Edinburgh. Winters are cold and can be very windy: you will need warm weatherproof clothes, footwear, hat and gloves if you're visiting at any time between October and April/May. When planning walks in winter, allow for the relatively restricted hours of daylight: in midwinter it is only seven hours between sunrise and sunset.

Overall, the best walking months are undoubtedly mid–May to late September, but bear in mind that the city centre and main attractions are at their busiest in August and September.

This book includes walks for every time of year and frame of mind, from long open-air hikes in open country to shorter strolls through the city centre, where museums, art galleries and cosy pubs offer a handy escape from wet or chilly weather. Some walks can be combined for a longer or more varied itinerary.

The City's History

Edinburgh is a city poised to reclaim its rightful place among the capitals of Europe, the seat once more of a Scottish Parliament which voted itself out of existence to unite with its English counterpart in 1707, only to be reborn with the referendum of 1998, when Scots voted decisively for devolution from London.

'Auld Reekie' ('Old Smoky'), as Edinburgh was once nicknamed, embodies at least two cities – the medieval Old Town, huddled around and beneath the crags and battlements of Edinburgh Castle, and the elegant terraces of the New Town, designed by the architect Robert Adam (1728–1792) during the eighteenth century, when union with England was bringing the city new prosperity. Meanwhile, the port of Leith, a couple of miles from the city centre on the shores of the Firth of Forth, is undergoing a twenty-first-century transformation from run-down dockland to vibrant waterfront district.

In the Beginning

While Britain south of Hadrian's Wall was part of the Roman Empire from the first century to the early fifth century, the land that is now Scotland was the unconquered territory of the Picts. Indeed, there is evidence that the Romans paid a form of tribute to the Pictish rulers of the region around Edinburgh to deter them from frontier raids.

Edinburgh's history begins in the seventh century, when the Angles of Northumbria, descendants of migrants to Britain from northern Europe, built a fort atop Castle Rock, a steep-sided 100m (330ft) crag and a superb natural defensive site. This fort may have been named Edinburgh (Edwin's Fort), after King and Saint Edwin (c. 585–633) of the Northumbrian Angles. More likely its name is an Anglo-Saxon translation of the Gaelic Dun Edin ('Fort of the Hill Slope') or of a Celtic British name, Mynyd Eidden (possibly 'Castle of the Virgins').

Until at least the ninth century, Scottish, Pictish and Anglo-Saxon rulers, as well as Viking raiders from Scandinavia, fought each other for control of the region. Then, in about 843, Kenneth Mac Alpin, King of the Scots of Dalriada (in modern Argyll), conquered the Pictish lands of eastern Scotland to become king of all the lands north of the Forth – a land which he decreed would henceforth be known as Alba and its people as Albannach. The Angles of Lothian and Edinburgh, however, successfully resisted until the mid-tenth century all attempts to absorb their lands. Then, in 1018, Mac Alpin's descendant, Malcolm II (b. c. 954), confirmed Scottish rule over the region with the defeat of an Anglo-Saxon army at Carham. By 1032 Scotland's frontiers stood roughly where they are now.

This expansion of Scottish rule inevitably brought the Scots into conflict with their southern neighbours, especially as the Norman conquerors of England pushed northward. In 1071 William I the Conqueror (1027–1087) briefly invaded Scotland in reprisal for Scottish border raids and forced Malcolm III Canmore (*c.* 1031–1093) to pay homage to him. This set the scene for some six centuries of dynastic struggle between the two kingdoms.

Heart of a Nation

Edinburgh did not become Scotland's capital until 1124, when Malcolm's son David I (*c.* 1080–1153) relocated his royal seat to Edinburgh from Dunfermline, on the north side of the Forth, and founded the Abbey of the Holy Rood which now stands in picturesque ruins next to the Royal Palace of Holyroodhouse.

Only about 80km (50 miles) from the English border, Edinburgh was always vulnerable to assault by English invaders. In the long struggle between English kings intent on subjugating the Scots and Scottish rulers equally intent on maintaining their independence, it was frequently sacked or occupied. Ironically, the Scots were often the besiegers of their own Edinburgh Castle and an English garrison the besieged, and on several occasions the castle was destroyed by the Scots to prevent the English using it.

The thirteenth and fourteenth centuries were turbulent times for Edinburgh and Scotland. Edward I (1239–1307) of England earned the sobriquet 'Hammer of the Scots' among his admirers for his determination to subjugate Scotland from 1296 onward (the Scots, less flatteringly, called him 'Langshanks' – 'Long Legs'). English forces occupied Edinburgh until 1311, during which time they carried off the treasures of Edinburgh Castle and even the Stone of Destiny, the ancient stone throne on which generations of Scottish kings had been crowned. (It was not to be returned to Edinburgh until 1998.) The English under Edward II (1284–1327) were decisively defeated at Bannock Burn (Bannockburn), near Stirling, in 1314; despite the signing of a peace treaty in 1328, the two countries were soon at war once more, and in 1333 Edinburgh was again briefly occupied by the English. For the next three centuries Scotland and England were at war as often as not; moreover, in the intervals between fighting the English, the Scottish kings had to contend with their own rebellious nobles and with the clans of the Highlands and the Isles, who fiercely resisted rule from Edinburgh.

In 1371, the last of the Bruce line, David II (1324–1371), was succeeded by his nephew, Robert II (1316–1390), the first of the Stewart dynasty, whose history was to be intertwined with Edinburgh's for the next four centuries.

An Unlucky Line

The Stewarts were plagued by bad luck. Robert II's successor, Robert III (*c.* 1340–1406), who came to the throne in 1399, was an invalid. For the first quarter of the fourteenth century Scotland was ruled by regents who were usually more concerned with strengthening their own position than with the good of the nation. Robert III's heir, James I (1394–1437), spent the first eighteen years of his reign as a hostage of Henry IV (1367–1413) of England. Returning to Scotland, James battled with Highland rebels and unruly nobles, in due course being assassinated by three of those nobles in 1437. His son James II (1430–1460) ruled for only eleven years before being killed by the explosion of one of his own cannons during the siege of Roxburgh Castle. James III (1451–1488) was murdered in 1488 after being defeated in battle with rebel nobles at Sauchiburn, near Stirling, and his heir James IV (1473–1513) – a Renaissance ruler who was the most capable and popular to date of the Stewarts – died at the head of his troops in the bloody disaster of Flodden Field.

Before this untimely death, however, James IV presided over a flowering of Scottish culture and the first long stretch of peace and prosperity Scotland had experienced. Literature, scholarship, music and architecture flourished, and Edinburgh began to be transformed from a medieval town of wooden buildings into a city where the nobles and the prosperous merchant class built in stone; the first printing press made its appearance in Edinburgh in 1507.

James IV's defeat and death at Flodden in 1513, alongside more than 10,000 Scots soldiers, was the greatest disaster ever to befall the kingdom, and it echoes through Scots history to the present day. The city had outgrown its medieval ramparts so, for fear of an English invasion, new city walls were built. Completed in 1560, the new walls formed the official perimeter of the city until the mid-eighteenth century, by which time Edinburgh's population had grown from 10,000 to more than 30,000.

This growth of population density within the fixed city limits gave birth to the characteristic 'lands' of old Edinburgh – perhaps the world's first high-rise, multi-storey apartment buildings – going up to eleven storeys high. Edinburgh became a city of apartment dwellers, and remains so to this day.

A Tragic Queen

James V (1512–1542), no luckier than his ancestors, died not by violence but of a broken heart after yet another defeat at the hands of the English, this time at Solway Moss in 1542. His early death – leaving as his only successor his infant daughter Mary (1542–1587), who as Mary Queen of Scots has become one of the most famous figures in world history – ushered in an era of near civil war between pro-English and pro-French factions among the Scottish aristocracy.

Henry VIII (1491–1547) of England wished to unite Scotland with England by marrying Mary to his son Edward. Thwarted by the French-aligned Scottish nobles, who had determined to wed her instead to a French prince, Henry sent the Earl of Hertford to ravage Scotland, burning much of Edinburgh and Leith in 1544 and initiating a reign of terror in southern Scotland that was ended only by the arrival of a French army in 1548. Mary herself was spirited off to France. When she returned, in 1561, she was more French than Scots (unable in her speech to deal with the letter 'W', she changed the spelling of the royal surname to 'Stuart'), and her reappearance triggered new divisions at court – and in the kirks and streets of Edinburgh.

Reformation and Revolt

The Reformation sweeping Europe added religious conflict to the witches' brew of political rivalries, with Catholic nobles seeking French support and the Protestant faction aligning itself with England. On the Protestant side, the towering, brooding figure of John Knox (c. 1513–1572), father of the Reformation in Scotland, still casts a long, dour shadow over Scotland's history.

Knox was a disciple of the radical reformer John Calvin (Jean Cauvin; 1509–1564) of Geneva. He and his followers utterly opposed all forms of the Catholic faith, and were set on replacing them with a sterner, puritanical Protestantism in which churches were stripped of all decoration and religion of its priestly ceremony. Knox's aim was to create a Protestant theocracy in Scotland, and from his pulpit he became a power to be reckoned with. The struggle between Protestant and Catholic would dominate Scottish politics for the next two hundred years.

Mary was spectacularly unfortunate in her marriages. Her first husband, the French King François II (1544–1560), died after only seventeen months on the throne. On her return to Scotland, she married her cousin Henry Stewart (c. 1545–1567), Lord Darnley, who was soon murdered, probably at the instigation of, perhaps even by, James Hepburn, Fourth Earl of Bothwell (c. 1537–1578), Scotland's Lord High Admiral, who became Mary's third husband only eight weeks after Darnley's death. Scandalized, the powerful Protestant Lords forced Mary to abdicate, crowned her baby son King James VI of Scotland, and imprisoned her in Lochleven Castle. Escaping from Lochleven, Mary raised an army to reclaim her throne but was defeated at Langside by the forces of the Protestant Regent, her half-brother James Stewart (1531–1570), Earl of Moray. In 1568, she fled to England, where Queen Elizabeth I (1533–1603) imprisoned her for nineteen years, then had her executed in 1587 on a trumped-up charge of treason.

Union of the Crowns
With Mary's flight, chaos descended on Scottish affairs. The 'Queen's Lords', her last supporters, seized Edinburgh Castle and held it until blasted out by heavy cannons in 1573. The first two regents, Moray and Lennox, were swiftly murdered by their rivals. The next, the Earl of Mar, died in office, and the fourth, James Douglas (c. 1516–1581), Fourth Earl of Morton, was toppled and executed by the machinations of Esme Stewart, Lord of Aubigny, a Franco Scottish noble who then became Lord High Chamberlain. His plan to raise James as a Catholic outraged the Protestant lords, who kidnapped the young king and forced Aubigny to flee to France, where he died soon after. In 1583, at the age of seventeen, James escaped his 'protectors' to assume full powers as king.

On the death of his unmarried and childless cousin, Queen Elizabeth I (1533–1603), James was invited to become King James I of England. He promptly decamped to London with his court, marking the end of Edinburgh as a royal capital, though it remained the seat of the Scottish Parliament.

James was the most competent of the Stewart kings of England, although he gabbled in his speech and ate messily – for this reason he was dubbed by his courtiers 'The Wisest Fool in Christendom'. He ruled for forty-two years, for the latter twenty-two of which he was King of England as well as of Scotland, and he presided over the longest period of peace the two countries had yet enjoyed.

It was not to last. His son, Charles I (1600–1649), was arrogant, stubborn and inept. His attempts to impose the Episcopalian forms of the Church of England outraged the Presbyterian Elders of the Scottish Kirk in Edinburgh, while his autocratic ambitions alienated the English Parliament.

Wars of Religion

In 1637, Edinburgh churchgoers rioted against the introduction of a reformed, Anglican-style book of prayer, and in 1638 the Protestant Lords of Congregation drew up a National Covenant, pledging to maintain the 'true religion'. In 1639, following a bloodless confrontation known as the First Bishops' War, the Scottish Parliament effectively declared itself free of royal control and a Covenanter army crossed the border and captured Newcastle and Durham. After civil war broke out in England, the Scots stood aside until 1643 when, following a series of Cavalier victories, the English Parliamentarians offered them £30,000 a month to attack the Royalists. Civil war now spread throughout the land, culminating in Charles's surrender to the Scots at Newark in 1646. By 1647, the Scottish Parliament had switched sides, sending an army to support the king. It was defeated by the Parliamentarians at Preston, and the more radical Covenanters, who had opposed this move, marched on Edinburgh and seized power, giving a hero's welcome to the English Parliamentarian general, Oliver Cromwell (1599–1658), when he visited Scotland.

But the execution of Charles I swung Scottish opinion against the English Parliamentarians. In 1650 Charles II (1630–1685) arrived in Scotland to claim his father's kingdom. Cromwell promptly crossed the border, inflicted a series of devastating defeats on the Scots, and crushed all resistance.

Only ten years later, on Cromwell's death, Charles II was back on the throne. He never again visited Scotland, although he did reinstate the Edinburgh Parliament, packing it with Royalist henchmen. A sensible and largely popular king, he was a shrewd politician who realized that, if the monarchy were to survive at all, there would have to be some tempering of the Divine Right of Kings. Previous Stewart/Stuart monarchs (and, indeed, those around them) had held the belief that kings were selected by God and thus infallible and empowered to do exactly what they saw fit: in other words, their contract was with God rather than with their subjects and could not be terminated except by God. This circumstance inevitably led to conflicts of interest. Charles had only to look to the example of his father's demise to recognize that others besides God might reckon they had a say in the matter. Obvious as it might sound to us, the fallacy of the Divine Right of Kings had by no means been so obvious to Charles's predecessors.

Scotland remained restive even during his reign, but the Covenanters took up arms against Charles's successor, James VII and II (1633–1701), and quickly rose in support of the Protestant Prince William (1650–1702) – the Dutch husband of James's daughter Mary (1662–1694) – who in 1689 was invited to supplant James, and who ruled as William III alongside his wife, Mary II, until her death. When William died in 1702 he was succeeded by his daughter, Anne (1665–1714).

An end of an old song

Rule from England rankled, but Scotland's economy was in a parlous state. After long negotiations, England offered to open its trade to Scots merchants and to award Scotland a subsidy of £398,085 and ten shillings in return for a Treaty of Union, which would unite the parliaments of the two countries while preserving Scotland's unique legal system and guarantee the position of the Presbyterian Kirk. The Scottish

Parliament reluctantly assented. 'There's ane end of ane auld sang [an end of an old song],' said one of the signatories, Lord Seafield, the Lord Privy Seal of Scotland.

But the song was not yet quite finished. England's main motive for promulgating the treaty was to secure, as successor to Queen Anne, a Protestant heir of the German House of Hanover – descendants, through the female line, of James VI and I – and thereby prevent the exiled Catholic heirs of James VII and II from using Scotland as a base to reclaim the thrones of both nations. 'We are bought and sold for English gold,' sang the Jacobite supporters of the Stuart pretenders to the throne.

In 1714, Anne died and George of Hanover (1660–1727), great-grandson of James VI and I, became King George I of England and Scotland. A year later an army of Jacobite Highlanders, led by John Erskine (1675–1732), Eleventh Earl of Mar, rose for James Edward Stuart (1688–1766) – the Old Pretender, son of James VII and II – and marched on Edinburgh.

The rising of 1715 was not anything so simple as a conflict between England and Scotland, nor even between Lowland and Highland Scots. There was support for James in England and in the Lowlands, and for the Hanoverians among many of the Highland clans, including the most powerful of all, the Campbells of Argyll. By the time James landed in Scotland, indecisive generalship had already lost the initiative, and by 1716 the rebellion had petered out.

Thirty years later, James's son Charles Edward Stuart (1720–1788) – Bonnie Prince Charlie, the Young Pretender – had better luck in a whirlwind campaign that began in 1745 with the defeat of the Hanoverian General Sir John Cope (d. 1760) at Prestonpans, just outside Edinburgh. The city fell to the Jacobites, and Charles proclaimed his father to be king and himself prince regent. But as Bonnie Prince Charlie marched south, his Highland levies became less eager for battle. Moreover, the French, who had backed the Stuarts to weaken England, failed to send troops. After reaching Derby, the Jacobite army turned back, retreating into the Highlands to final defeat in 1746 at Culloden, where Highland broadswords and bravery proved no match for Hanoverian discipline, muskets and bayonets.

'The Athens of the North'
The second half of the eighteenth century, by contrast, was a golden age for Edinburgh, with rapid developments in industry, commerce and literature. Symbolic of this new era of the 'Scottish Enlightenment' was the New Town, planned by James Craig (1744–1795) and executed by the Adam brothers, James (1730–1794) and Robert (1728–1792). Edinburgh and its university became a centre of learning to rank with the greatest in Europe, and revelled in the sobriquet 'The Athens of the North'. The leading lights of the age included the philosopher David Hume (1711–1776), the painters Allan Ramsay (1713–1784) and Sir Henry Raeburn (1756–1823), the poet Robert Burns (1759–1796) and the novelist Sir Walter Scott (1771–1832), whose work romanticized Scotland's past and present culture.

The Nineteenth Century
By the early nineteenth century, social, political and economic change were transforming Edinburgh. In 1822, King George IV (1762–1830) visited the city; in 1832,

political reform gave the vote to many more of the city's by now 170,000 citizens. The Union Canal, connecting Edinburgh with the Forth and Clyde Canal, was completed in 1822. In 1842, the first railway was completed between Edinburgh and Glasgow, and by 1846 trains were running all the way from London. The Forth Railway Bridge, completed in 1890, was one of the greatest engineering achievements of the age. With easier access, Edinburgh began to become a tourist destination, its popularity increased by Queen Victoria's fondness for all things Scottish.

If the eighteenth century was a golden age for the arts, the nineteenth was a more pragmatic era, with Edinburgh becoming famous as a centre of finance and medical knowledge.

The Twentieth Century

By the early twentieth century, Edinburgh had spread to its present limits, absorbing what had been separate communities, such as Colinton and Corstorphine to the south and west and Leith, Granton, Newhaven and Musselburgh on the Forth coast.

Between the two world wars, new commercial and residential building began to change the face of the city, and in the second half of the twentieth century this dramatically altered much of Princes Street, the western part of the city, and the University quarter south of the Old Town.

In 1947, the Edinburgh Festival was inaugurated as part of a concerted bid to recreate the city as a modern cultural capital. Since then the Festival – held each year in August and September – has grown into the greatest single multicultural event in the world, celebrating everything from mime and street theatre, traditional and classical music and stand-up comedy to poetry, drama, ballet, opera, film, television, books and the visual arts. More hedonistic but now no less important a part of Edinburgh's celebratory calendar is Hogmanay, when the Castle, the Old Town and the Royal Mile become the venue for a New Year street party that attracts up to 200,000 revellers.

A Nation Once Again?

Demands for some kind of home rule for Scotland began to be voiced in the 1960s – 1967 saw the election to the British Parliament of the first Scottish Nationalist Party MP, Winnie Ewing, who was elected member for Hamilton – and gathered pace into the 1970s. Edinburgh's planners looked forward to converting the gracious old Royal High School building on Calton Hill into the seat of a new Scottish Parliament. However, when a referendum on devolution was held in 1979, only 33 per cent of the Scottish population voted in favour. This balance of opinion was to change radically as time passed. Between 1979 and 1997, Scots were alienated by a series of Conservative governments which were seen as mulishly unresponsive to Scotland's needs and aspirations, and in the general election of 1997 the Conservatives, who suffered nationally an electoral disaster, won not a single Scottish seat. A new referendum, held by the freshly elected Labour government, made it clear that 'the settled will of the Scottish people' was for devolution.

So Edinburgh greets the twenty-first century as the seat, once again, of a Scottish Parliament, and some believe this is the first step towards a Scotland that will enjoy a new independent status within the European Union.

Key Dates and People

Seventh century: Foundation of the first settlement by the Angles of Lothian.

685: The Angles of Lothian and Northumbria are defeated by the Picts at the Battle of Nectansmere.

843: Kenneth Mac Alpin conquers the Pictish kingdom to create the kingdom of Alba, north of the Forth.

Mid-tenth century: Mac Alpin defeats Indulf, the last Anglian ruler of Lothian, and takes Edinburgh.

1018: Malcolm II (b. *c*. 954), King of the Scots, defeats the Angles of Northumbria at Carham to cement Scottish rule over Lothian.

1128: David I (*c*. 1080–1153) endows the Abbey of Holy Rood.

1174: Edinburgh Castle handed over to Henry II (1133–1189) of England as ransom for William I the Lyon (1143–1214), King of Scots, captured on a raid into England. The Castle was returned to the Scots in 1186.

1296–1328: Edward I (1239–1307) and Edward II (1284–1327) of England attempt to conquer Scotland. Edinburgh and other Scottish cities periodically occupied and retaken. In 1314 Edinburgh Castle, recaptured by the Scots, is destroyed to prevent its use by the enemy.

1329: Edward II recognizes Scottish independence.
King Robert I the Bruce (1274–1329) grants Edinburgh its royal city charter.

1333: Edward III (1312–1377) invades Scotland and seizes Edinburgh.

1335: Edward III rebuilds Edinburgh Castle.

1341: The Scots again recapture and destroy Edinburgh Castle.

1357: David II (1324–1371) rebuilds the Castle around King David's Tower.

1385: Richard II (1367–1400) of England invades Scotland and sacks Edinburgh, but fails to take Edinburgh Castle.

1498: Palace of Holyroodhouse founded.

1507: First printing press arrives in Edinburgh.

1513: The Scottish army, led by James IV (1473–1513), is annihilated at Flodden.

1561–1710: 'The Maiden' (guillotine) is used for public executions in Scotland.

1567: Murder of Lord Darnley (*c*. 1545–1567), husband of Mary Queen of Scots (1542–1587), at Kirk o' Field.

1573: King David's Tower is destroyed by English bombardment.

1583: Edinburgh University founded.

1603: Union of the Crowns. James VI of Scotland and I of England (1566–1625) moves his court to London.

1637: The introduction of the Anglican Revised Prayer Book leads to riots in Edinburgh.

15

1640: Parliament Hall built next to St Giles Cathedral.

1707: Treaty of Union abolishes Scottish Parliament.

1715–16: The first Jacobite rising against House of Hanover is quickly defeated.

1745: The Battle of Prestonpans, outside Edinburgh, begins a new Jacobite rising against the Hanoverian dynasty. Edinburgh falls to the Jacobites before the latter's defeat at Culloden (1746).

1767: Building of Edinburgh's New Town begins.

1810: New Town is completed.

1846: Opening of the railway to connect Edinburgh to London.

1890: The Forth Railway Bridge is completed.

1947: The first Edinburgh International Festival is held.

1964: The Forth Road Bridge is completed.

1979: An apathetic response to a national Scottish referendum on devolution produces low polls with only about one-third of the population voting in favour.

1998: A new Scottish referendum sees a decisive vote to restore the Scottish Parliament to Edinburgh.

1999: The new Scottish Parliament sits for the first time.

Categories of Walks

Historic Buildings
Battlements and Banners: Edinburgh Castle
The Royal Mile (1): from the Castle to the Tron
The Royal Mile (2): the Canongate from the Tron Kirk to Holyrood Palace
The New Town Stride: Georgian Edinburgh
The Auld Toun Shuffle: Around the Old Town
Lauriston Castle to Cramond
Cramond to South Queensferry
North Queensferry to Blackness Castle
Stirling and Bannockburn

Museums and Art Galleries
Battlements and Banners: Edinburgh Castle

The Royal Mile (1): from the Castle to the Tron
The Royal Mile (2): the Canongate from the Tron Kirk to Holyrood Palace
The New Town: Georgian Edinburgh
The Water of Leith: Dean Village, Stockbridge and the Botanic Garden
Around Stockbridge

Parks and Gardens
Monuments and Follies: Calton Hill
Blackford Hill and the Braid Hills
The Heart of the City: Along Princes Street
The Water of Leith: Dean Village, Stockbridge and the Botanic Gardens
Heriot's to the Zoo

Hills and Seaside
Wilderness in the City: Around
    Arthur's Seat
Cramond to South Queensferry
Leith to Prestonpans
North Queensferry to Blackness Castle
Linlithgow to Bo'ness

Architecture
The New Town Stride: Georgian
    Edinburgh
Monuments and Follies: Calton Hill
Museums and the University
Around Stockbridge

Battlefields
Leith to Prestonpans
Stirling and Bannockburn

Circular Walks
Monuments and Follies: Calton Hill
Museums and the University

Canal and River Walks
Water of Leith
Linlithgow to Bo'ness

Lengths of the Walks

Under 3km (2 miles)
Battlements and Banners: Edinburgh
    Castle
The Royal Mile (1): from the Castle
    to the Tron
The Royal Mile (2): the Canongate
    from the Tron Kirk to Holyrood
    Palace
The Heart of the City: Along Princes
    Street
Monuments and Follies: Calton Hill
Ghosts and Galleries: Waverley Station
    to the Tron
The Auld Toun Shuffle: around the
    Old Town
Museums and the University
St Andrews

3–3.5km (around 2 miles)
The New Town Stride: Georgian
    Edinburgh
Around Stockbridge
Lauriston Castle to Cramond
Dunfermline

4–5km (around 2½–3 miles)
Around Leith and Newhaven
Linlithgow to Bo'ness
Stirling and Bannockburn

6–8km (4–5 miles)
Wilderness in the City: Around
    Arthur's Seat
Heriot's to the Zoo
The Water of Leith: Dean Village,
    Stockbridge and the Botanic Garden
Leith to Prestonpans
Cramond to South Queensferry
Forth Coast Castles: Tantallon to
    Dirleton
The East Neuk

Over 8km (5 miles)
Blackford Hill and the Braid Hills
North Queensferry to Blackness Castle

Public Transport

Buses:

The main bus terminal is in St Andrew Square. Local bus companies include:
- Lothian Region Transport (LRT). Tel: (0131) 554 4494.
- SMT. Tel: (0131) 663 9233.
- Lowland. Tel: (0131) 653 3104.
- Midland Bluebird. Tel: (01324) 613 777.

Details of all public transport timetables are available from Traveline, 2 Cockburn Street, Edinburgh. Tel: (0800) 232 323, which can also provide details of accessible transport for people with special needs.

Trains:

Edinburgh has two railway stations:
- Waverley. Tel: (0131) 556 2451, the main station, with trains in all directions.
- Haymarket, where the lines for Glasgow and Stirling diverge from the main east-coast line to Fife. There is no direct telephone number for this station, but all train information can be obtained from National Rail Enquiries. Tel: (0345) 484 950.

Taxis:

Taxis are inexpensive and can be flagged down on the street or taken from ranks at stations and large hotels. 24-hour radio taxi firms include:
- Capital Castle Taxis, 2 Torphichen Street. Tel: (0131) 228 2555.
- Central Radio Taxis, 163–65 Gilmore Place. Tel: (0131) 229 2468.

Key to Route Maps

Each of the walks in this book is accompanied by a detailed map on which the route of the walk is shown in blue. Places of interest along the walks – such as historic buildings, museums and churches – are clearly identified. Addresses and telephone numbers for museums and art galleries are given in the Further Information section at the back of the book (see pages 161–162) and opening times are listed walk by walk, starting on page 163.

The following is a key to symbols and abbreviations used on the maps:

Symbols		*Abbreviations*			
	route of walk	APP	Approach	PH	Public House
	railway line	ARC	Arcade		(Pub)
	major building	AVE	Avneue	PK	Park
		BR	Bridge	PL	Place
✝	church	CL	Close	R	River
		CRES	Crescent	RD	Road
	public toilets	CT	Court	S˙	South
	park	DR	Drive	ST	Saint
	view	E	East	ST	Street
		GDNS	Gardens	TER	Terrace
		HO	House	WK	Walk
		LA	Lane	W	West
		N	North		

Map of Edinburgh and Surrounds

Cramond Island

Granton Point

Granton Harbour

Newhaven

A901

N

Granton

Trinity

New Burnshot

A90

Muirhouse

Silverknowes

Pilton

A902

Warriston

R. Almond

Cramond

Lauriston Castle to Cramond
see page 110

B9085

Inverleith

Royal Botanic Garden

Water of

Braepark

Barnton

Davidson's Main

Drylaw

Around Leith and Newhaven
see page 98

Cramond Bridge

A90

Cramound to South Queensferry
see page 115

Clermiston

Blackhall

Craigleith

The New Town Stric
see page 62

A902

Waverly Sta. to the Tron
see page 50

A701

Zoological Park

Ravelston

A90

Around Stockbridge
see page 84

New Town

Edinburgh Castle
see page 23

Murrayfield

Castle

Corstorphine

A8

Royal Mile 1
see page 28

Old Town

North Gyle

Murrayfield Rugby Ground

A71

Heriot's to the Zoo
see page 88

A8

South Gyle

The Water of Leith
see page 93

A702

A720

Gogar Green

Stenhouse

Gorgie

Merchiston

A70

Sighthill

A71

Longstone

Craiglockhart

Morningside

M8

East Hermiston

A71

Wester Hailes

Braid

Baberton Mains

Juniper Green

Colinton

B701

Oxgangs

Fairmilehead

Currie

Torphin

Dreghorn Mains

A720

Swanston

A70

A702

1000m (1060yd)

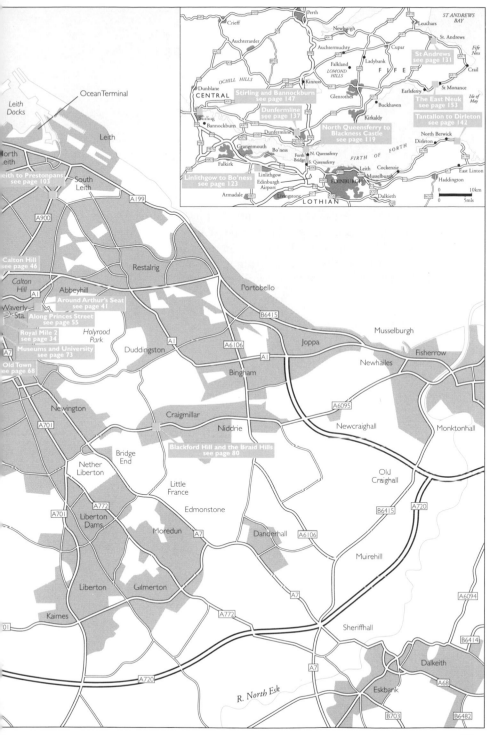

OceanTerminal

Leith
Docks

Leith

North
Leith

Leith to Prestonpans
see page 103

South
Leith

A900

A199

Restalrig

Portobello

B6415

Musselburgh

Calton Hill
see page 46

Calton
Hill

A1

Abbeyhill

Around Arthur's Seat
see page 41

Along Princes Street
see page 55

Royal Mile 2
see page 34

Holyrood
Park

Duddingston

A1

A6106

Joppa

Fisherrow

Newhailes

Waverley
Sta.

Museums and University
see page 73

A7

Old Town
see page 68

Bingham

A1

A6095

Newington

Craigmillar

Niddrie

Newcraighall

Monktonhall

A701

Blackford Hill and the Braid Hills
see page 80

Bridge
End

Nether
Liberton

Old
Craighall

Little
France

Edmonstone

B6415

A720

A772

Liberton
Dams

Moredun

A7

Danderhall

A6106

Muirehill

Liberton

Gilmerton

A7

A6094

Kaimes

01

A772

Sheriffhall

B6414

A720

A7

Dalkeith

R. North Esk

Eskbank

A68

B703

B6482

St Andrews
see page 131

Stirling and Bannockburn
see page 147

Dunfermline
see page 137

The East Neuk
see page 153

North Queensferry to
Blackness Castle
see page 119

Tantallon to Dirleton
see page 142

Linlithgow to Bo'ness
see page 123

ST ANDREWS
BAY

Crieff

Perth

Newburgh

Leuchars

St. Andrews

Auchterarder

Auchtermuchty

Cupar

Fife
Ness

Crail

Falkland

Ladybank

F I F E

OCHILL HILLS

LOMOND
HILLS

Kinross

Glenrothes

Earlsferry

St Monance

Dunblane

CENTRAL

Buckhaven

Isle of
May

Stirling

Bannockburn

Kirkcaldy

North Berwick

Dunfermline

Dirleton

Grangemouth

Bo'ness

N. Queensferry

FIRTH OF FORTH

East Linton

Falkirk

Forth
Bridge

S. Queensferry

Cockenzie

Haddington

Leith

Musselburgh

Linlithgow

Edinburgh
Airport

EDINBURGH

Armadale

Livingston

Dalkeith

L O T H I A N

0   10km
0   5mls

21

Edinburgh

Edinburgh stands on the south shore of the Firth of Forth, hemmed in to the south by the rolling Pentland Hills, which form a natural rampart between the city and the farmlands of Lothian and the Scottish Borders. The ramparts of Edinburgh Castle on its mighty rock are visible from all over the city, with the Old Town – the original core of the medieval city – huddled around and below. The many steeples which are a feature of the city skyline are clues to a history dominated by deep religious conviction; the domes of great public buildings of the eighteenth and nineteenth centuries highlight the city's role as a centre of learning and culture.

Another landmark is Arthur's Seat, the hill which looms over the eastern part of the city and whose surrounds offer an expanse of wide open country in the heart of the city.

Battlements and Banners: Edinburgh Castle

Summary: The ideal place to start your exploration of Edinburgh is the Castle, Edinburgh's most obvious central landmark located on a natural defensive site which attracted local rulers at least as early as the fifth century AD. Without the Castle (which, at the dawn of the twenty-first century, is still garrisoned by the British Army) there would be no city. Starting at the Castle provides a good introduction to Edinburgh's frequently gory history. It also provides you with a preview of what is to come, for a walk around its ramparts gives you a panoramic view of the city and its surroundings, including the start and finish points of almost every walk in this book.

Start:	Corner of Princes Street and The Mound.
Finish:	Castle Esplanade.
Length:	2km (1¼ miles).
Time:	3hr.
Refreshments:	Choice of a dozen pubs, cafés and restaurants on Castle Esplanade.
	Large restaurant within the Castle.
Which day:	Any day.
To visit:	Edinburgh Castle.
	Attractions within the Castle, same hours, same ticket, include:
	St Margaret's Chapel.
	King's Lodging.
	Crown Room.
	Great Hall.
	Scottish United Services Museum.
	Scottish National War Memorial.
	Edinburgh Tattoo – performances nightly on the Castle Esplanade, last three weeks in August.

Leave Princes Street by The Mound, a winding street which connects Princes Street with the Royal Mile. The Castle on its beetling crag looms large as you approach. Just before The Mound bends sharply to the left, turn right into Princes Street Gardens and follow the steep, zigzagging stepped path which leads you to Castle Esplanade and the entrance to Edinburgh Castle. The climb will give some appreciation of how daunting a prospect an assault on the Castle must have been to any prospective attacker, and the battlemented gatehouse which now faces you is almost as daunting.

Steeped in frequently bloody history, Edinburgh Castle is the most potent symbol of the city and its past, and its treasures and fortifications are well worth a morning's or an afternoon's exploration. From its ramparts and gun batteries there are superb panoramic views over Edinburgh and its surroundings, with the Firth of Forth and the Fife coast to the north, the Pentland Hills on the southern horizon and Arthur's Seat and the monuments of Calton Hill to the east and southeast. The views do not stop there: on a clear winter's day, you can even see the snow-capped peaks of the Central Highlands.

Occupied as often as not by Scotland's enemies, the Castle has been besieged and betrayed, taken by storm or stealth and demolished or rebuilt many times. It is still a British Army garrison – some military buildings are closed to the public.

The earliest fortress on the site was reputedly built by King (and Saint) Edwin (*c.* 585–633) of Northumbria in 626. No trace of it remains. Much of what you see today dates from the seventeenth and eighteenth centuries, when the Castle served as much to remind the unruly citizens and nobles of Edinburgh of the power of the Crown as to defend the city against outsiders.

Heroes and Villains

The gatehouse entrance is flanked by statues of Robert the Bruce (1274–1329) and William Wallace (1270–1305), the two greatest leaders of Scotland's struggle with England in the thirteenth and fourteenth centuries. The gatehouse is a Victorian addition, while the statues themselves date from as recently as 1929.

Wallace, immortalized in the eyes of an international audience by the Mel Gibson film *Braveheart* (1995), is a near-legendary figure, although recently revisionist historians have taken to pointing out the atrocities he perpetrated, and certainly some of his actions would seem to modern eyes to border on the psychopathic. We first hear of him as a young knight involved in a fight with English soldiers at Lanark in 1297, a year after the English King Edward I's seizure of Edinburgh and conquest of Scotland. According to one version of the story, Wallace was defending a girl, perhaps his wife, who helped him to escape but was herself caught and executed by the Sheriff of Lanark. The vengeful Wallace in turn killed the sheriff, went on the run and raised a force of freedom fighters who wiped out a large English army at Stirling Bridge, before driving the English from most of southern Scotland. But Edward I (1239–1307) quickly hit back; Wallace's guerrillas were lured into a pitched battle at Falkirk in July 1298 and scattered. Wallace remained on the loose for seven years, but never managed to rebuild his army. In 1305 he was captured, brought to London and executed by hanging, drawing and quartering. His head and parts of his body were displayed throughout the kingdom.

This bloody example failed to quell Scots resistance: a year after Wallace's death, the Norman-Scots noble Robert Bruce had himself crowned King of Scots and again raised the Scottish Royal Standard against the English. For four years his fortunes were mixed, but by 1311 he had driven the English from Edinburgh and the rest of Scotland, with only a small garrison left in Stirling Castle, which guarded the strategic route between southern and northern Scotland. Edward II (1284–1327) himself led a huge army to relieve the Stirling garrison, and the English once again

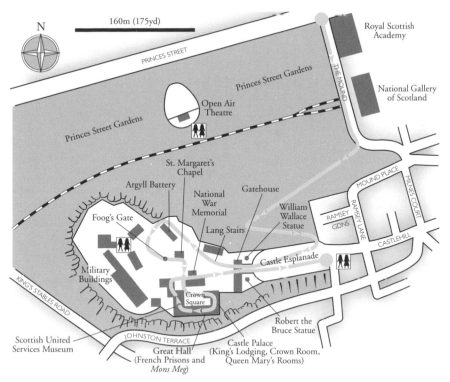

occupied Edinburgh Castle. Outnumbered three to one, lacking heavy cavalry or archers, the Scots nevertheless in 1314 inflicted a decisive defeat on Edward at Bannock Burn (Bannockburn), near Stirling. The Edinburgh garrison was taken by surprise by Sir Thomas Randolph (d. 1332) and his men, who scaled the steep cliffs at night to retake the Castle, and the threat of English conquest was temporarily over. Bruce died the following year.

The Oldest Building

Entering the Castle, you pass between the inner and outer ramparts, up a steep, ramp-like cobbled street and through a second arch – Morton's Gateway – to emerge within the Castle proper, on the Argyll Battery, where a row of cannons point northward over Princes Street and the New Town. Above you, to your left and standing on the highest point of the rock, is St Margaret's Chapel, built in about 1100, by either Malcolm III Canmore (*c.* 1031–1093) or his son David I (*c.* 1080–1153) in memory of Malcolm's queen, later beatified as Saint Margaret (*c.* 1046–1093). To reach the chapel, follow the road upward through Foog's Gate. The oldest building in the Castle (and in Edinburgh), the chapel was the only building spared when, to prevent another English occupation, Randolph destroyed the Castle in 1314. It was rebuilt over the following centuries, and last saw action during the 1745 Jacobite rebellion, when its garrison held out for George II (1683–1760) against the Jacobite troops occupying the rest of the city.

In Royal Footsteps

Follow the signposted route round to your left to enter the Castle Palace and the King's Lodging. The royal quarters form the east wing of the Castle's inner quadrangle, Crown Square. The Castle did not become the principal royal seat until the time of James III (1451–1488), and his successors preferred the more comfortable surroundings of the Palace of Holyroodhouse (see page 39).

From the entrance to the palace pass into the Crown Room. This houses the crown, sword and sceptre used at the coronations of the kings and queens of Scotland until the Treaty of Union in 1707, when they were unceremoniously stored away in the Castle and forgotten for more than a century. At the urging of Sir Walter Scott (1771–1832) they were eventually rediscovered in 1818.

Also on display is the Stone of Destiny, stolen by Edward I in 1296 and not returned to Edinburgh until a full six centuries later. This block of granite was the ancient coronation stone of Scotland, and was kept at Scone, near Perth, one of the capitals of the Pictish kingdom.

But is the stone you see in front of you here the real thing? In 1950 Scottish Nationalists 'liberated' the Stone of Destiny from its place in Westminster Abbey, and some believe that what was returned to London and eventually to Edinburgh was in fact a copy.

Next to the Crown Room are Queen Mary's Rooms, royal apartments which include the Queen's Bedchamber, the birthplace of James VI and I (1566–1625). The pretty oak coffered ceiling is decorated with the initials of Mary Queen of Scots (1542–1587) and James. The gorgeous canopied bed is a genuine period piece, though it may not have been Mary's. The conjoined initials of Mary and her ill-fated second husband, Lord Darnley (*c.* 1545–1567), are on the entrance doorway.

Arms and Armour

Continuing clockwise around Crown Square, enter the Great Hall. This was the meeting place of the first Scottish Parliament until the building of the Parliament House on the High Street in 1640, and was also the banqueting hall used by James IV (1473–1513) and his successors. Two of the many eminent figures who once dined here were Charles I (1600–1649) and, fifteen years later, his arch-enemy Oliver Cromwell (1599–1658).

From the late seventeenth century until 1887, when it was lavishly restored at the expense of the Edinburgh publishing magnate William Nelson (1816–1887) – son of the firm's founder, the great Thomas Nelson (1780–1861) – the Great Hall was used only as an army barracks. The restoration probably has more to do with Victorian notions of medieval grandeur than with the original interior. Its most striking feature is the arching hammer-beam roof; the beams are supported by elaborately carved stone corbels and display human and animal faces. Suits of armour stand guard along the walls, and displays of savage-looking swords, pikes and battleaxes hang on each wall.

Beneath the Great Hall are the Castle vaults, built so as to create a level foundation for the structure above. French prisoners were incarcerated here during the Napoleonic Wars, and their graffiti can be seen cut into the walls – the vaults are still known as the French Prisons. Pride of place here, however, goes to the mighty *Mons Meg*, an enormous cannon made in 1449 for Philip the Good (1396–1467), Duke of Burgundy, and given by him to his nephew James II (1430–1460). Capable of demolishing the strongest walls, *Meg* could have been a decisive weapon in the long-running power struggle between Crown and aristocracy, but James never got a chance to try it out. He was killed by the explosion of another, smaller cannon at the siege of Roxburgh Castle in 1460. There is no record that *Mons Meg* has ever been used in anger, though it was fired in salute to mark the birth of the future James V (1512–1542) and has been fired on various ceremonial occasions since. In 1758 it was hauled off to the Tower of London, to be returned only after the intervention of Sir Walter Scott in 1829.

The crash of artillery still reverberates every weekday over the Castle with the firing of the One O'Clock Gun, a tradition which dates back to 1848 – though nowadays a modern field gun is used rather than one of the ranks of cast-iron muzzle-loading cannons which you can see poking out from the embrasures.

From the vaults, retrace your steps back into Crown Square and continue clockwise to the west wing, which houses the Scottish United Services Museum, a fine collection of regimental honours, uniforms, banners, trophies, decorations and weapons which reflects Scotland's long military tradition.

Military Honours

As early as the fourteenth century, Scottish soldiers of fortune were fighting in France against the English, and over the centuries Scots have served under many foreign flags, including those of Sweden, Russia and the Hanseatic League. Within a generation of the defeat of the Jacobite cause, clan-based Highland regiments had become a most effective part of the British Army, as they remain today. The last stop on this walk, the Scottish National War Memorial, was designed in 1927 by Sir Robert Lorimer (1864–1929) and commemorates the role of the Scottish soldier in every British Imperial conflict up to World War I (in which the kilted Highland Regiments earned the nickname 'the Ladies from Hell' from their German adversaries).

To leave the Castle, follow the signs to the Lang ('Long') Stairs, which will lead you back to Castle Esplanade. This terrace at the top of the Royal Mile is the venue for the annual Edinburgh Tattoo, a spectacular display of military pageantry held each August. Highlights of the event are the massed pipes and drums of the Highland regiments, but there are also displays by almost every unit of the British Army and each year there is a guest demonstration by members of one foreign army/navy/air force or another.

Memorials to numerous British military commanders and their regiments – including Earl Haig, commander in chief of the British Forces during World War I – are placed along both walls of the Esplanade.

From the Esplanade you can either walk back down to Princes Street or begin our second walk, down the Royal Mile to the Tron Kirk.

The Royal Mile (1): from the Castle to the Tron

Summary: This walk takes you from the Castle through the historic heart of Edinburgh and provides an introduction to the city.

The Royal Mile runs downhill from the Castle to the Palace of Holyroodhouse. Every inch of it, every narrow wynd or close to either side, and almost every building has its story to tell — uncanny, gory, tragic or romantic. Since there is so much to see and explore, the Royal Mile has for the purposes of this book been divided into two walks, connecting at the historic Tron Kirk, midway between the Castle and the Palace. (For the start of the second Royal Mile walk see page 34.)

Start:	Castle Esplanade.
Finish:	Tron Kirk.
Length:	2.5km (1½ miles).
Time:	3hr.
Refreshments:	Pubs, restaurants and cafés at every step along the way.
	Scotch Whisky Heritage Centre self-service restaurant.
	The Witchery, 352 Castlehill, Edinburgh EH1 2NE, Tel (0131) 225 5613, offers fine Scottish cuisine in an historic building next to the Castle, and has an award-winning wine cellar.
	Deacon Brodie's, corner of Lawnmarket and Bank Street, is a traditional Edinburgh pub associated with one of Edinburgh's many villains.
	City Café, Blair Street, is a young and trendy watering hole.
Which day:	Not Sunday.
To visit:	Scotch Whisky Heritage Centre.
	Outlook Tower and Camera Obscura.
	Gladstone's Land.
	Lady Stair's House (Writers' Museum).
	St Giles Cathedral (the High Kirk).

Leaving Castle Esplanade, walk onto Castlehill. Notice, opposite the northeast corner of the esplanade on Ramsay Gardens, the striking red-and-white complex of flats, designed in 1893 by the pioneering town planner and architect Sir Patrick Geddes (1854–1932) in mock-baronial style.

Books, Scotch and a Certain Faraway Look . . .

The poet Allan Ramsay (1684–1758) built a house here in about 1740; its unusual eight-sided shape earned it the nickname of the Goose Pie. Ramsay, a wigmaker turned bookseller, set his hand to writing essays and poetry in both standard English and the Scottish vernacular. He scandalized Edinburgh's puritanical Calvinist establishment by establishing Britain's first circulating library, making the latest books and plays from London available to the citizens of Edinburgh for tuppence a night at a time when religious works were virtually the only writing approved by the powerful Kirk authorities. He also campaigned for the legalization of the theatre in Edinburgh, such frivolities being, of course, mightily frowned upon by the pious. The theatre was eventually licensed in 1764, six years after Ramsay's death. His son, the painter Allan Ramsay (1713–1784), many of whose portraits of the great men of the period may be seen in the Scottish National Portrait Gallery (see page 63), also lived here.

On your right, at 354 Castlehill, is the Scotch Whisky Heritage Centre, dedicated to three hundred years of Scotch whisky history. In its bar you can sample the hundreds of blended and single malt whiskies distilled in Scotland, from the pale, dry malts of the northeast to the dark, peaty whiskies of the islands of Islay and Jura.

Carry on down the north side of Castlehill to the corner of Ramsay Lane, where you will find the Outlook Tower and the Camera Obscura. The Camera Obscura, built in the nineteenth century, uses a combination of lenses and mirrors to project the image of the outside world, and can be swivelled to offer different views. The original lens and mirror apparatus were replaced in 1945. The device provides startlingly detailed panoramas of central Edinburgh, appearing as if by a miracle on the walls of a darkened chamber. The experience is quite fascinating – don't miss it.

Some 50m (65yd) south of the Outlook Tower, cross to the south side of Castlehill and Tolbooth St John's. Easily spotted with its octagonal Gothic spire – at 74m (240ft) the tallest in Edinburgh – the Tolbooth Kirk was built between 1842 and 1844 to house the General Assembly of the Church of Scotland, the Kirk's presiding body. The architects were Augustus Pugin (1812–1852) and James Gillespie Graham (1777–1858), both of whom were noted exponents of the Gothic style.

A Medieval Market Place and a Vile Massacre

Castlehill now blends into the Lawnmarket, originally the 'Landmarket' and the medieval town's main market place. Shortly after the beginning of the Lawnmarket, turn left to glance into Milne's Court – a fine restoration of late-seventeenth-century planned housing which now accommodates students from Edinburgh University – before turning right into Riddle's Close, a narrow alley which offers a glimpse into a pretty double courtyard where James VI (1566–1625) held a great feast for nobles of a Danish embassy in 1593.

In the inner of the two courts is Bailie McMorran's House; easy to recognize because of its outside wooden staircase, it dates from the sixteenth century. Bailie John McMorran (a bailie or bailiff was a city official) died in a celebrated incident on 15 September 1595, when, after being refused a holiday, the boys of the Edinburgh High School took up arms and barricaded themselves in the school building. Bailie McMorran was sent to bring them to order, but one of the schoolboys shot him dead. The panicky pupils then surrendered and, remarkably, got off more or less scot free after the intervention of the killer's uncle, Lord Sinclair.

Continue down Lawnmarket and turn left into Gladstone's Land, where there is a merchant's home and shop, dating from earlier in the same century and now restored by the National Trust for Scotland. Such 'lands' are typical of Old Town Edinburgh. The original building dates from 1550. It was taken over in 1617 by a merchant and burgess of the city, Thomas Gledstanes, said to have been an ancestor of the nineteenth-century Liberal Prime Minister, Thomas Ewart Gladstone (1809–1898). Six storeys high, the building accommodated the merchant and his family, while four of the apartments were rented respectively to another merchant, a minister, a knight and a guild officer – a good example of the wide span of social classes who might live in one of these early high-rises.

Walk past Gladstone's Land into an inner courtyard rich in literary associations. The flats surrounding James Court were a fashionable place to live during Edinburgh's eighteenth-century Enlightenment. The philosopher David Hume (1711–1776) was one tenant, while Dr Samuel Johnson's biographer and associate, the Edinburgh-educated James Boswell (1740–1795), entertained Johnson here during their tour of Scotland in 1773.

Continue into Lady Stair's Close. Here, clearly signposted, is Lady Stair's House, an elegant townhouse dating from the early seventeenth century. Today it houses the Writers' Museum, which is packed with memorabilia of three of Scotland's greatest writers – Robert Burns (1759–1796), Sir Walter Scott (1771–1832) and Robert Louis Stevenson (1850–1894).

The townhouse which houses the Museum was built in 1622 for an Edinburgh baronet, Sir William Gray of Pittendrum, whose initials, linked with those of his wife, Gidia Smith, may be seen on the mantel above the front door. Lady Stair, widow of John Dalrymple (1648–1707), first Earl of Stair, bought the house in 1719 and lived here until her death 12 years later.

As Secretary of State for Scotland under William II (1650–1702), Dalrymple was the instigator of the Massacre of Glencoe. On 13 February 1693, eight hundred troops of the Earl of Argyll's Regiment of Foot murdered men, women and children of the clan of MacIan MacDonald of Glencoe, burning their houses and leaving many more to die in the snow. Ostensibly, the MacDonalds were being punished for their tardiness in taking the oath of allegiance to King William. In fact, Stair intended to make an example of them. 'The winter time,' he wrote to William, 'is the only season in which we are sure the Highlanders cannot escape, and carry their wives, bairns and cattle to the hills . . . This is the proper time to maul them in the long dark nights.' Captain Robert Campbell of Glenlyon, the commander of the attackers, was ordered '. . . to fall upon the McDonalds [sic] of Glencoe and put all to the sword under seventy . . .'

The massacre was a little too much even for the hardened sensibilities of seventeenth-century Scotland, and William was forced to dismiss Dalrymple from office. But when the furore had died down, Dalrymple was rewarded with an earldom for his services, while Glenlyon received promotion to colonel. William could not have realized that the names of the two men would be cursed for this crime even today, over three hundred years later.

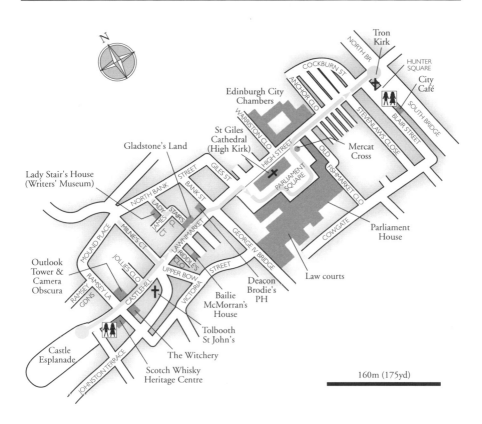

A Notorious Criminal

Retrace your steps to the Lawnmarket, turn left and continue downhill. At the corner of Bank Street and the Lawnmarket stands Deacon Brodie's, a cavernous and venerable pub – but one with villainous associations, for here it was that Deacon William Brodie, respectable citizen, skilled cabinet-maker and Town Councillor by day, robber and burglar by night, is claimed to have planned his exploits. Brodie was betrayed by one of his accomplices after the particularly daring burglary of the General Excise Office, and fled to Amsterdam. However, he was caught, convicted and hanged – on a gallows that, ironically, was of his own design.

After a pint of Eighty Shilling Ale (so named for the original dutiable value of a barrel), cross diagonally to the corner of George IV Bridge and Parliament Square, where you'll find one of Edinburgh's most outstanding buildings, the High Kirk of Edinburgh (St Giles Cathedral). The statue on the square immediately west of the church is of Walter Francis Montagu Douglas Scott (1806–1884), fifth Duke of Buccleuch and seventh Duke of Queensberry. No relation to the more famous writer, he financed several important public building works in Edinburgh, notably Granton Harbour, and was rewarded with a statue and an honorary degree from Edinburgh University.

31

Before entering the High Kirk, note outside the main entrance the cobblestones shaped into a heart. This is the Heart of Midlothian, and marks the site of the Tolbooth; it gives its name to one of Edinburgh's two famous football teams, the other being the Hibernians. Built in 1561, the Tolbooth was the customs house where merchants and carriers paid toll for the use of roads, streets and market spaces. Eventually it grew to become the Town Hall, a meeting place for the Privy Council, the College of Justice, and for a time the Scottish Parliament. From the mid–seventeenth century it was also a prison and place of execution, and the heads of the executed became hideous ornaments on its north wall. It was demolished in 1817, and a pattern of brass plates marks its outline on the roadway.

An Historic Cathedral

The High Kirk is Edinburgh's most imposing church. Some form of church has stood on the site since the ninth century. The oldest parts of the existing building are four central pillars which date from 1120. Burnt during an English raid in 1385, the church was rebuilt and expanded, and in 1460 it was again enlarged, with a higher roof and the addition of clerestory windows. In 1495, the crown spire was added.

Named for a sixth-century French saint, the church underwent drastic change during the Reformation, when Calvinist followers of the radical reformer John Knox (*c.* 1513–1572) stripped it of much of its Catholic paraphernalia, leaving the far less ornate interior that we see today. A statue of Knox stands just within the main entrance to the kirk.

When Charles I (1600–1649) reintroduced bishops to the Presbyterian Scottish Church, the High Kirk became a cathedral, and, though it lost its bishop during the 'Glorious Revolution' of 1688, it is still referred to as St Giles Cathedral.

In 1637 the High Kirk was the scene of an incident which spilled over into wider rioting and eventually full-scale civil war. One of the clergy appointed by King Charles I to bring the Presbyterian Scottish Church into line with the Episcopalian Church of England attempted to read from the newly published book of prayer. Outraged by this departure from Presbyterian forms of worship, Jenny Geddes (*c.* 1600–*c.* 1660), a market stall-holder, threw her folding stool at the preacher. From there things went rapidly downhill, to such an extent that the members of the Privy Council, responsible for governing Scotland on behalf of the king, had to take refuge from the mob in the Palace of Holyroodhouse.

Seats of Government

As you exit the cathedral, turn left and walk anti-clockwise around Parliament Square. Occupying the south side of the Square is the former Scottish Parliament Hall, now the High Court.

Completed in 1639, this was the seat of Scotland's Parliament until it was extinguished by the Treaty of Union in 1707, and is now part of a complex of buildings which includes also the Court of Session (which, with the High Court, forms Scotland's Supreme Court) and the District Court. The neo-Classical façade is a later addition, dating from 1808.

Leaving Parliament Square behind you, carry on down the south side of the

Plate 1: *Atop a superb natural defensive site in use for more than two millennia, Edinburgh Castle dominates the city centre and is still a military garrison (see page 23).*

Plate 2: *A kilted sentry stands guard at the Castle gate (see page 23).*

Plate 3: *The unicorn crowning the Mercat Cross is Scotland's royal symbol (see page 33).*

Plate 4: *Gladstone's Land, in the Lawnmarket, is a finely preserved example of a typical Edinburgh tenement building (see page 30).*

Plate 5: *Statue of philosopher David Hume outside St Giles Cathedral (see page 32 and 79).*

Plate 6: *The arms of King James V adorn the Palace of Holyroodhouse (see page 39).*

Plate 7: *The Tolbooth, on the Royal Mile, was Edinburgh's courthouse and prison (see page 36).*

Plate 8: *A view down the Royal Mile towards the Palace of Holyroodhouse (see page 34).*

Plate 9: *John Knox House, on the Royal Mile, is the finest remaining example of a sixteenth-century Edinburgh townhouse. Knox reputedly died here in 1572 (see page 35).*

Lawnmarket, passing on your right the Mercat ('Market') Cross. This was the official hub of the city market and a landmark for merchants and citizens. From it, royal proclamations and other official announcements were read. The existing Mercat Cross dates from only 1885, but it has part of the original fourteenth-century cross built into its shaft.

Immediately opposite the Mercat Cross, on the north side of the Lawnmarket, is the impressive, arcaded façade of the Edinburgh City Chambers, designed by John Adam (1730–1794) and completed in 1761. The building was originally intended as the Royal Exchange and Custom House but failed to find favour with Edinburgh merchants, who preferred to meet in the less formal surroundings of the coffee house, the tavern or the street. In 1811 it was taken over by the Town Council, and it is now the meeting place of the City of Edinburgh Council. The equestrian statue of Alexander the Great (*c.* 356–323 BC), in the forecourt, dates from 1916.

The Tron Kirk

Finally, cross the street once again and walk down what is now the High Street to Hunter Square and the junction of North Bridge, South Bridge and the High Street. Your landmark here is the Tron Kirk, a seventeenth-century church whose present steeple was added in 1829, after the original wooden spire had been destroyed by fire. Edinburgh owes the Tron Kirk, indirectly at least, to Charles I, whose misguided attempts to re-impose an episcopal structure on the Scottish church, with appointed bishops outranking the elected elders of the Kirk, led to the so-called 'Bishops' Wars' and, ultimately, to the king's downfall. Charles decreed that St Giles should become a cathedral and seat of the Bishop of Edinburgh, and the outraged congregation decamped *en masse* and commissioned a new church to be built downhill from St Giles. This was the Tron Kirk, begun in 1636 and completed in 1647. The Tron traditionally was the focus for Edinburgh's Hogmanay (New Year's Eve) celebrations, when hundreds of inebriated revellers gathered to hear its clock ring out the old year and ring in the new, but now that the city's Hogmanay festival has become a much more organised and commercialised affair, the focus has moved away from the old church, towards live entertainment elsewhere.

'The Tron' was the name of the weighing scales which stood here in medieval times and survived into the eighteenth century. The kirk has a well preserved hammer-beam roof. No longer a church, it functions instead as a visitor information centre during the tourist season.

From the Tron, you can carry on to the end of the High Street and the beginning of the next walk, which continues to the end of the Royal Mile and the Palace of Holyroodhouse; or you can turn left and cross North Bridge to the beginning of our Princes Street walk (see page 55).

The Royal Mile (2): the Canongate from the Tron Kirk to Holyrood Palace

Summary: This walk leads through the Canongate – originally a separate burgh, becoming a part of Edinburgh proper only in 1856 – to the splendid Palace of Holyroodhouse, the official residence of the Royal Family when in Edinburgh. This lower section of the Royal Mile has for many years been much quieter than the busy, tourist-oriented Lawnmarket and High Street but, with the opening of the new Scottish Parliament building at a site near the Palace in 2000, it is poised for a renaissance.

Start:	Tron Kirk.
Finish:	Palace of Holyroodhouse.
Time:	3hr.
Length:	1km (1100yd).
Refreshments:	The bar and restaurant in the Netherbow Arts Centre.
Which day:	Not Saturday or Sunday.
To visit:	Museum of Childhood.
	Brass Rubbing Centre.
	John Knox House.
	Netherbow Arts Centre.
	People's Story Museum (Canongate Tolbooth).
	Canongate Kirk.
	Huntly House Museum.
	Palace of Holyroodhouse.
	Holyrood Abbey.

Leaving the Tron Kirk, cross South Bridge and walk down the south side of the High Street to No. 42, which is the home of the Museum of Childhood.

Playthings and Puritans

Opened in 1955, this was the first museum in the world to specialize in the history of childhood. It now has five galleries crammed with toys and games from all over the world. In the era of Nintendo, Sega and the personal computer game, the toys and games of decades as recent as the 1950s and 1960s look quaintly obsolete. Of special fascination is a collection of 'teacher torturers' – ingenious gadgets which can produce irritating repetitive noises during class and yet which are small enough to escape, with luck, the searches of a maddened teacher.

From the Museum, cross the High Street to Chalmers Close and Trinity Apse, the only surviving part of Trinity College Church, which was founded in 1460. The building now houses the Brass Rubbing Centre, where you can make (or buy, ready-made) rubbings from Pictish standing stones and medieval church brasses.

Walk down the north side to John Knox House at 43–5 High Street. Originally built in the mid-fifteenth century, it was extensively rebuilt in the mid-sixteenth century by James Mossman, goldsmith and Queen Mary's Keeper of the Royal Mint. This is the finest extant example of an Edinburgh townhouse of that era, with its overhanging, wooden upper storeys and typical 'crow-step' gable ends. Its connection with John Knox (*c.* 1513–1572) is precarious; the great reformer may have died there in 1572, but even that is uncertain. It was saved from demolition and restored in 1853, and subsequently, a century afterwards, in 1953, was even more painstakingly and extensively restored. These new restorers discovered many original features which had been concealed by later building. It now belongs, appropriately, to the Church of Scotland.

Next to John Knox House is the Netherbow Arts Centre, the arts centre of the Church of Scotland, which is designed in a style meant to echo that of its venerable neighbour. It has a small theatre, an art gallery with a changing schedule of exhibitions and a courtyard restaurant, and it is a popular performance venue during the Edinburgh Festival. Features of the courtyard include a carving from the Netherbow Port, one of the original medieval gates into the city, and the Netherbow Port Bell, dating from 1621. In Scots, the common street suffix '-gate', as in Canongate, was more properly spelt 'gait' and meant 'way', while the city gates were known as 'ports'.

Leaving John Knox House and the Netherbow Arts Centre, look out for the brass slabs set into the road at the very end of the High Street. These mark the site of the Netherbow Port, one of six gates in the Edinburgh city walls. Built in 1513, the arched gateway was demolished during the English assault on the city in 1544. Reconstructed, it stood until 1764, when it was again demolished, this time to improve access between the High Street and Canongate (which, in a way, had been the purpose of the earlier demolition as well!). Like other prominent sites, the Netherbow was used to exhibit the severed heads of criminals, traitors and opponents of whoever happened to be in power at the time. It fell to the Jacobites without a struggle in 1745, and Bonnie Prince Charlie (1720–1788) entered the city through it, only to be refused entrance to the Castle by the Hanoverian garrison.

The Friars' Street

The Canongate, which begins here, gets its name from the Augustinian canons of Holyrood Abbey, who were granted land here by David I (*c.* 1080–1153). Until 1500, when King James IV (1473–1513) built the Palace of Holyroodhouse, this area was little more than a village outside the city walls, but when royalty moved in it became prime real estate, and Scottish nobles built fine townhouses along the road. This was not necessarily a bright idea: being outside the protection of the city walls,

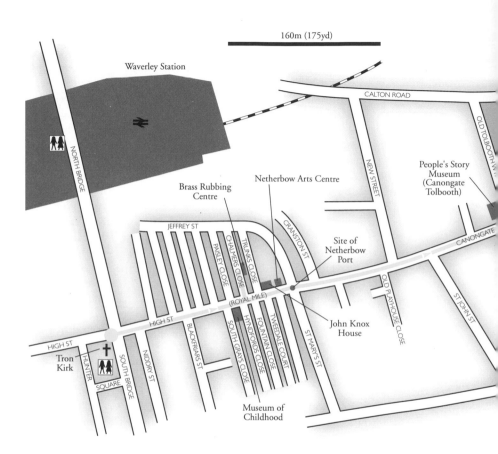

160m (175yd)

Waverley Station

CALTON ROAD

OLD TOLBOOTH W

NORTH BRIDGE

People's Story
Museum
(Canongate
Tolbooth)

Netherbow Arts Centre

NEW STREET

Brass Rubbing
Centre

JEFFREY ST

CRANSTON ST

CANONGATE

PAISLEY CLOSE

CHALMERS CLOSE

TRUNK'S CLOSE

Site of
Netherbow
Port

ST JOHN ST

OLD PLAYHOUSE CLOSE

(ROYAL MILE)

HIGH ST

BLACKFRIARS ST

SOUTH GRAY'S CLOSE

HYNDFORD'S CLOSE

FOUNTAIN CLOSE

TWEEDALE COURT

ST MARY'S ST

John Knox
House

HIGH ST

HUNTER

Tron
Kirk

SOUTH BRIDGE

NIDDRY ST

SQUARE

Museum of
Childhood

the buildings were the first to be ransacked when English armies rolled into town, as they frequently did throughout the sixteenth century. With the Union of the Crowns in 1603, King James VI's noble toadies decamped *en masse* for the rich pickings of London, and the Canongate declined in popularity.

Follow the north side of the Canongate past the junctions with Jeffrey Street, Cranston Street and New Street until you reach the Canongate Tolbooth. Like the Edinburgh Tolbooth on the Lawnmarket, this was the burgh's customs house, council house, courtroom, prison and place of execution; unlike the Edinburgh Tolbooth, it escaped demolition and today houses the People's Story Museum, which recounts the history of Edinburgh since the eighteenth century with the aid of sights, sounds and even smells from the past – mind you, if it truly recreated the powerful reek of the medieval Canongate there would be few enough visitors who would choose to linger.

Built in 1591 in Franco-Scottish style, the Tolbooth is decorated with the Coat

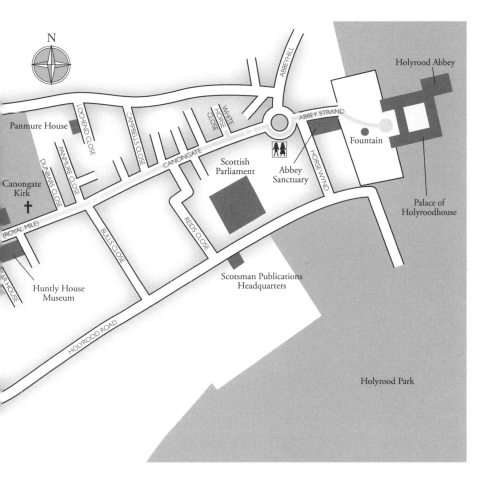

of Arms of the burgh, a stag's head bearing a cross between its antlers which recalls the legend of the founding of Holyrood Abbey (see page 40), and the Latin motto *Sic itur ad astra* ('This way to the stars'). The original burgh clock, attached to the façade in the late seventeenth century, was replaced in 1820.

Opposite the Tolbooth stands another fine seventeenth-century building: Huntly House, built in 1570, restored in 1932 and now housing a fascinating local history museum which has a fine collection of Edinburgh crystal and silverware. Pride of place is given to the National Covenant, the petition signed by Presbyterian nobles and commoners opposing Charles I's attempt in 1638 to impose his bishops and the Episcopalian form of worship on the Scottish Kirk.

Huntly House itself, with its plastered, wood-framed upper floors and triple gables projecting over the two lower storeys, is typical of the houses that once stood in the old Canongate. On the front of the building are five Latin tags – four dating from the sixteenth century, when Huntly House was built, and the last from 1932, when it was restored. The first of them is attributed to Sir Thomas Whitson, Lord Provost of Edinburgh in 1932:

Anti qua tamen, juven esco
('I am old, but renew my youth.')

The other inscriptions are:

Hodie mihi crastibi, cur igitur curas
('Today me, tomorrow you, therefore why care you?')

Ut tu linguae tuae, sic ego mear auriu dominus sum
('As you are master of your tongue, so am I master of my ears.')

Constanti pectori, res mortalium umbra
('To a constant mind, the affairs of mortals are a shadow.')

Spes altera viae
('[There is] hope of another life.')

Poets, Parliamentarians and Penmen
Mulling over these pithy sayings, and doubtless becoming a wiser and better person for so doing, recross the Canongate and continue down its north side to the Canongate Kirk and Kirkyard, built in 1688. Standing to the right of the front door is the Canongate Mercat Cross, previously located at the midpoint of the Canongate. After the Jacobite victory at Prestonpans in 1745, soldiers of General Sir John Cope's defeated Hanoverian army were imprisoned in the church.

In the cemetery is buried the Scots poet Robert Fergusson (1750–1774). Fergusson died of a head injury incurred during rowdy election-night celebrations, and is far less famous than Robert Burns (1759–1796), who found his poetry an inspiration and, in 1787, paid for a tombstone to mark Fergusson's grave, carved with Burns's own memorial verse:

No sculptured Marble here nor pompous lay
No storied Urn nor animated Bust
This simple Stone directs Pale Scotia's way
To pour her Sorrows o'er her Poet's Dust.

Also interred here is Adam Smith (1723–1790), author of *The Wealth of Nations* (1776), the father of modern political economics and the first proponent of the theory of the free market. From 1778 to 1790, Smith lived at Panmure House, an unassuming seventeenth-century townhouse on Lochend Close, about 50m (65yd) east of Canongate Kirk on the south side of the street. Panmure House is now used as a youth centre.

Carrying on down the Canongate, note the attractive buildings of White Horse Close, a seventeenth-century coaching inn and stables which has been converted into apartments. Almost immediately opposite, on a site between the Canongate and Holyrood Road, is the new Scottish Parliament building.

The Scottish Parliament, scheduled for completion by 2001 at a cost of about £50 million, is the work of the Barcelona architect Enric Miralles, whose design was selected from international competition in July 1998. The design, resembling a series of up-turned boats, changes the face of the Canongate, and indeed the presence of the Scottish Parliament is revitalizing this part of the Royal Mile.

Close to the Parliament stands another dramatic new building, the headquarters of Scotsman Publications, which has, after more than a century, left its original building on the North Bridge for a site nearer to Scotland's new corridors of power. Costing £20 million, the new structure was completed in 1999 and features a glass atrium and an entrance reached by a bridge extending almost the full height of the building.

The Palace of Holyroodhouse

The final stop on this walk is the Palace of Holyroodhouse and the ruins of its neighbouring abbey, which now face you at the foot of Abbey Strand, a short extension of the Canongate.

The Abbey Sanctuary buildings on the south side of the street were built in the sixteenth century and were a refuge for nobles who had fallen into debt. Within the sanctuary, they were immune from arrest and, since its boundaries encompassed the whole of Holyrood Park and Arthur's Seat, they had plenty of room to stretch their legs.

The Palace of Holyroodhouse was originally the guesthouse of the Augustinian Abbey, founded by David I in 1128, but as he and later kings were among its most frequent guests – finding it more congenial than the dour and draughty Castle – it was gradually transformed into a residence fit for royalty. James IV was the monarch who began turning it into a palace proper, so that it would be more in keeping with his own Renaissance ambitions. Sadly, nothing remains of this original structure; the oldest part of the building that you now see – the northern tower, on your left as you enter the grounds – dates from 1528–33 and is the work of James V (1512–1542).

In 1544, the Palace was burned by Henry VIII's army during the so-called 'Rough Wooing', when Henry tried to coerce Scotland into an English royal marriage for the young Princess Mary, later to be Mary Queen of Scots (1542–1587). Instead, thanks to French arms and the influence of Mary's mother and regent, Mary of (Marie de) Guise (1515–1560), her hand went to the young Dauphin of France, later François II (1544–1560), who died soon after coming to the French throne.

Mary made her home in the North Tower here when she returned, a young widow, to Scotland and it was here that her secretary and favourite, David Rizzio (or Riccio; *c.* 1533–1566), was murdered in a frenzied stabbing attack by a group of Protestant nobles who resented this Italian Catholic's influence over their Queen. Mary's second husband, Lord Darnley (*c.*1545–1567), was among their supporters; when Darnley in turn was killed by a gunpowder blast, it was rumoured that Mary and James Hepburn, Earl of Bothwell (*c.* 1537–1578), who soon became her third husband, had connived at his death. When Mary was dethroned and imprisoned, Bothwell took to a life of piracy, was captured by the Danes and died, mad, in prison; his mummified remains may be seen at Dragsholm Castle in Jutland.

Royal Towers

Unlike Mary's first two husbands, the North or James IV Tower is a survivor; it again escaped burning in 1650, when Cromwell's Parliamentarian troops sacked Edinburgh and burned the rest of the Palace.

The remainder of the present building is to the design of Sir William Bruce (1630–1710), commissioned by Charles II (1630–1685), and of the master mason Robert Mylne, an ancestor of the famous architect Robert Mylne (1734–1811), and was built between 1671 and 1676. Bruce added a second four-turreted tower, a copy of the first, to balance the front of the building. A low, single-storey front connects the two towers, and a Classical columned gateway leads to an elegant arcaded court-yard within.

Inside the Palace, the main attraction is the Picture Gallery, lined with portraits commissioned by Charles II from the Dutch painter Jacob de Wit (1649–1681). De Wit's brief seems to have been to create and depict an implausibly long pedigree for the Stuarts; of the 111 portraits, ostensibly of Scottish monarchs, only that of Charles II can conceivably have been painted from life, while many of the earlier kings por-trayed here may have lived only in legend. In 1745, these portraits looked down on the king that Scotland never had but whom most people have heard of, Charles Edward Stuart (1720–1788) – better known as Bonnie Prince Charlie – who held banquets and balls here during his brief occupation of the city.

Adjoining the northeast corner of the Palace, Holyrood Abbey is Edinburgh's most picturesque ruin. The story goes that David I, hunting in the woodland that once covered the area, narrowly escaped being gored by a splendidly antlered stag. Grasping its horns, he discovered that it bore a gold crucifix between them. That night a dream told him to build a monastery on the spot, and in 1128 he did so, naming it the Holy Rood (Cross), and making his father confessor, the Augustinian Canon Alwin, the first abbot.

The Abbey flourished under royal patronage until the Reformation, when it was looked on with disfavour by Protestants, and during the violence that in 1688–1689 accompanied the overthrow of James II and the accession of William of Orange it was severely damaged, losing its roof, windows and interior. A new roof, installed in 1758, collapsed within ten years, taking sections of the walls with it.

From here you can, if you're feeling energetic, start on the next walk. Otherwise, return to Abbey Strand and hence Canongate.

Wilderness in the City: Around Arthur's Seat

Summary: Arthur's Seat, the lion-shaped, 275m (823ft) mount that dwarfs the city's other hills and is its most prominent landmark, offers a chance to stretch your legs, get away from the city streets and take in a splendid panorama of the city and its surroundings, with tremendous views over the Firth of Forth to the Fife coast and, on a clear day, even as far as the southern Highlands. For bird watchers there is Duddingston Loch, bordered by a bird sanctuary and a nature reserve; for the rest of us, Edinburgh's oldest pub, the Sheep Heid Inn, in quaint Duddingston Village, is a good enough reason to work up a thirst and an appetite.

'The views from Arthur's Seat are preferable to dozing inside on a fine day, or using wine to stimulate wit ...', said the poet Robert Burns (1759–1796), who often walked to the top just for the pleasure of it. Coming from a man as firmly committed to wine and comfort as Burns, this is high praise indeed.

Start:	Dynamic Earth, corner of Holyrood Road and The Mall.
Finish:	Sheep Heid Inn, Duddingston Village.
Length:	8km (5 miles); height climbed to summit 210m (710ft).
Time:	3hr.
Refreshments:	Sheep Heid Inn, The Causeway, Duddingston Village, tel (0131) 661 1020. Edinburgh's oldest inn offers lunches and dinners in the restaurant and bar.
	Food Chain restaurant and Iso-Bar café at Dynamic Earth.
Which day:	Any day April–October; during November–March, this walk is only for those fully prepared for cold, wet, winter conditions.
To visit:	Dynamic Earth.
	Holyrood Park Visitor Centre.
	Bawsinch Nature Reserve and Duddingston Loch Bird Sanctuary.
	Duddingston Kirk.

Geologically, Arthur's Seat is a volcanic plug, the relic of a small volcano which was last active about 325 million years ago. The hill's connection with the legendary King Arthur is tenuous. For a time during the fifth century AD, Edinburgh and the surrounding regions formed part of the short-lived British kingdom of Rheged, settled by refugees from the ruins of Roman Britain. Arthur, or the Romano-British king on which the legend is based, ruled at about the same time, so perhaps the name was given to the hill by the refugees to honour the monarch of whom they had heard tell; more likely, some medieval romantic was the one responsible. Certainly the site was inhabited as early as 2500 years ago, when Pictish villagers lived behind defensive ramparts on the higher slopes and farmed the hillsides below.

Where We All Began

The first stop on this walk is Edinburgh's newest and one of its most spectacular purpose-built visitor attractions, the multi-million-pound Dynamic Earth at the corner of Holyrood Road and The Mall, next to Holyrood Park. Dynamic Earth, a multi-media exhibition held here, is a journey through space and time that starts with The State of the Earth, monitoring volcanoes, earthquakes and extreme weather events around the globe on giant video displays. From this exhibit you walk into the Time Machine section, where displays take you back through recent and ancient history, through the ages of the dinosaurs and even earlier primitive life, to the dawn of time itself. Walk on from here to find yourself on the bridge of a starship, watch the Universe form in a spectacular Big Bang, and see the Earth begin as a ball of swirling gases bombarded by meteors.

The next stop is the Restless Earth display, recreating a world of volcanoes and earthquakes, followed by Shaping the Surface, which takes you on a mock flight over glaciers, mountains and icebergs as they shape the face of the planet. The following display, Casualties and Survivors, looks at the great extinctions which have periodically swept the Earth. From here, you pass through displays that recreate all the planet's environments and climate zones, from the deep ocean trenches to the polar regions and tropical rainforests, before winding up in the auditorium, where the tour comes to a climax with a dazzling audiovisual presentation featuring everything from exploding volcanoes to the effects of global warming.

Dynamic Earth is an appropriate beginning to this walk, because the cliffs and crags of Arthur's Seat, heaved from the depths by volcanic action and smoothed and carved by glaciers, have experienced everything that rock can experience – including the massive quarrying that in the nineteenth century seemed poised almost to flatten Edinburgh's proudest landmark.

Quarrymen and a Great Geologist

To walk around Arthur's Seat, go first to the foot of Holyrood Road and turn right, into the 260ha (640 acre) Holyrood Park. Here the paths are well maintained, but you will need sensible footwear and rainwear as there is little shelter within the park.

Leaving the Palace car park, cross Queen's Drive and walk up a short flight of steps, then turn right onto a clearly marked walking track, Radical Road, which curves around the foot of the 173m (567ft) Salisbury Crags. In 1820, a committee headed by Sir Walter Scott (1771–1832) hired a group of labourers who had been sacked for their radical politics to build a safe walking path here. The imposing basalt cliffs show the scars of nineteenth-century quarrying which was fortunately halted before it destroyed one of Edinburgh's finest landmarks. North Quarry, Long Quarry and finally South Quarry take great bites out of the cliff face as you follow the track round.

At South Quarry, a stretch of rock face known as Hutton's Section and a nearby

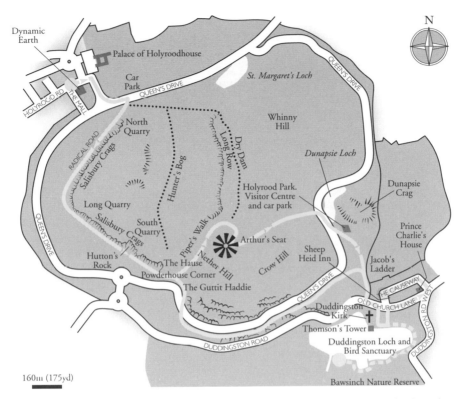

N

Dynamic Earth

Palace of Holyroodhouse

Car Park

St. Margaret's Loch

QUEEN'S DRIVE

HOLYROOD RD

THE MALL

North Quarry

RADICAL ROAD

Salisbury Crags

Whinny Hill

Hunter's Bog

Dry Dam
Long Row

Dunapsie Loch

Dunapsie Crag

Long Quarry

South Quarry

Salisbury Crags

QUEEN'S DRIVE

Holyrood Park.
Visitor Centre
and car park

Piper's Walk

Prince Charlie's House

Hutton's Rock

The Hause

Nether Hill

Arthur's Seat

Crow Hill

Sheep Heid Inn

Jacob's Ladder

Powderhouse Corner

The Guttit Haddie

QUEEN'S DRIVE

THE CAUSEWAY

OLD CHURCH LANE

DUDDINGSTON RD WEST

Duddingston Kirk

Thomson's Tower

DUDDINGSTON ROAD

Duddingston Loch and
Bird Sanctuary

160m (175yd)

Bawsinch Nature Reserve

monolith, Hutton's Rock, are named for James Hutton (1726–1797), a leading figure of the Scottish Enlightenment and one of the fathers of modern Earth science. Hutton was the champion of the Plutonian theory of geology, which proposed that certain types of rock (now known as 'igneous') were formed from molten material beneath the Earth's crust. Hutton demonstrated that the relevant rock formations, like the ones on show here, could only have been formed in this way, and not, as his opponents suggested, as sediment from an ancient ocean.

But Hutton's even greater claim to fame is as the founder of that theory of geology known as Uniformitarianism, which holds that all geological and landscape formations are the product of processes that we can see in operation today, but acting over vast periods of time. Because of the huge timescales involved, Uniformitarianism earned the wrath of the religious, who maintained that the Earth had come into existence at the instigation of God much more recently, with 4004 BC being a popular date for Creation. A more logical argument was that between the Uniformitarians and the Catastrophists, the latter maintaining that many of the Earth's features could have come about only through catastrophic events, some of unimaginable ferocity. Today, a slightly modified version of Uniformitarianism is generally accepted as the correct explanation of the formation of the landscapes we can see.

At the point known as Powderhouse Corner – where the powder magazine of the nineteenth-century quarry operation stood – a path leads uphill towards the summit of Arthur's Seat.

At this point this walk splits into soft and tough options:

1. Round Arthur's Seat: the soft option
If you are daunted by the walk to the summit, turn right, walk down to and cross Queen's Drive, and follow the footpath which runs beside it for about 1km (1100yd) to the signposted path to Duddingston Village, on your right, and the flight of steps known as Jacob's Ladder. At the foot of this, turn left along Old Church Lane into Duddingston Village.

2. Arthur's Seat the hard way: to Duddingston via the summit
Energetic walkers should turn left at Powderhouse Corner and follow the rougher track known as Piper's Walk, which heads almost due north below the steep west face of Arthur's Seat. Ignore the first two paths turning off to your right and take the third one, some 400m (440yd) along, following a path which curves steadily round to ascend to the summit by the gentler east face. At the next path junction, turn right and continue a bit over a hundred metres uphill on a clearly marked path to the top, where the rock has been polished smooth by generations of climbers.

After pausing to get your breath back and admire the view, retrace your steps to the junction of the paths and carry on straight downhill, ignoring turnoffs to right and left, to Queen's Drive, which encircles Arthur's Seat, and to the car park and Holyrood Park Visitor Centre south of Dunsapie Loch, a crescent of water over-looked by the cliffs of Dunsapie Crag. Bonnie Prince Charlie's army camped on the slopes here before their victory at Prestonpans in September 1745.

The loch is artificial, formed when Queen's Drive was built in 1844, and is fre-quently dotted with wildfowl which nest and shelter at the nearby Duddingston Loch and Bird Sanctuary.

From the information centre at the south end of the car park, follow the sign-posted path downhill to Duddingston via Jacob's Ladder, a flight of steps which delivers you to the north shore of Duddingston Loch; by now you will have been joined by those walkers who took the soft option. At the foot of the steps, cross Duddingston Road and follow the path, Old Church Lane, that leads to Duddingston Kirk and Kirkyard.

An Ancient Kirk
To the left of the gate as you enter, an eight-sided tower stands guard over the Kirkyard. During the eighteenth and nineteenth centuries, anatomists unable legal-ly to acquire bodies for dissection paid well for freshly exhumed corpses, and grave-robbers like the notorious Burke and Hare (see page 69) did a profitable trade in digging up the dead. At Duddingston, two of the Kirk Elders were assigned to stand watch in the tower at night for three weeks after each burial, by which time the corpse was useless for dissection.

Duddingston Kirk is one of the oldest buildings in Edinburgh, dating from as early as 1120, although it has been rebuilt so many times that relatively little of the original structure remains. Duddingston's best known minister, the Reverend John Thomson (1778–1840), was a friend and contemporary of Sir Walter Scott, who became an Elder of Duddingston Kirk in 1860. Thomson saw himself as a true father to his flock, who in turn coined the expression 'we're a' Jock Tamson's bairns' ('we're all John Thomson's children'), still occasionally used by Scots to evoke a largely spurious egalitarianism.

The tiny window in the north wall of the chancel may have been a lepers' peep-hole, used in medieval times to allow those afflicted with leprosy (who were barred from entering the church with the congregation) to take part in the service from a distance.

Just south of the church, on the shore of the loch, is Thomson's Tower, an octag-onal building erected in the second half of the eighteenth century, perhaps as a shot tower for making lead bullets. The Reverend John Thomson was, as well as a min-ister, a talented landscape painter – a member of the Royal Scottish Academy, no less – and during his tenure as minister he used the upper part of the tower as a studio.

The lower floor was used by the Duddingston Loch Curling Society, which was founded in 1195. In 1803, this society did for this game of sliding stone weights over polished ice at a target what the Royal and Ancient did for golf and the MCC for cricket: it standardized the rules that are now in use wherever curling is played. Sadly, this failed to ensure the society's immortality, and it was disbanded in 1948.

Those with an interest in birds should continue round the shore of the loch to the entrance to the Bawsinch Nature Reserve and Duddingston Loch Bird Sanctuary, an area of woodland, bog and reedbed around the loch which provides refuge for up to a hundred bird species, among them Fulmar, various migrant and feral geese, Mute and Whooper swans, Short-eared owl and other owl species, and Great spotted wood-pecker.

Alternatively, retrace your steps to Old Church Lane and walk anticlockwise around Duddingston Village, now a charming enclave of sought-after houses and cottages. About 100m (110yd) from the church the road turns sharply left, and on this corner stands a building known as Prince Charlie's House. It was a coaching tavern when Charles Edward Stuart (1720–1788) and his officers stayed here two nights before routing the Redcoats under General Sir John Cope (d. 1760) at Prestonpans on 21 September 1745. It is now a private home.

Turn left, go left again at the next corner and walk up the Causeway to one of Scotland's most venerable pubs, the superb Sheep Heid Inn. There has been an inn here since the fourteenth century; the present building is a mere upstart, having been built in the eighteenth century. The pub also has Scotland's oldest skittle alley, and until the 1970s had the distinction of being the only pub in Edinburgh where drinks might be consumed outdoors. The Sheep Heid gets its name from the nour-ishing soup it once served, of which a sheep's head was the main ingredient. This delicacy is no longer on the menu – a fact you may either rue or take comfort in as you relax with a pint of heavy (bitter) and congratulate yourself on your long and perhaps strenuous tramp.

Monuments and Follies: Calton Hill

Summary: Calton Hill, looming 100m (330ft) above the east end of Princes Street, is crowned with monuments, including the columns of a nineteenth-century folly intended to reinforce Edinburgh's claim to be the 'Athens of the North'.

Start/finish:	The corner of North Bridge and Waterloo Place.
Length:	2km (1½ miles).
Time:	2hr.
Refreshments:	The Restaurant, New Balmoral Hotel, 1 Princes Street. Tel (0131) 556 2414.
	NB's Bar, also in the New Balmoral Hotel.
	Numerous restaurants and cafés within Waverley Market shopping centre.
	Café Royal, 17A West Register Street. Tel (0131) 556 4124.
Which day:	Any day (unless you wish to visit the General Register House, which is open only Monday–Friday 09.00–16.45).
To visit:	Nelson Monument.
	Observatory and Edinburgh Experience.
	General Register House.

Starting at the corner of North Bridge and Waterloo Place, walk approximately 100m (100yd) up the north side of Waterloo Place, cross the small street called Calton Hill, and follow the steps, signposted 'Calton Hill', to the foot of the Nelson Monument, an unmissable lighthouse-like tower built in 1815 and rising to a turret which allows superb views of the entire city and its surroundings.

Leaving the Nelson Monument, follow the path as it doubles back sharply uphill until you get to the Dugald Stewart Monument. Built in 1831, this eight-columned Doric pavilion commemorates Dugald Stewart (1753–1828), professor of moral philosophy at Edinburgh University; it offers an excellent view of Princes Street and the Castle. Stewart was a friend of Sir Walter Scott (1771–1832) and numbered several future prime ministers – including Lords Palmerston (1784–1865), Russell (1792–1878) and Lansdowne (1780–1863) – among his acquaintances.

A path now leads directly to the green copper dome of the Observatory complex, comprising the Old Observatory, built by James Craig (1744–1795) in 1776, and the New Observatory, designed by William Playfair (1789–1857), who also designed Stewart's monument, in 1818. The New Observatory now houses the Edinburgh Experience, an audiovisual show which tells in twenty minutes or so the story of the city from prehistoric times to the present day. This is a fast gallop through history by any standards, and the 3D slide technology seems somewhat dated, but it is quite a useful briefing for those new to the city.

The 'Athens of the North'

Leaving the Observatory it is impossible to miss, some 50m (55yd) east, the columns of the National Monument. Inspired by the city's nickname, the architect, Charles Robert Cockerell (1788–1863), meant this imitation of the Parthenon to be the crowning glory of the 'Athens of the North'. Intended as a monument to the Scottish dead of the Napoleonic Wars, the project ran out of money in 1822 and was never completed. Arguably, it's more picturesque (and truer to the Athenian original) as an incomplete folly.

Edinburgh was first compared to Athens by the painter and architect James Stuart (1713–1788) in his work *The Antiquities of Athens*, in which he claimed to have been struck by the similarities between the two cities. In 1751, Stuart was commissioned by a club of aristocratic connoisseurs calling themselves the Society of Dilettanti to visit Athens and bring back an exact record of the ancient monuments of the Classical era. *The Antiquities of Athens*, published in parts from 1762 to 1814, inspired the first imitations of Classical Greek architecture in London and subsequently throughout eighteenth- and nineteenth-century Britain, not least in Edinburgh. But when Stuart visited Athens in 1751, it was little more than a village of shepherds and farmers squatting beneath the shattered ruins of the Acropolis, so the comparison between the two cities may not be quite as flattering as the inhabitants of Edinburgh later took it to be.

The real father of 'Athenian' Edinburgh was William Playfair (1789–1857), architect of the Dugald Stewart Monument, the New Observatory and of much of the New Town, the National Gallery of Scotland and many of the fine Victorian buildings of Edinburgh University. You will see more of his work later on during this walk.

Parliament Manqué

Follow the footpath round to the right of the monument to the vehicle road which circles the summit of Calton Hill. Turn right onto this road and follow it for about 200m (220yd) (turning sharply to your right after the first 100m [110yd] or so) to the point at which it joins Regent Road. Turn sharply left here and walk along Regent Road in front of the fine Royal High School building.

Designed in 1825 by Thomas Hamilton (1784–1858), this grandiloquent confection of Doric porticoes and colonnades is one of the finest relics of the Scottish Greek Revival school of architecture. When devolution of the Scottish government from London to Edinburgh first seemed a reality in the mid-1970s, the building, from which the Royal High School itself has long departed, was designated to become the seat of the new Scottish Parliament. After the hopes for devolution ran into the sand, this plan was shelved. The Scottish Parliament, which finally becomes a reality in 2000, will sit not here but in a new Parliament Building close to the Palace of Holyroodhouse (see page 39). The building you currently see in front of you is now the Scottish headquarters of the Crown Office.

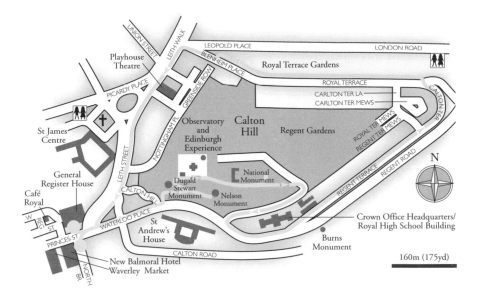

Scotland's Favourite Son

Just below the east end of the Crown Office buildings, turn off Regent Road and onto Regent Terrace, which runs parallel to it. Laid out by William Playfair, this elegant row of townhouses is among the finer examples of Edinburgh New Town architecture.

Before you leave the junction, look down and to your right to the Burns Monument, erected in 1830 to the memory of Scotland's most famous poet.

Robert Burns (1759–1796), born at Alloway in southwest Scotland, is universally known for his most popular works of poetry, 'Tam o' Shanter' and 'Address to the Haggis', read every year at Burns' Night celebrations all over the world, 'Auld Lang Syne', sung by Scots and others wherever Hogmanay is celebrated, and 'Scots Wha Ha'e', set to a traditional air to celebrate Scotland's heroic fight for freedom. Originally a farm labourer, the self-educated Burns worked as a surveyor and as a farmer while writing songs and poetry, before finding success with the publication of a book of verses, *Poems, Chiefly in the Scottish Dialect* (1786), the income from which he intended to use to pay his passage to Jamaica, where he had been offered the post of plantation overseer. Instead, however, he stayed in Scotland, gained a literary reputation as a lyricist and satirist matched only by his notoriety as a hard-drinking scallywag and womanizer, and died at the age of 37 of a chill caught after passing out drunk by the roadside one night.

Detection and Genealogy

Follow Regent Terrace for some 300m (330yd), at which point it becomes Calton Terrace; walk along this as it curves to your left, then cross Royal Terrace to walk through Royal Terrace Gardens for some 750m (820yd). The Gardens end at the junction of Blenheim Place, Leopold Place and Leith Walk; turn left and walk up Leith Walk, past the Playhouse Theatre on your left, to Picardy Place, where Leith Walk joins Leith Street. A statue of Sherlock Holmes presides over this busy junction; Sir Arthur Conan Doyle (1859–1930), creator of 'the world's greatest consulting detective', was born at an address in Picardy Place in 1859. Ignoring as best you can the hideous late-1960s/early-1970s excrescence of the St James Centre, continue up Leith Street to the south side of Waterloo Place, where it joins Princes Street.

The General Register House, which occupies the south side of the place, is guarded by an equestrian statue of the Duke of Wellington (1769–1852), one of many generals to respect and employ the fighting talents of the Scottish regiments. It was erected in 1852. The elegantly proportioned Register House itself, designed by Robert Adam (1728–1792) in 1852, houses the Scottish Record Office and the Scottish National Archives and thereby offers a valuable resource for those hoping to trace their Scots ancestry. An exhibition area houses changing displays relating to the history of Scotland and Edinburgh.

Leaving Register House, walk over to the corner with North Bridge, which is where you started.

Ghosts and Galleries: Waverley Station to the Tron

Summary: This walk loops through some of the back streets of the Old Town either side of the Royal Mile and visits four excellent art galleries as well as a spine-chilling, haunted underground street. On the way it passes the former headquarters of Scotland's most venerable national newspaper, *The Scotsman*. Be warned: there are steep ups and downs along the route.

Start:	The corner of Waverley Bridge and Princes Street.
Finish:	The Tron Kirk, the High Street.
Length:	1.6km (1 mile).
Time:	2hr.
Which day:	Not Sunday.
Refreshments:	Cafés and restaurants in the City Art Centre and Fruitmarket Gallery. A fine selection of pubs, including the Half Way House and Jinglin' Geordie's in Fleshmarket Close, and Bannerman's, in Cowgate.
To visit:	Mary King's Close, tours daily 10.30, 11.30, 14.30, 15.30, 16.30, 20.30 and 21.30, except Sunday morning and Tuesday evening. City Art Centre. Fruitmarket Gallery. St Cecilia's Hall and Russell Collection of Early Keyboard Instruments. 369 Gallery.

From Princes Street, turn onto Waverley Bridge and walk to the corner of Cockburn Street and Market Street. Above Market Street, just west of North Bridge, stands the impressive former headquarters of *The Scotsman* newspaper, which regards itself as Scotland's leading national broadsheet – a title that is hotly contested by the Glasgow-based *Herald*. The seven-storey baroque building is a veritable press baron's castle, with turrets, pediments and allegorical statues decorating the four upper levels above North Bridge. It has fine views over Calton Hill, Princes Street and the New Town. *The Scotsman* moved its operations into a new building (see page 39) opposite the new Scottish Parliament at Holyrood in 1999, and the old *Scotsman* building was converted into a luxury hotel.

Death Beneath the Streets
Walk up Cockburn Street, which winds steeply up towards the High Street and the Tron Kirk. Above you on your right is the back of the City Chambers, with a far longer drop to street level here than at its front on the High Street above. Beneath the City Chambers lies one of Edinburgh's more ghoulish and until recently better kept secrets.

In 1645, Edinburgh suffered its last and worst epidemic of bubonic plague. Schools were closed, the University fled to Linlithgow and Parliament moved to Stirling. Prisoners in the Tolbooth and the Castle dungeons were freed because there were not enough warders left to guard them. The city came to a standstill while Death himself, it seemed, stalked the streets. Those who concealed a sick friend or family member could be executed, and the sick were quarantined in huts outside the city centre, for in those days no one knew that the plague was carried by infected fleas and rats, of which old Edinburgh had plenty. The death toll was huge; it is known that, for example, more than half the population of Leith perished.

Mary King's Close, leading off the High Street, was one of the most severely affected streets. Believing the plague lay in the fabric of the buildings, the city magistrates ordered the survivors to move out and sealed off the entire close.

Five years later, people who had moved back into the deserted buildings began to tell horrid tales of hauntings by disembodied hands and by the victims of the pestilence, and many fled in terror. Soon no one at all would live in Mary King's Close, and for a century it stood empty, but still there persisted the stories of 'ghoulies and ghostics and things that go bump in the night' including a lady in black, a child, and a headless dog. As recently as 1993, it is claimed by the credulous, the ghost of a blonde-haired girl aged about eight and dressed in rags was seen in one of the derelict rooms.

When the City Chambers were built (completed 1761), what had been Mary King's Close was simply sealed off, built over and forgotten about, until it was accidentally rediscovered during building work in the early 1990s. If you want to test the limits of your scepticism, or enjoy having your spine chilled, you can take one of the guided tours of the haunted vault, 12m (40ft) below street level, by arrangement.

Entry to Mary King's Close is via the City Chambers on the High Street; to reach this building, turn right off Cockburn Street and walk up Warriston Close to the High Street.

Encyclopedia Britannica's **Birthplace**
After your visit to Mary King's Close, turn left and take the steeply sloping Anchor Close, the first on your left, back down to Cockburn Street. This close is typical of the enclosed alleys that until the mid-nineteenth century made the older parts of Edinburgh either side of the Royal Mile resemble a Middle Eastern casbah. It is named after the Anchor Tavern, where the Crochallan Fencibles, nominally a militia company but in fact a congenial drinking and dining club, met during the eighteenth century, when Robert Burns (1759–1796) was among its members.

Anchor Close is also where the first-ever edition of the *Encyclopedia Britannica* was published, in 1771, by the printer, antiquarian and naturalist William Smellie

(1740–1795). Smellie really deserves to have a street named after him, but perhaps renaming this thoroughfare Smellie Close was felt to be a bit too accurate for comfort. The Old Town was notorious for its powerful stink, the result of the custom of dumping kitchen and market refuse and the contents of chamberpots into the street, and visitors often hired guides or 'caddies' to lead them through the odorous maze and warn householders not to let fly until the visitor had passed, with a cry of 'Haud yer haunde!' ('Hold your hand!').

Cockburn Street, named after Lord Henry Cockburn (1779-1854), the prominent advocate and judge, is much newer than the closes above and below it, despite the self-consciously mock-medieval style of many of its buildings, with their corner turrets and other baronial embellishments. It was built in 1859 to provide a thoroughfare between Waverley Station and the High Street, cutting through an area of slums ripe for clearance. It is to Cockburn that Edinburgh owes one of its most attractive parks, Princes Street Gardens, for he campaigned to keep it as a public space. Edinburgh's important conservation organization, the Cockburn Society, is named after him.

Galleries Galore

Cross Cockburn Street, walk briefly downhill, then turn right into Craig's Close, a narrow alley which slopes steeply down to Market Street. Here, turn right and walk about 50m (55yd) down to the City Art Centre, at 2 Market Street. This is the home of Edinburgh's own art gallery, housed on six floors of a converted warehouse with a rotating programme of exhibitions from the municipal fine art collection, as well as visiting exhibitions.

Immediately opposite the City Art Centre, at 45 Market Street, is the Fruitmarket Gallery, one of Scotland's leading spaces for exhibitions of contemporary work by Scottish and international artists.

Leaving the Fruitmarket Gallery, cross back over Market Street once again and, at the east side of the City Art Centre, take a deep breath and set off up the long, steep steps of Fleshmarket Close (promising yourself a rest and a pint in the sensibly named Half Way House pub as an incentive). At the top, you emerge once more on Cockburn Street; turn left into the unassuming North Bridge Arcade and walk through to North Bridge. Turn right to the crossroads of North Bridge, South Bridge and High Street. Cross to the south side of the High Street and turn left, walking down the High Street briefly before turning right up Blackfriars Street.

This was the scene in 1520 of the celebrated scrap known as 'Cleanse the Causeway', between the Douglas and Hamilton families, the two most powerful Lowland dynasties, who were locked in a struggle for control of Scotland during the minority of James V (1512–1542). There were several hundred on each side; before the Douglas faction – led by Archibald, the sixth Earl of Angus (*c.* 1489–1557), who in 1574 had married Margaret Tudor (1489–1541), the widow of James IV (1473–1513) – had defeated the Hamiltons there were up to a hundred dead.

Walk to the end of Blackfriars Street and turn right on the Cowgate, a rather canyon-like street sunk beneath the level of the surrounding streets and buildings, and cast into gloom most of the time by the shadow of South Bridge and George IV Bridge. Almost immediately on your right, at the corner of Cowgate and Niddry Street, is St Cecilia's Hall. This is Scotland's oldest concert venue, designed by Robert Mylne (1734–1811) for the Edinburgh Musical Society in 1762.

Mylne was a bit of a jack-of-all-trades, being an engineer as well as architect, designer of Blackfriars Bridge in London and surveyor of St Paul's Cathedral. His concert hall, which has undergone several changes of use since then (it was by turns a Baptist chapel, a workshop, a dance hall and, in the early nineteenth century, the headquarters of a masonic lodge, as the inscription above the lintel indicates), has been beautifully restored. An oval room with fine acoustics, it was based on the opera house at Parma in Italy and is regularly used for concerts, especially during Festival time.

Now owned by Edinburgh University, it houses the important Russell

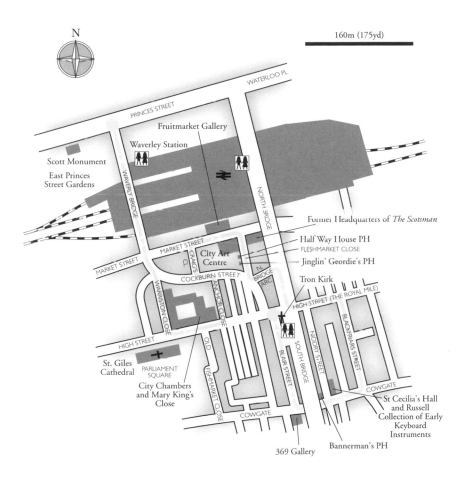

Collection of Early Keyboard Instruments. The collection includes more than fifty superbly made and beautifully decorated harpsichords, virginals and claviers, all between two and four hundred years old and many still in playing condition. If you can't time your visit to Edinburgh to coincide with one of the recitals, you can buy recordings on compact disc or cassette tape of many of the instruments displayed here and choose among a range of specialist books.

Continue along the Cowgate, under the gloomy arches of South Bridge, to the 369 Gallery, at 233 Cowgate, immediately after the bridge on your left. This small commercial gallery has new exhibitions every month. After visiting the gallery, cross the Cowgate and walk up Blair Street into Hunter Square and to the Tron Kirk, the High Street and the end of this walk.

The Heart of the City: Along Princes Street

Summary: Princes Street is Edinburgh's main thoroughfare and its busiest shopping street, and although the architectural mishaps of the second half of the twentieth century mar its original gracious appearance, it still has sights worth seeing – including the grand hotels at either end built by rival nineteenth-century railway companies, the world's oldest department store, a monument to one of Edinburgh's most famous sons, and two magnificent art galleries.

Start:	Outside the New Balmoral Hotel at the east end of Princes Street, on the corner with North Bridge.
Finish:	St Cuthbert's Church, at the north end of Lothian Road.
Length:	About 1.6km (1 mile).
Time:	2-3hr, depending on how long you spent in the Royal Scottish Academy and the National Gallery of Scotland.
Refreshments:	New Balmoral Hotel bar and restaurant; many cafés and restaurants in the Waverley Market shopping centre; Caledonian Hotel bar and restautant.
Which day:	Any day except Sunday.
To visit:	Scott Monument.
	Royal Scottish Academy.
	National Gallery of Scotland.
	St John's Church.
	St Cuthbert's Church.

In this one valley, where the life of the town goes most busily forward, there may be seen, shown one above and behind another by the accidents of the ground, buildings in almost every style upon the globe. Egyptian and Greek temples, Venetian palaces and Gothic spires, are huddled one over another in a most admired disorder; while above all, the brute mass of the Castle and the summit of Arthur's Seat look down upon these imitations with a becoming dignity, as the works of Nature may look down upon the monuments of Art.

So wrote Robert Louis Stevenson (1850–1894) of Edinburgh in 1878. Today, mundane chain stores dominate virtually all of the north side of Princes Street at street level, but this walk avoids most of the crowds and traffic by detouring into Princes Street Gardens, the attractively landscaped park which runs along the south side of Princes Street for almost its entire length. Looking up and to your left, you will have fine views of Edinburgh Castle, while to the east the monuments of Calton Hill and the slopes of Arthur's Seat dominate your view.

A Palatial Hotel

Begin at the east end of Princes Street, outside the magnificent New Balmoral Hotel. Built at the turn of the nineteenth century, this was originally the North British Hotel, owned by the North British Railway Company, which brought the east-coast railway line to Edinburgh. The hotel was built at the same time as the adjoining Waverley Station (between 1895 and 1899) and, although it thereafter changed hands several times, with the nationalization of the private railway companies in the late 1940s it was taken over by the state-owned British Railways and lost some of its former grandeur. With re-privatization in the 1980s it once more joined the private sector. The present management has restored it to luxury status; the new name offers something of a tip of the hat to tradition in that it retains the initials of the hotel's original owners.

Waverley Station, which adjoins the hotel, is virtually underground, submerged by the Waverley Market shopping centre, whose interior can perhaps best be described as of the 'Elderly Futuristic' school of design but which at least has a number of places where you can eat and drink. At street level, the Edinburgh Tourist Board's information office offers a wide range of services, including tours and accommodation booking.

Reclamation and Exploration

In medieval times the area now occupied by the station, the main railway line and East Princes Street Gardens was a marsh for most of the year, watered by the Craig Burn, which flowed from a hollow in the north side of Castle Rock. This made the Castle and the town difficult to approach from the north, supplementing its other natural defences, and in 1440 the Craig Burn was even dammed in order to create the Nor' (North) Loch, an artificial lake. In 1759, with Scotland once and for all at peace with England and itself, work began on draining the Nor' Loch and opening what is now Princes Street and the New Town for development (see page 62), providing much-needed space for the city to expand beyond its ancient limits. In 1768, work began on a bridge to connect the Old Town with this virgin territory, and it opened as a footbridge in 1769 – only to collapse shortly afterwards, killing five people. What is now Waverley Bridge was finally completed in 1772.

With the Waverley Market to your left, walk along Princes Street for about 150m (165yd), cross Waverley Bridge (there is usually a bagpiper busking on the corner during the day) and turn right into East Princes Street Gardens. At the corner, as you enter the park, stands a statue of David Livingstone (1813–1873), the Scottish missionary and explorer who was the first European to see the Victoria Falls.

Monument to an Author

This statue is dwarfed by the spiky Gothic stone spire of the Scott Monument, built between 1840 and 1846 in honour of the city's most famous son. A white marble statue of Sir Walter Scott (1771–1832) is complemented by sixty-four statuettes adorning the monument, each representing a character from one of his novels. Scott's historical romances helped to rekindle interest in all things Scottish among

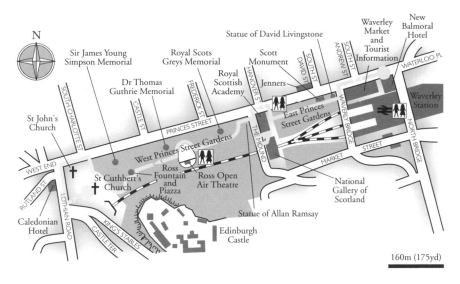

readers – Queen Victoria (1819–1901) among them – and he was influential in rediscovering elements of Scotland's lost heritage, including the ancient regalia which were stored away after the Treaty of Union. However, he must also, largely through stirring the enthusiasm of Victoria's husband Albert (1819–1861), bear much of the blame for the plague of tartan kitsch which began in the nineteenth century and afflicts Edinburgh and Scotland to this day.

Just before you explore the Monument, should you decide to do so, look over to the opposite side of Princes Street where, at No. 48, you will see Jenners, Edinburgh's answer to Harrods and purported to be the oldest department store in the world. It was opened in 1834 by Charles Kennington and Charles Jenner, and became simply 'Jenners' on Kennington's death in 1862. The original store burned down in 1892, and Jenner commissioned William Hamilton Beattie (1852–1912) to design a new building. Its front, which you can see clearly from here unless there is a bus in the way (which there may well be, because Princes Street's traffic flow is not good), is a copy of the Bodleian Library building in Oxford. Jenner died in 1893, two years before the reopening of the store that still bears his name.

If you are visiting the Scott Monument in summer you will probably find a long queue of visitors waiting to climb the 65m (200ft) Monument; in any case, there are better views of the city to be had with less hassle from other viewpoints (see pages 23 and 46 for examples), so walk on through the Gardens for 200m (220yd) or so, passing on the way statues of Adam Black (1784–1874), the respected Liberal politician who was twice Lord Provost of Edinburgh, and John Wilson (1785–1854), professor of moral philosophy at the University of Edinburgh who, under the *nom de plume* Christopher North, was also a respected journalist and essayist.

Now turn right to exit from the Gardens onto Princes Street, then enter the Royal Scottish Academy, which stands on the corner of Princes Street and The Mound (entrance on Princes Street).

Two Fine Collections

Like much of early-nineteenth-century Edinburgh, the Academy building is self-consciously in the style of the Greek Revival and is the work of William Playfair (1789–1857) – see page 47. Built between 1822 and 1826, it houses a series of mainly commercial exhibitions, mostly of contemporary Scottish artists, throughout the year. Like London's Royal Academy, it also hosts a yearly Summer Exhibition, usually timed to overlap with the Edinburgh Festival. Amateurs, beginners and students as well as established artists may submit works for this exhibition, and as a result it is an excellent showcase for sometimes surprising pieces by as yet unrecognized artists, as well as for works by Academicians. Many of the smaller pieces are within the budget of the less well-heeled collector.

Leaving the Royal Scottish Academy, turn left and walk about 75m (80yd) up The Mound; immediately south of the Academy and separated from it by a piazza which during the summer is a venue for all manner of street performers and buskers, is the National Gallery of Scotland.

This is a gem of a collection, housed within a building which harmonizes with that of the Royal Scottish Academy and rated as one of the finest smaller art museums in Europe. Its collection has a far wider span than its name might suggest, with works by Constable, El Greco, Raphael, Rembrandt, Titian, Velasquez, Van Gogh and Gauguin as well as by some of Scotland's finest Classical masters, most notably its superb collection of paintings by Sir Henry Raeburn (1756–1823).

Sometimes called The Scottish Reynolds, after his contemporary and tutor, the great English portraitist Sir Joshua Reynolds (1723–1792), Raeburn began painting miniature portraits of his friends in water colours at the age of 16 and thereafter studied painting in Rome. From the time of his return to Edinburgh in 1787 until his death he was the most fashionable portraitist in Scotland and an associate of the wealthy, aristocratic and famous. Raeburn captured in paint almost every single one of his notable Scottish contemporaries, the only person of any significance to escape his brush being Robert Burns (1759–1796). A founder of the Royal Scottish Academy, he was knighted in 1822. Many of his portraits remain in the private collections of the aristocratic families whose ancestors commissioned them, but this collection contains some fine examples, as does the Scottish National Portrait Gallery (see page 63).

In a sense, the National Gallery does Scotland's own painters few favours, for its collection includes such an array of works by Europe's greatest painters, spanning more than four centuries, that the works of Ramsay and Raeburn are perhaps a little diminished by comparison. They are still the greatest Scottish artists of their time, and therefore something special by the standards of even the most discriminating connoisseur, but the Gallery takes them out of that context and invites you to compare them with a number of the finest painters of all time. Ramsay versus his English rival Reynolds, yes; but ranked against Rembrandt . . . no.

For that reason, you should first visit the Gallery's New Wing, where the Scots artists are hung on the ground floor, to see them with an unclouded eye before going on to view the rest of the collection at your leisure. Look out for Raeburn's best known work, *The Reverend Robert Walker Skating on Duddingston Loch*, and for

Ramsay's *The Painter's Wife*, a loving portrait of the artist's second wife, Margaret.

Then return to the entrance hall and view the rest of the collection clockwise, starting by turning left into Rooms 1 and 2, where there are fine works by sixteenth-century Italians. The finest are the four superb Titians which greet you as you enter this section of the gallery. These impress first of all by their sheer size – the two largest are some 210cm by 270cm (7ft by 8ft) – and only then by Titian's grasp of colour, composition and, above all, the nude female form. They are *Diana and Actaeon* and *Diana and Callisto*, painted in the mid-sixteenth century for King Philip II (1527–1598) of Spain, and flanked here in the National Gallery by two smaller and earlier paintings, *The Three Ages of Man* and *Venus Anadyomene*.

Continuing clockwise around the ground floor, Room 3 is hung with smaller canvases by German medieval painters, Room 4 is more arresting, with seventeenth-century French, Spanish and Italian masters, including El Greco and Velasquez, and you must pause in Room 5 where Poussin's seven *Sacraments* hang, before passing on to view the collection's three paintings attributable to Rembrandt: *Self Portrait*, *Woman in a Bed* and *Young Woman with Flowers in her Hair*. Rooms 6 and 7 house seventeenth-century Dutch painters, Room 8 a changing exhibition of drawings and prints, and Room 9 larger paintings by Rubens, Van Dyck and other Flemish and Dutch masters.

Upstairs is the Gallery's collection of French Impressionists, mostly smaller works by Gauguin, Monet, Cezanne and van Gogh, together with an assortment of eighteenth-century painters in Room 10, a number of works by Turner and Constable in Room 11, and more works by Raeburn in Room 12.

Statuary in the Gardens

On leaving the National Gallery, you can either turn left and walk up The Mound to begin the Edinburgh Castle walk (see page 23) or you can cross The Mound, walk up to the corner of Princes Street and turn left into West Princes Street Gardens. Assuming you've taken the latter option, you are immediately greeted by a statue, put up in 1848, of the ubiquitous Allan Ramsay (1684–1758), poet and publisher (see page 28). The open-air theatre in the centre of the Gardens is used in summer for live music performances, especially during the Edinburgh Festival.

Continuing through the Gardens, walking parallel to Princes Street, you pass by three more monuments: a bronze of a mounted trooper of the Royal Scots Greys, commemorating the regiment's part in the South African War of 1899–1902; a memorial to Dr Thomas Guthrie (1803–1873), the Edinburgh preacher, teacher and philanthropist; and a memorial to Sir James Young Simpson (1811–1870), obstetrician and gynaecologist, whose pioneering use of chloroform makes him the father of anaesthetics and one of the most important figures in the development of modern surgery.

A Voluptuous Statue and Two Fine Churches

The most prominent landmark at the western end of Princes Street Gardens is the Ross Fountain, overlooking the Piazza, a florid cast-iron set-piece whose bosomy allegorical figures were quite at odds with respectable Victorian sentiment. It was given to the city by Daniel Ross, an Edinburgh gunsmith whose admiration for the metallurgical skill used in casting it may have shaded his appreciation of its voluptuous, scantily veiled subject matter – what might have been acceptable for the International Exhibition in Paris in 1862, where Ross bought the piece, was perhaps less acceptable to straitlaced Edinburgh. At any rate, the statue was deposited in this relatively inconspicuous location, where it caused the Dean of nearby St John's Church grave offence; he thought it 'grossly indecent and disgusting'. It seems tame enough, however, to the modern eye.

From the Fountain and Piazza, follow the path for about 100m (110yd). From here, take the path to your right and, once you are back on Princes Street, turn left and go for another 100m (110yd) to enter St John's Church, at the corner of Princes Street and Lothian Road.

This very attractive, small church dates from 1818, when it was designed by William Burn (1789–1870). Its exterior, in Perpendicular style, is perhaps less immediately striking than some of Edinburgh's more muscular Gothic churches of the later nineteenth century, but the interior, for which Burn's inspiration was St George's Chapel at Windsor Castle, is well worth a closer look. The very attractive woodwork dates from the mid-nineteenth century but imitates the elaborately figured stalls and screen of Scottish medieval church decoration. Sir Henry Raeburn (1756–1823), the finest Scottish portraitist of the late eighteenth and early nineteenth centuries, is buried in the graveyard of St John's Church.

Turn left into Lothian Road and pass the palatial red sandstone front of the Caledonian Hotel, opposite St John's. This grand pile was built by the Caledonian Railway Company to rival the North British Hotel at the east end of Princes Street. The tall Corinthian-columned arches on the ground floor were the entrance to the company's station, from which trains ran to Glasgow and around which the hotel was built in 1903. The Caledonian is still one of Edinburgh's grandest hotels, and its foyer is a fine example of Edwardian interior decoration.

Turn left and walk through the churchyard to St Cuthbert's Church. A massive, clumsy structure, the present church was built in 1890 on the site of a much older church, founded in the twelfth century by Saint Margaret (c. 1046–1093) and named after the great Augustinian abbot of Lindisfarne ('Holy Isle'), Saint Cuthbert (c. 635–687). The architect, Hippolyte Blanc (1844–1927), although an Edinburgh man himself, was of French descent, and perhaps that is why he seems to have had only a shaky grasp of the vernacular of Scottish religious architecture; his church would look more at home in the centre of a French provincial town than in the capital of Scotland. The church had already been rebuilt twice, in the eighteenth and nineteenth centuries, so there is nothing to be seen of the original building. The spire, which is all that remains of the 1790 building, is visibly at odds with Blanc's design, which consists of two Baroque towers, one on each side of a domed apse.

The interior is more attractive, and its decoration is lavish by the standards of Scottish Presbyterian church architecture, which tends to be spartan in the extreme. With a mosaic floor, a marble communion table with inlays of porphyry, mother-of-pearl and turquoise and a green marble pulpit supported by red marble columns, as well as plentiful stained glass and a white marble font which is copied from one in Siena Cathedral, St Cuthbert's would seem to be an indication that by the end of the nineteenth century the stern shadow of John Knox (*c.* 1513–1572) was lifting from the Kirk, and that a certain amount of colour in church decoration was no longer seen automatically as a turning towards the pernicious doctrines of Rome.

This is where the walk ends, but if it's a sunny day, you might want to stroll back to Princes Street Gardens, perhaps for a picnic or just to wander around watching the people go by. Alternatively, since you are hard by Edinburgh's major shopping area, you could choose to go and divest yourself of some of your holiday spending money. As well as the big-name shops, Princes Street has an array of establishments peddling tartan wares to visitors seeking an authentic Caledonian souvenir. For more upmarket shopping, you can walk south about 200m (220yd) to George Street, which runs parallel to Princes Street, and has recently become Edinburgh's most stylish place to spend your money.

The New Town Stride: Georgian Edinburgh

Summary: Edinburgh's New Town, a rectangle of elegant Georgian and Regency streets and terraces that begins north of Princes Street, is one of the first and finest examples of town planning in Europe. Compared with the higgledy-piggledy wynds and closes of the Old Town, which grew up over centuries along and around the Royal Mile and the Castle, the New Town is a model of orderly design that reflects its birth during the Age of Reason. Its streets bear the names of local notables and contemporary royalty: George Street for King George III (1738–1820), Charlotte Street for his Queen, Princes Street for the Prince of Wales and Frederick Street for Frederick Louis (1707–1751), Prince of Wales and father of George III. Frederick died nine years before George II (1683–1760) causing the crown to skip a generation. Hanover Street, of course, genuflects to the whole Hanoverian dynasty.

Start:	St Andrew Square.
Finish:	West Register House, Charlotte Square.
Length:	3.2km (2 miles).
Time:	3hr.
Refreshments:	Numerous pubs, bars and cafés along the way.
Which day:	Not Saturday or Sunday.
To visit:	Scottish National Portrait Gallery.
	St Andrew's and St George's Church.
	New Town Conservation Centre.
	Georgian House.
	West Register House.

First planned in 1767 by James Craig (1744–1795), the New Town was initially bounded by Princes Street in the south and Queen Street in the north, with George Street running through its centre. Symmetrical garden squares stand at each end of George Street: Charlotte Square at the west end and St Andrew Square at the east end.

Illustrious Men

Start at St Andrew Square, where your landmark is the 37m (121ft) column of the Melville Monument, atop which stands a statue of Henry Dundas (1724–1811), first Viscount Melville, the arch-Tory, ally of William Pitt the Younger (1759–1806) and political fixer who at the turn of the eighteenth century had managed to make himself – in the words of one of his fiercest Whig opponents, Lord Henry Cockburn (1779–1854) – 'the absolute dictator of Scotland'. His downfall came in 1805, when he was impeached for corruption in the handling of public funds; he was judged guilty of negligence, and although he was restored to office, his influence was never the same. The Monument was erected in 1823.

Occupying the east side of the square at No. 36, next to the ugly bus terminus, is the Royal Bank of Scotland headquarters. Built in 1774, it was designed by Sir William Chambers (1726–1796) for Sir Lawrence Dundas, a relative of Viscount Melville, as a private home. The statue standing in front of the bank is of John Hope (1765–1823), fourth Earl of Hopetoun, a distinguished officer of the French Revolutionary and Napoleonic Wars, whose family home is near Queensferry on the Firth of Forth and can be visited on a later walk (see page 121).

Leave St Andrew Square by its northeast corner, continue along North St Andrew Street, then turn left onto Queen Street and enter the Scottish National Portrait Gallery. Built in 1885, in French Gothic style, the gallery was the gift of J. R. Finlay, proprietor of *The Scotsman*, Scotland's national newspaper, and contains an extensive collection of portraits of influential Scots from the eighteenth century onward, including a number by Sir Henry Raeburn (1756–1823) and Allan Ramsay (1713–1784).

The National Portrait Gallery's collection, however, is every bit as interesting for its historical associations as for its artistic merit. Here are portraits of all the heroes, heroines and villains who have tripped or stumbled across the crowded and frequently bloody stage of Scotland's past: the stubbornly determined Mary of Guise (1515–1560) and her doomed daughter Mary Queen of Scots (1542–1587); Mary's second husband, Henry Stewart (*c.* 1545–1567), Lord Darnley, as a 17-year-old fop and Flora Macdonald (1722–1790), the Jacobite sympathizer who helped Bonnie Prince Charlie escape Scotland after Culloden in 1746 (according to legend she slipped him past the Hanoverian troops in transvestite disguise as her maidservant, and certainly the portrait of Prince Charles Edward Stuart here shows him as a pretty boy who would have looked convincing in drag). *George IV's Entry into the Palace of Holyroodhouse*, painted by David Wilkie (1785–1841) to commemorate the first royal visit to Scotland in more than a century, is a fine example of painterly sycophancy; still, it earned Wilkie his knighthood in 1836. Raeburn gets a whole room to himself on the top floor.

God and Mammon
On leaving the Scottish National Portrait Gallery, turn left onto Queen Street, walk west for one block, and turn left again into North St David Street, which returns you briefly to St Andrew Square. From the west side of the square, turn right onto George Street and walk halfway along the first block on the north side to the prominent St Andrew's and St George's Church. Dedicated to the patron saints of Scotland and England, the church was built in 1784 and was the New Town's first place of worship. It has a 52m (168ft) steeple, added in 1787, and within is a delightful Adam-style ceiling, one of the finest pieces of eighteenth-century interior decoration in the city. The architect was Major Andrew Frazer (d. 1792), an officer of the Royal Engineers who served with distinction during the Seven Years' War.

Opposite the church is a dignified Victorian building, the Royal Society of Scotland, built on the site of the former Royal College of Physicians (which the

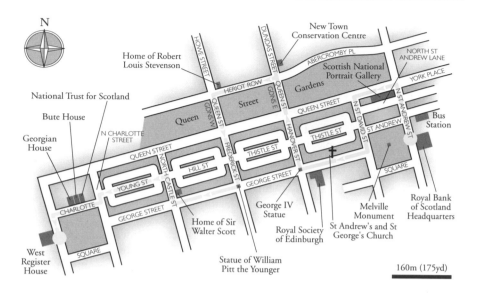

N

New Town Conservation Centre

Home of Robert Louis Stevenson

Scottish National Portrait Gallery

NORTH ST ANDREW LANE

YORK PLACE

National Trust for Scotland

Bute House

Georgian House

Bus Station

Royal Bank of Scotland Headquarters

George IV Statue

Melville Monument

Home of Sir Walter Scott

Royal Society of Edinburgh

St Andrew's and St George's Church

West Register House

Statue of William Pitt the Younger

160m (175yd)

bank bought and demolished) and designed by David Rhind. It opened in 1847.

Continue along George Street to Hanover Street, next on your right. A statue of George IV (1762–1830), erected in 1831, stands at the intersection. Turn right, and after about 150m (165yd) cross Queen Street and walk down Queen Street Gardens East, with its elegant private gardens on each side, to the junction of Abercromby Place – named after the Edinburgh-educated Napoleonic War general Sir Ralph Abercromby (1734–1801) – and Heriot Row. George Heriot (1563–1624), who lends his name to this street, was the court jeweller of King James VI of Scotland and I of England (1566–1625) and a favourite of the king, who granted him the revenue of the sugar tax for three years from 1620 (in those days it was usual for the collection of certain taxes to be 'farmed' to aristocrats, financiers or other royal favourites who kept a percentage of the revenue, passing the balance to the Exchequer). He left a large fortune and endowed one of Edinburgh's most prestigious schools – George Heriot's – as well as the Heriot Trust and Heriot-Watt University.

Conservation in Action

Continue straight on down Dundas Street – another tribute to Melville – to the New Town Conservation Centre at No. 13A. This is the headquarters of the committee which oversees conservation of the Georgian buildings of the New Town. An exhibition area highlights the committee's work and the projects that are currently under way, and there is a reference library and bookshop for those with a more than superficial interest in architecture and design.

A Master Storyteller

Double back now to Heriot Row, turn right and walk 150m (165yd) or so along the north side of the street to No. 17, the home of Robert Louis Stevenson

Plate 10: *The Palace of Holyroodhouse and its ruined Abbey, viewed here from Holyrood Park, is the royal family's residence in Edinburgh (see pages 39 and 42).*

Plate 11: *Salisbury Crags, below Arthur's Seat, loom above central Edinburgh (see page 42).*

Plate 12: The Tron Kirk, on the Royal Mile, traditionally the focus for Hogmanay celebrations (see pages 33, 34 and 54).

Plate 13: The Ross Fountain, one of Princes Street Gardens' many memorials (see page 59).

Plate 14: Princes Street, looking east to the New Balmoral Hotel and Calton Hill (see page 55).

Plate 15: *The Scott Monument dominates Princes Street, commemorating one of Edinburgh's most famous literary men, nineteenth-century novelist Sir Walter Scott (see page 56).*

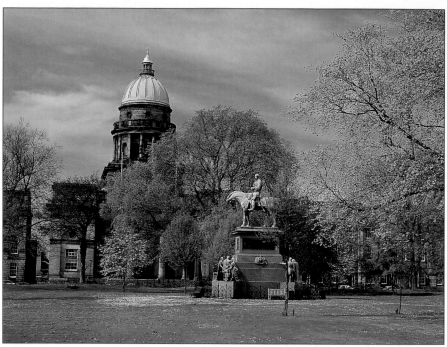

Plate 16: The green copper dome of the West Register House overlooks Charlotte Square, with its equestrian Albert Memorial (see page 66).

Plate 17: Sections of the old city walls still stand in The Vennel (see page 70).

Plate 18: Statue of Greyfriars Bobby, canine hero canonised by Walt Disney (see page 71).

(1850–1894). Stevenson's adventure tales, such as *Kidnapped* (1886) and *Treasure Island* (1883), remain popular today, and he is also known for historical romances set during the turbulent eighteenth century, such as *Catriona* (1893) and *The Master of Ballantrae* (1889), and spine-chillers of which the most famous is surely *The Strange Case of Dr Jekyll and Mr Hyde* (1886), the story of a respectable Edinburgh doctor, who, through meddling in experimental chemistry, releases his uncontrollable, evil *alter ego*. Stevenson was also a talented travel writer, bringing news of places as diverse as the French Cevennes and the islands of the South Pacific to his stay-at-home audience. He suffered from tuberculosis for most of his life, and travelled widely in search of a warmer climate than Edinburgh's. He finally went to live in Samoa, where, at the age of only 44, he died of the disease. He is buried there beneath a headstone which bears the epitaph he wrote for himself:

> *Under the wide and starry sky*
> *Dig the grave and let me lie.*
> *Glad did I live and gladly die,*
> *And I laid me down with a will.*

> *This be the verse that you grave for me:*
> *Here he lies where he longed to be;*
> *Home is the sailor, home from the sea,*
> *And the hunter home from the hill.*

The house is now a private home.

A Prolific Romancer
Cross Heriot Row and turn immediately left into Queen Street Gardens West. Cross Queen Street, walk two blocks up Frederick Street to George Street. A statue of William Pitt the Younger, second Earl of Chatham, stands at the crossroads. Walk one block west and turn right into North Castle Street and No. 39, home of Sir Walter Scott (1771–1832) between 1802 and 1826.

Son of an Edinburgh lawyer, Scott was born and educated in Edinburgh and trained as a barrister. He is vastly more famous as an author, and was hugely influential in creating a romantic, tartan-tinged myth of Scotland that survives to this day and is the powerhouse of the Scottish tourism industry, which owes Scott a great debt. The tartan fakery of Princes Street and the Royal Mile (both the kilt and the notion of a separate tartan for each clan are nineteenth-century inventions), the cacophonous drone of the pipes, the garish rugs, hideous gewgaws, phony genealogy and the transformation of the image of the Highland clansman from thieving barbarian to noble savage – all of these we can lay at Scott's door.

He is best known for novels such as *Rob Roy* (1817), in which he turned an outlawed brigand and cattle-thief into a romantic hero (the tale was filmed in 1953 starring Richard Todd and in 1990 starring Liam Neeson); *Waverley* (1814), which gave its name to Edinburgh's main station, in honour of the author, and to a brand of pen supposedly endorsed by him; *The Heart of Midlothian* (1818), which gave its name to one of Edinburgh's two football teams, Hearts; *Ivanhoe* (1820), filmed in 1952 starring Robert Taylor, George Sanders and Elizabeth Taylor, and adapted in 1996 as *Young Ivanhoe* with Stacy Keach and Margot Kidder; and *Guy Mannering* (1815). Scott gained huge popularity for his tales of medieval derring-do, evil barons, heroic knights and pure maidens.

His literary career was in fact largely a by-product of his failure in business. After the collapse of his printing and publishing company, Scott set out to write his way out of bankruptcy and pay off his debts with the earnings of his pen. He was astonishingly prolific. His first major book, *Border Minstrelsy*, a collection of ballads, had been published in three volumes in 1802 and 1803. In 1813 he had been offered the post of Poet Laureate but turned it down, proposing that Robert Southey (1774–1843) be offered it instead – Southey accepted. So Scott – made a baronet by George IV (1762–1830) in 1820 – was already an established author when in 1826 he was ruined by the failure of the publishing company Constable and Ballantyne in which he was partner.

Spurred on by this financial disaster, he churned out a dozen books over the next six years and had published almost forty by the time of his death. Not only the leading literary figure of the early nineteenth century, he was also Scotland's first great modern writer, his works bridging the gap to the folk ballads and poems of an older tradition and evoking a vanished or vanishing world in a market hungry for romance and nostalgia.

The house is, alas, not open to the public. Those with an interest in Scott memorabilia will find plenty at the Writer's Museum on the Royal Mile (see page 30).

Scotland's Past Recorded

Walk on down North Castle Street, take the first left onto Young Street and continue to the north side of Charlotte Square. Like Queen Street, this is named for George III's queen, Charlotte Sophia (1744–1818). Walk along the north side, past the National Trust for Scotland to Bute House. This imposing building was the residence of John Stuart, third Earl of Bute (1713–1792), the eighteenth-century politician, and of his successors. Stuart rose to power as a courtier of King George III, playing a leading part in the political intrigues of the 1760s. The house later became the official residence of the Secretary of State for Scotland. Continue to the Georgian House.

Completed at the end of the eighteenth century and designed by the Edinburgh-educated Robert Adam (1728–1792), Charlotte Square is one of the most harmonious examples of European architecture of that era, and this gracious building has been restored and furnished with period pieces as it would have been by its first owners.

Now walk round to the west side of the square, which is dominated by the splendid, copper-green dome of the West Register House. Originally built in 1811 as St George's Church, this now contains the overspill from the Scottish Record Office at the General Register House (see page 49) on Princes Street, mainly nineteenth- and twentieth-century documents. For the visitor the most interesting section is the permanent exhibition of Scottish historical documents, including the Declaration of

Arbroath. Signed in 1320 by King Robert the Bruce (1274–1329) and the nobles, clergy and commons of Scotland, it is a stirring and defiant document, affirming Scotland's independence after more than thirty years of continuous armed struggle against its much mightier neighbour. They wrote:

We fight not for glory, nor riches, nor honour, but only for that liberty which no true man relinquishes but with his life. . . . for so long as an hundred [of us] remain alive we are minded never a whit to bow beneath the yoke of English dominion.

The walk is now over, but you may wish to spend some time among these fascinating records of past glories.

The Auld Toun Shuffle: Around the Old Town

Edinburgh toun has a nice distinction
Edinburgh toun gets a nice abuse
But everybody knows when the east wind up and blows
Edinburgh toun's reduced
to two conditions that might be described
as the Auld Toun Shuffle and the New Town Stride

So cast a canny eye at the South Side Swagger
Don't be taken in by the New Town taste
Edinburgh toun wears a bib above a goun
Baith above a bib and brace
But don't mistake it for Jekyll and Hyde
It's the Auld Toun Shuffle and the New Town Stride.[1]

So sings local bard Rod Paterson in 'The Auld Toun Shuffle and the New Town Stride', contrasting the still-wide gulf between genteel middle-class Edinburgh and the working-class traditions of the old town around and south of the Royal Mile. Unlike London (but like many mainland European cities) Edinburgh still has long-standing communities of working-class flat dwellers living in its historic heart, within a stone's throw of its main tourist beat, in solidly build stone tenements. This walk goes through what was the heart of medieval Edinburgh, the Grassmarket, and ends at the beginning of the museum and University district.

Start:	Usher Hall, Lothian Road.
Finish:	Sandy Bell's, on the corner of Forrest Road and Forrest Hill.
Length:	1.6km (1 mile).
Time:	1hr.
Refreshments:	Numerous pubs, restaurants and cafés along the route, especially on the Grassmarket, including the Burke and Hare pub, the Last Drop Tavern, the Beehive Inn, and Sandy Bell's Bar.
Which day:	Any day.
To visit:	Usher Hall.
	Traverse Theatre.
	Royal Lyceum Theatre.
	Greyfriars Kirk and kirkyard.

[1] Copyright © Rod Paterson, 1987: 'The Auld Toun Shuffle and the New Town Stride'.

This walk starts in Edinburgh's theatreland, outside the Usher Hall on Lothian Road. A solid, domed building reflecting the city's early-twentieth-century prosperity, the Hall is the city's main concert venue and was the gift of Andrew Usher of the Usher brewing dynasty. Completed in 1913, the Usher Hall is the winter home of the Scottish National Orchestra, and during the Festival its amphitheatrical auditorium and 2900 seats are in almost continuous use. The sturdy eight-sided building is capped by a green copper dome, and equally sturdy Doric columns support the entranceways. All in all, it gives the appearance of being a solid, businesslike piece of work, an impression enhanced by the grime of Lothian Road.

Next to it, at the corner of Cambridge Street, stands the new Traverse Theatre, which has a long and honourable career of fostering new and avant-garde drama and performance in Scotland and internationally and which has played a central part in the development of Edinburgh as an international centre for theatre and the arts. The Traverse opened in 1957 in a building on the Grassmarket, and relocated to this striking new building in 1996.

From the front of the Usher Hall, walk along Grindlay Street, passing a theatre beside which the Traverse is something of an upstart. The Royal Lyceum Theatre, which was built in 1883, is the home of the Edinburgh Repertory Theatre Company and, like the Usher Hall, reaches a peak of thespian frenzy during the Festival.

From the end of Grindlay Street, turn right on Spittal Street and then left on Bread Street, and walk down to the West Port. This road junction, as its name implies, was once the west gate through the city wall into the old town of Edinburgh.

Grave Concern

On the West Port, in the acute angle formed by the junction of Bread Street and Fountainbridge, stands a pub with a gruesome history: the Burke and Hare. William Burke (1792–1829) and his co-conspirator William Hare (1790 *c.* 1860) began their unsavoury career as 'resurrectionists', the nickname for graverobbers who supplied the medical profession with cadavers for dissection or other purposes. Burke and Hare's main client was the surgeon and lecturer in anatomy Dr Robert Knox (1791–1862), and they brought him freshly disinterred corpses exhumed from the city's cemeteries for anatomical study. At the time, very few people were willing to leave their bodies to medical science, and Knox was cynically prepared to ask no questions as to where the bodies came from, and to pay well.

All went smoothly until the demand for bodies began to exceed the number of people dying of natural causes. Burke and Hare, who are said to have met in the tavern which stood here at the time, hit on a simple solution: murder. Well, it saved a lot of digging. They killed between sixteen and thirty people before one of their victims was recognized on the dissecting table by a relative. Dr Knox fingered his unpleasant associates; Hare – in fact if anything the more culpable of the two, although there was little to choose between them – turned King's Evidence and set up his partner to save his own neck, and Burke went to the gallows. Their skeletons and death masks are preserved in the Anatomy Department of Edinburgh University – poetic justice indeed.

The scandal forced Knox to leave Edinburgh for London, where he became a noted ethnologist – and a Fellow of the London Ethnological Society, no less.

Medieval Walls
After enjoying a pint and a shudder in the Burke and Hare, walk down the steeply sloping West Port towards the Grassmarket. At the foot of the West Port, turn sharply right up The Vennel, a narrow stepped street, to view the only surviving fragment of the medieval city wall.

Like city walls throughout Europe, this was as much a means of controlling trade and raising revenue as a defensive rampart, forcing merchants and traders to enter and leave the city through its gates, where their goods and commerce could be taxed. By the mid-eighteenth century the city was already outgrowing its older limits and, after the failure of the Jacobite rebellion of 1745–6, there was no longer a perceptible outside threat. The walls were demolished bit by bit and the stone used in newer buildings. None of the city gateways survive.

Penned within the walls, the citizens of Edinburgh were forced to build ever higher, and the typical city housing from the Middle Ages onward was in tall tenement buildings called 'lands' – perhaps the world's first high-density, high-rise housing. Each land might house people from a wide range of social classes, from commoners to tradesmen, professional men and even the lower ranks of the nobility. The ground floor might be occupied by a shop or a workshop and the rooms above by the shopkeeper or craftsman, while the wealthier folk lived as high up as they could get – and as far as possible from the stink of the streets, into which the contents of chamberpots might be emptied from on high with the cry of 'gardie loo' (from the French *gardez à l'eau* or 'Watch out for water!').

Flying into the Midden
Walk back down The Vennel and turn right into the Grassmarket. This long, cobbled rectangle below Castle Rock with stone tenement buildings on each side lies directly south of the Castle; until the early sixteenth century it lay just outside the city boundaries.

In 1477, James III (1451–1488) granted a charter for a market, originally mainly for farm produce, to be held here. James's court alchemist, Damien – who clearly fancied himself as the Scottish Leonardo da Vinci – attempted to fly from Castle Rock wearing a pair of wings he had made. Naturally, he failed, plummeting from the crag into the Grassmarket midden (dunghill) below, as a result of which fortunate if malodorous happenstance he amazingly survived the fall. His glib explanation for the failure was that he had made the wings from chicken feathers 'which sought the midden' as their natural habitat. His next pair of wings, he said, would be made from eagle feathers, which by their nature would seek to soar to the heavens. The image of eagle-winged Scots warriors swooping on the English invader from above is an attractive one but, sadly, history tells us no more of this medieval pioneer in aviation.

The oldest surviving buildings, however, date from the early eighteenth century. Today, shops – mostly quasi-bohemian boutiques – pubs and restaurants occupy the

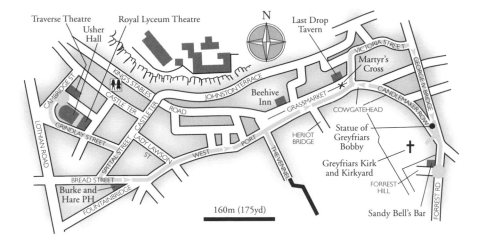

ground floor of most buildings, with flats above.

Towards the east end, a cross of pink-coloured setts (cobbles) marks the site of the gallows. Opposite, the sardonically named Last Drop Tavern – gallows humour at its most literal – recalls the days when the Grassmarket was a common place of public execution.

At the east end of the Grassmarket, Victoria Street is a striking, steeply curving street lined by tall tenement buildings, some up to nine storeys high, with a plentiful assortment of antique and designer shops at street level. If you are keen on shopping you will want to check this street out; either walk up one side to the top, where it joins George IV Bridge, and back down the opposite side to the Grassmarket, or at the top turn right on George IV Bridge and walk 150m (165yd) to the statue of Greyfriars Bobby and Greyfriars Kirk.

If you choose the first option, on your return to the Grassmarket leave it by Cowgatehead (so called because it was the route by which cattle were driven into the market) and walk up the steeply curving Candlemaker Row (where tallow candles were made out of the fat rendered down from cattle slaughtered nearby) to George IV Bridge and Edinburgh's most nauseatingly heart-warming landmark, the statue of Greyfriars Bobby.

Faithful to the Last

This twee, life-sized monument immortalizes the Skye terrier who, after the death in 1858 of his master, Police Constable John Gray, stood guard over his grave in the nearby kirkyard for fourteen years until his own death, thereby becoming a legend of canine devotion. Fed on scraps from a local tavern, the faithful Bobby became a Greyfriars fixture; his dog licence was paid for by the Lord Provost in a startling departure from the usually flinty-hearted attitude of such men, and the year after his death a public subscription paid for his statue, by the sculptor William Brodie, to be put up at the junction of George IV Bridge and Candlemaker Row. In 1961, the film *Greyfriars Bobby*, based on the tale, was released by Disney, the combination delivering to the stomach a double dose of tweedom that packed quite a punch – but this was as nothing compared to an earlier movie that was derived from the legend, *Challenge to Lassie* (1949).

Cross back to the west side of Candlemaker Row to enter Greyfriars Kirk and its kirkyard. The first kirk on this site was dedicated on Christmas Day, 1620. Within is the National Covenant, signed here on 28 February 1638. This is a document that rivals the Declaration of Arbroath as a testimony to the cross-grained, stubbornly independent will of the Scottish people to determine their own affairs. It is ironic that in 1679 the kirkyard was used as a prison for some fourteen hundred Covenanters captured after the Battle of Bothwell Brig.

The kirk and kirkyard stand on the site of a Franciscan friary built in the fifteenth century. Sacked by Cromwell's troops in 1650, the church was rebuilt in 1721 but burned down in 1845. The present building dates from the mid-nineteenth century, although it was again extensively restored in 1938.

Many of Edinburgh's best known citizens are buried in the churchyard, among them Greyfriars Bobby's master, PC Gray. Others include: James Craig (1744–1795), planner of the New Town; James Douglas (*c.* 1516–1581), fourth Earl of Morton, executed for his part in the murder of David Rizzio (or Riccio; *c.* 1533–1566), Mary Queen of Scots' Italian secretary; and Sir George Mackenzie of Rosehaugh (1636–1691). Lord Advocate of Scotland under James VII and II (1633–1701), Mackenzie was known as 'Bluidy [Bloody] Mackenzie' for his ruthless hounding of the Covenanters and other opponents of the Crown. Over the quarter century of the 'Killing Time', some 18,000 were executed for treason in Edinburgh alone. They are commemorated in Greyfriars Kirkyard, by the Martyrs' Monument, which stands at the Burial Gate in the northeast corner.

Turn right as you leave the kirkyard and find, on the corner of Forrest Road and Forrest Hill, Sandy Bell's Bar, which has been for generations a gathering place and a second home for Scottish traditional musicians. It's not unlikely that on any given afternoon or evening there will be some form of impromptu performance going on. Until the 1980s it was officially the Forrest Hill Bar, and known as Sandy Bell's only to regulars who remembered a long-ago landlord who – unlike most Edinburgh publicans in those days – actually welcomed musicians. To avoid confusion, it now bears the name Sandy Bell's above the door, a change deplored by many of its longer-standing aficionados, who maintain that the old system helped to keep the riffraff out.

Museums and the University

Summary: This walk takes us through Edinburgh's University and museum quarter, where there are some fine museum collections and public buildings. Edinburgh University has since the eighteenth century had an international reputation as a centre of learning in fields as diverse as law and divinity, philosophy, medicine, history and anatomy. Its alumni include the historian Thomas Carlyle (1795–1881), the authors Robert Louis Stevenson (1850–1894) and Arthur Conan Doyle (1859–1930), the father of evolutionary science Charles Darwin (1809–1882), the first president of Tanzania, Julius Nyerere (1922–), and the present British Chancellor of the Exchequer, Gordon Brown (1951–). The Royal Museum and the magnificent new Museum of Scotland are among the nation's finest.

Start/finish:	North end of George IV Bridge (corner of High Street).
Length:	2km (1¾ miles)
Time:	4hr.
Refreshments:	Café Couronne, Petite Couronne Tearoom, and Tower Restaurant, all at the Museum of Scotland.
	Nicolson's Restaurant, 6A Nicolson Street.
	Sandy Bell's Bar
Which day:	Tuesday to Friday.
To visit:	National Library of Scotland.
	Scottish Genealogy Society Library and Family History Centre.
	Museum of Scotland.
	Royal Museum.
	Talbot Rice Art Gallery.
	Sir Jules Thorne Historical Museum, Royal College of Surgeons.
	Reid Concert Hall, which holds the Edinburgh University Collection of Historic Musical Instruments.

Leaving the High Street, turn left onto George IV Bridge and walk a little under 100m (110yd) south, down the east pavement, to the National Library of Scotland.

A Bibliophile's Paradise
The National Library was founded in 1689 and, with the nation's finest collection of works and original documents (more than one million of them) covering every aspect of Scottish history and culture, it is one of the four largest libraries in Britain.

Books and documents are available for research; for the casual visitor, the changing programme of exhibitions is likely to be of greatest interest .

The institution began as the Advocates' Library. It was founded by Sir George Mackenzie of Rosehaugh (1636–1691), Lord Advocate of Scotland under James VII and II (1633–1701) and execrated by opponents of the Crown as 'Bluidy [Bloody] Mackenzie' (see page 72). Despite his ruthless crushing of dissent, he was a cultured and learned legal scholar, bequeathing his own collection of some 1,500 books as the core of the library.

He was, in fact, probably less bloody-minded than his Covenanter adversaries suggested: he was one of the first to begin to soften the law on witchcraft. Medieval Scots believed in witchcraft as a matter of course, but between 1560 and 1707 Scotland, like a number of other countries, including much of continental Europe, was seized by a witch craze. Accusations of witchcraft resulted in up to four and a half thousand people – mostly old women innocent of any sin more grievous than ugliness and/or senility – being tortured and then strangled, pressed (having heavy weights loaded onto their prone or supine bodies until they died of broken bones, internal injuries and suffocation), drowned, hanged (if they were lucky) or, rarely in Scotland, burned at the stake. Mackenzie was among the first to suggest that the practice of torturing anyone accused of witchcraft into confessing and naming her accomplices might not be the best legal practice – might indeed be contributing to the paranoid hysteria that surrounded accusations of witchcraft. But that is by the by.

The library that Mackenzie inaugurated became the National Library of Scotland only in 1925, and moved into its present building in 1956.

Family Trees and a Focus of Knowledge

Those with an interest in tracing their Scottish ancestry can now cross George IV Bridge to the Scottish Genealogy Society Library and Family History Centre, at 15 Victoria Terrace, where a large collection of books, microfilm and microfiche may help you to untangle the roots and branches of your family tree. Judging by surnames, there are tens of millions of people living abroad who can claim Scots descent to some degree, compared with only five million or so in Scotland itself.

Carry on up George IV Bridge, crossing over the deep trench of the Cowgate below, for 200m (220yd), then turn left into Chambers Street.

This broad, dignified street was built during the 1870s to connect George IV Bridge and South Bridge. With the brand new Museum of Scotland at its west end, the Royal Museum next to it and the grand, domed quadrangle of the Old College of Edinburgh University, housing the faculties of law and divinity, at its east end, Chambers Street has since the nineteenth century been a focus of knowledge and study. It is named after the famous publisher William Chambers (1800–1883), who was Lord Provost at the time and whose pet project it was.

The Museum of Scotland

Cross to the south side of Chambers Street and enter the Museum of Scotland, an award-winning modern building whose design echoes Scottish baronial architecture and which opened in 1998, appropriately enough on St Andrew's Day, 30 November.

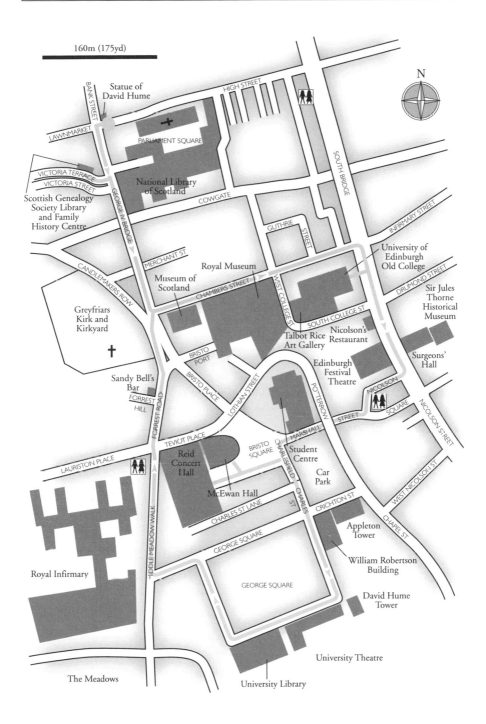

160m (175yd)

N

Statue of
David Hume

HIGH STREET

PARLIAMENT SQUARE

BANK STREET

LAWNMARKET

SOUTH BRIDGE

VICTORIA TERRACE

VICTORIA STREET

Scottish Genealogy
Society Library
and Family
History Centre

National Library
of Scotland

COWGATE

GEORGE IV BRIDGE

CANDLEMAKERS ROW

MERCHANT ST

GUTHRIE STREET

INFIRMARY STREET

University of
Edinburgh
Old College

Royal Museum

Museum of
Scotland

CHAMBERS STREET

WEST COLLEGE ST

DRUMOND STREET

Sir Jules
Thorne
Historical
Museum

Greyfriars
Kirk and
Kirkyard

SOUTH COLLEGE ST

Nicolson's
Restaurant

Talbot Rice
Art Gallery

Surgeons'
Hall

Sandy Bell's
Bar

BRISTO PORT

BRISTO PLACE

LOTHIAN STREET

Edinburgh
Festival
Theatre

NICOLSON

NICOLSON SQUARE

NICOLSON STREET

FORREST HILL

FORREST ROAD

POTTERROW

STREET

TEVIOT PLACE

LAURISTON PLACE

Reid
Concert
Hall

BRISTO SQUARE

Student
Centre

Car
Park

WEST NICOLSON ST

McEwan Hall

CHARLESFIELD

CHARLES ST

CRICHTON ST

CHAPEL ST

CHARLES ST LANE

Appleton
Tower

MIDDLE MEADOW WALK

MARSHALL

GEORGE SQUARE

William Robertson
Building

Royal Infirmary

GEORGE SQUARE

David Hume
Tower

The Meadows

University Library

University Theatre

75

You will need at least an hour and preferably two for even a cursory look at this superb, brilliantly laid-out collection covering every aspect of Scotland's fascinating past.

The Museum of Scotland covers seven floors, ascending in chronological order. Start at the basement (Level 0), where there are displays devoted to Scotland's geology and archaeology. Imaginatively displayed exhibits range from wonderful Iron Age jewellery, including gold brooches and arm-rings, to the hoard of Roman silver found at Traprain Law and the Roman statue of a lioness mauling her victim found in the River Almond at Cramond. The first floor highlights the creation of the Kingdom of the Scots and the fusion of Saxon, Scot, Pict, Viking and Norman into a Scottish identity, with displays of tools and weapons, including the huge, two-handed swords known as claymores (from the Gaelic, meaning 'big sword'); they make the much shorter, basket-hilted Highland broadsword (often mistakenly called the claymore) look like a toy.

Exhibits on the third floor highlight Scotland's transformation from medieval times through to the Union, with superb displays of clothing, furniture, tools and documents. One of the more gruesome highlights is the Maiden, the Scottish forerunner of the French Revolutionary guillotine; an interactive computer display shows how it works. Grim though it is, the Maiden was, like the guillotine, actually intended to be more merciful than the executioner's axe. Unlike the headsman, the Maiden never missed, guaranteeing its victims a rapid demise.

The fourth and fifth floors cover the Industrial Revolution and the heyday of the British Empire, and the sixth floor takes you up to the present day.

The Royal Museum

Completing your tour of the Museum of Scotland here, take the lift down to the first floor and cross by the connecting walkway into the adjoining Royal Museum, a striking Victorian building built in 1861 and distinguished by its huge, glass-roofed atrium which ascends the full 21m (69ft) height of the building, with displays on mezzanine floors at each level. The walkway connects with the Royal Museum's first floor and its ancient-Egyptian collection.

Walking clockwise around the first-floor mezzanine takes you through the Royal Museum's gallery of modern Western decorative art, ceramics and glass. From the ceramics section, turn left into the collection of European art, which dates from 1200 to the present day. Highlights include German woodcarving, French eighteenth-century silverware, and religious objects, many of which date from the early Middle Ages.

Walk straight on through the door at the south end of the gallery, turn right through the plaster-cast gallery and take the lift to the ground floor. Exiting the lift, turn left into the Museum's science and industry section, which has a fascinating collection of working model steam engines as well as the world's oldest locomotive – George Stephenson's *Rocket* – and the world's oldest glider.

Turn right at the north end of this hall, go through the sculpture display and the café, and leave the Royal Museum by the main door on your left. Turn right along Chambers Street and cross West College Street. Continue to the corner of South Bridge and turn right.

Into Old Varsityland

Edinburgh University Old College occupies the entire block bounded by Chambers Street, South Bridge, West College Street and South College Street. Kirk o' Field, where Mary Queen of Scots' second husband Lord Darnley (*c.* 1545–1567) was strangled and his lodgings blown up in 1567, stood in what is now the southeast corner of the quadrangle. Begun by the ubiquitous Robert Adam (1728–1792) in 1789 and completed by William Playfair (1789–1857) between 1817 and 1824, it replaced the crumbling buildings of the university which, by the mid-eighteenth century, were in poor condition – although, paradoxically, Edinburgh's standing as a centre of academic brilliance had never been greater.

Old College is a grand building – perhaps Adam's finest. It deserves to be seen from a distance, amid open space; unfortunately it is surrounded by narrow streets and is, sadly, impossible to see in proportion. The long entrance frontage has a central arch flanked by two smaller arches, each of which is enclosed within a massive Doric portico with two columns that match those either side of the main arch. Almost 1m (3ft) thick and 7m (22ft) high, each column is a single piece of Craigleith stone. A high, domed vault and a large semicircular window crown the central archway.

Walk through this and across the quadrangle to the southwest corner and the Talbot Rice Art Gallery. This gallery houses the University's permanent Torrie Collection – mainly of Dutch and Flemish seventeenth-century painters – and has a changing schedule of exhibitions.

The Royal College of Surgeons

Leave by the grand archway, turn right, and walk down the west side of Nicolson Street, past the fine new Edinburgh Festival Theatre. Immediately opposite is another building by William Playfair, the Ionic-columned Surgeons' Hall, completed in 1832. Not open to the public, this is the headquarters of the Royal College of Surgeons in Scotland; next to it is the inconspicuous Old Surgeons' Hall which it replaced, and where the notorious William Burke (1792–1829) and William Hare (1790–*c.* 1860) brought the bodies of their victims to sell to the anatomist Robert Knox (1791–1862).

At the rear of the Royal College of Surgeons, at 18 Nicolson Street, is the Sir Jules Thorne Historical Museum. Here there is an exhibition outlining Edinburgh's contribution to medicine and surgery, with artefacts connected with notable Edinburgh medical men including Sir Charles Bell (1774-1842), the Edinburgh professor of surgery who discovered the distinct functions of the nerves, and Joseph Lister (1827–1912), pioneer of antiseptics and thus – with another Edinburgh medical man, James Young Simpson (1811–1870), who introduced chloroform as an anaesthetic – one of the fathers of modern surgery. There is also a grisly collection of early medical and surgical instruments which is guaranteed to make you feel profoundly grateful to both men.

Matters Musical

Walk on and turn right into Nicolson Square, walk across this, and leave by Marshall Street, crossing Potterrow to the main campus of the University of Edinburgh. Walk to the end of Marshall Street, and cross Charlesfield to Bristo Square and the McEwan Hall.

Like the Usher Hall on Lothian Road, the McEwan Hall was the gift of one of the great Edinburgh brewing families, and like the Usher Hall it impresses more through size than through grace. It is used mainly for concerts and for University graduation ceremonies.

Walk around the McEwan Hall to Reid Concert Hall, behind it, and the Edinburgh University Collection of Historic Musical Instruments, housed within. The collection contains more than fifteen hundred musical instruments from all over the world, including seven hundred woodwinds, three hundred brass and two hundred and fifty stringed instruments in addition to the percussion and other acoustic sections. There are also, of course, bagpipes, often thought of as uniquely and typically Scottish, but in fact found all over Europe and the Middle East, as far afield as Tunisia and the Epirus region of Greece.

Palaces of Learning

Unlike the rest of Britain's most venerated universities, Edinburgh University did not grow up out of a medieval cathedral school, but came into being as the result of a 1582 charter of James VI and I (1566–1625). Even in Scotland, it is junior to St Andrews and Glasgow, but it made its reputation as the home of the Scottish Enlightenment during the second half of the eighteenth century.

Two boxy modern buildings dating from the 1960s – the William Robertson Building at the corner of George Square and Crichton Street, and the Appleton Tower next to it – greet you as you approach George Square.

The first is named for the historian William Robertson (1721–1793), principal of the University 1762–1793, and houses the faculty of social sciences. Highly regarded by fellow scholars, Robertson had the misfortune to have as a contemporary the great Edward Gibbon (1737–1794), author of *The Decline and Fall of the Roman Empire* (1776–1788), so perhaps he has not been accorded the reputation he deserves.

The Appleton Tower is named after the physicist and Nobel prize winner Sir Edward Appleton (1892–1965), principal of the University in 1949, whose research proved integral to the development of both radar and the atom bomb.

George Square was one of the most fashionable addresses in Edinburgh during the late eighteenth century, being only gradually replaced in this respect by the New Town. Among those who lived there was Sir Walter Scott (1771–1832), whose father built No. 25, where the family lived from 1774 until 1797. Henry Dundas (1742–1811), first Viscount Melville and Baron Dunira, was another famous resident, as was Scotland's notorious hanging judge, Lord Braxfield (1722–1799), still remembered in the legal annals for his grim response to a radical brought before him for sentencing. The accused pointed out that 'even our Saviour Jesus Christ himself' had been a radical reformer. 'Muckle [much] he made o' that,' said Braxfield dourly. 'He was hanget [hanged].' Braxfield was also said to have pronounced sentence of death on an old chess opponent with the words: 'And there's check to you, Jeemy.' Charming man.

Today the square is surrounded by rather starkly functional 1960s buildings, notably the bunker-like University Library, a six-storey glass and concrete monster which until the opening of the new British Library in London in 1998 had the distinction of being Europe's largest library.

At the southeast corner of George Square, the David Hume Tower is a monument to the philosopher and historian David Hume (1711–1776), sceptic, champion of empirical metaphysics and leading light of the Scottish Enlightenment of the late eighteenth century. Hume's rigorously empirical approach, exemplified in his *Philosophical Essays* (1748), *Enquiry concerning Principles of Morals* (1751), *Political Discourses* (1752), *Four Dissertations* (1757) and *Dialogues on Natural Religion* (1779), indicated a landmark in the disciple of metaphysics. An inept and unconvincing modern statue of Hume, incongruously draped in the robes of a philosopher of ancient Greece, sits on the High Street next to the junction with George IV Bridge, opposite St Giles Cathedral, near your start/finish point for this walk.

Walk around George Square to the northwest corner, turn left, then right on Middle Meadow Walk, which connects The Meadows park with Teviot Place. Cross Teviot Place and walk along Forrest Road back to George IV Bridge to return to your starting point.

Blackford Hill and the Braid Hills

Summary: South of the University of Edinburgh campus at George Square is the broad green expanse of The Meadows. Like the Nor' Loch (see page 56) on the other side of town, this was marshland until the eighteenth century, when it was drained and turned into a park where the city's gentry paraded in their finery until the New Town supplanted George Square as Edinburgh's most fashionable quarter. South of The Meadows are the genteel nineteenth-century middle-class suburbs of Marchmont, Newington and Morningside. Blackford Hill and its observatory, and beyond that the Braid Hills, rise above the serried ranks of solidly respectable sandstone tenements, all with the Pentland Hills as a distant backdrop.

Start:	The crossroads of Peffermill Road, Niddrie Mains Road, Craigmillar Castle Road and Duddingston Road West.
Finish:	Blackford Avenue.
Length:	11km (3¾ miles).
Time:	3–4hr.
Refreshments:	Pubs and cafés are thin on the ground in these residential suburbs, so schedule your walk such that you can return to the city centre at an appropriate time for sustenance.
Which day:	Any day.
To visit:	Craigmillar Castle.
	Royal Observatory Visitor Centre.

Leave the bus (number 14, 42 or 46 from the city centre) at the crossroads of Peffermill Road, Niddrie Mains Road, Craigmillar Castle Road and Duddingston Road West. Turn right and walk for about ten minutes along Craigmillar Castle Road, which leads you, predictably enough, to the picturesque ruin of Craigmillar Castle in its own grounds on your right.

A Quondam Stately Home

Craigmillar Castle is, like so many Scottish castles, a fortress in miniature. It has a dramatic history. Its L-plan tower, typical of medieval Scottish baronial castles, dates from 1374, and its defences were strengthened in 1427 when it was surrounded by a curtain wall. This failed to deter the Earl of Hertford's army from taking and burning it in 1544, during the 'Rough Wooing', after which it was strengthened still further. Mary Queen of Scots (1542–1587) took refuge here after the murder of her Italian secretary, David Rizzio (or Riccio; c. 1533–1566), at Holyrood, it being the most strongly fortified castle outside the city, with corner towers, gunports, projecting parapets that can still be seen today and walls that are up to 4m (13ft) thick.

Craigmillar was not just a garrison stronghold, however, but an aristocratic home, and the alterations that gradually made it more homely also weakened its defences. The walls were pierced in several places to provide greater ease of access, and this no doubt made it a much simpler matter for the English to take it in 1544.

It took again the status of a stately home rather than a fortress as southern Scotland became a more peaceable place in the late seventeenth century, but like many similar small castles it was abandoned by its owners after the defeat of the Jacobite cause in 1745, and the final pacification of Scotland meant it was no longer necessary for Scottish lairds to live within walls that could be easily defended from attack. By the early 1800s, Craigmillar Castle was a roofless ruin, and it is likely to remain so.

Liberton Tower and a Lot of Golf

Leaving the Castle, turn right and walk 200m (220yd) along Craigmillar Castle Road to Old Dalkeith Road, turn right again, cross the road and take the first left, Kingston Avenue. Follow Kingston Avenue along the north side of Liberton Golf Course to Gilmerton Road. Cross this and continue along Mount Vernon Road for 600m (650yd) to Kirk Brae. Turn right, and continue to the foot of Kirk Brae and its junction with Liberton Road. Cross Liberton Road and turn left on Blackford Glen Road, signposted 'Hermitage of Braid'. Follow this along the south boundary of the private Craigmillar Park Golf Course and turn left, crossing the Braid Burn, towards the steeply rising north slope of the Braid Hills, on Howe Dean path, following signposts to the public Braid Hills Golf Course. The path climbs steeply out of the valley of the Braid Burn to Braid Hills Drive. Turn left here and walk for a further 500m (550yd).

On your left, the next landmark is Liberton Tower, a bleak-looking contemporary of Craigmillar Castle, built in or around 1500. Liberton, like these other former villages on the southern fringe of the city, was a separate community as recently as 1920, when Edinburgh suffered an attack of urban sprawl that absorbed a crescent of separate villages that ran from Juniper Green in the southwest round through Corstorphine, Colinton, Swanston, Liberton and Gilmerton.

The interior of the Tower holds little of interest, so cross Braid Hills Drive and follow the footpath up the shallow slope, along the east edge of the Braid Hills Golf Course, for 500m (550yd) more before turning right to walk along the ridge. Below you on your left as you walk, beyond the golf driving range, are disused gun emplacements dating from World War II. Beyond them, in turn, is Liberton House, built in a typical L-plan by the laird of Liberton around 1600 and noticeably more civilized-looking than its neighbours.

A City Built on Seven Hills, Like Rome . . .

The path along the crest of the hills passes between the Braid Golf Course and the much more expensive and exclusive Mortonhall Golf Course for about something over a kilometre (½ mile) before you come to the Seven Hills Outlook Indicator. From this hilltop beacon – 207m (680ft) above sea level – there is a fine view of the city and the seven hills on which it stands.

These seven hills – in clockwise order, Calton Hill, Arthur's Seat, Blackford Hill, Braid Hill, Craiglockhart Hill, Corstorphine Hill and Castle Rock – make up the circuit of the annual Seven Hills Race, held in June and starting and finishing on Calton Hill. Entry is open to all, and the challenge is to complete the 24km (15 mile) course in less than four hours. The course record is a startling 1 hour 32 minutes.

Reaching for the Stars

From the indicator, keep along the path for 200m (220yd) west, and then turn right to follow it as it zigzags downhill, around the edge of the golf course and back to Braid Hills Drive. Leave the golf course by the gate at the west side of the car park, cross Braid Hills Drive once again, and take Lang Linn Path down into the Braid Glen. Cross the stream and follow the signposted footpath around the flank of Blackford Hill to the Royal Observatory, just below the crest of the hill.

The original Royal Observatory was on top of Calton Hill, but by the end of

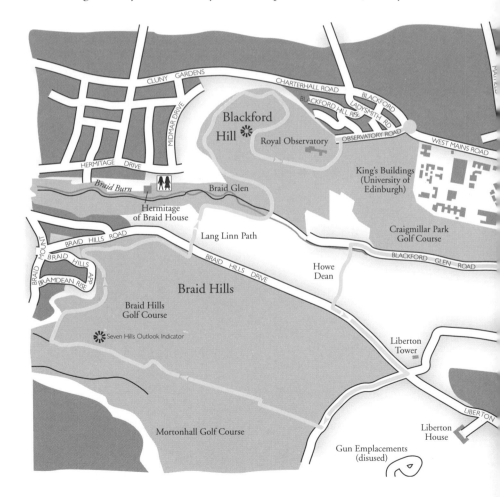

the nineteenth century, Edinburgh's rapid growth, coupled with advances in the technology of street and domestic lighting, made that site less suitable. The Observatory's 36in (91cm) telescope is the largest in Scotland. Displays in the visitor centre include hands-on exhibits, CD-ROMs about space and astronomy, striking computer-enhanced pictures from deep-space probes like *Mariner* and *Voyager* and from the orbital Hubble Telescope, and exhibits highlighting the Observatory's ongoing collaboration with other observatories, including institutions in Hawaii and Australia. Permanent exhibits include: The Universe, a journey through time from the Big Bang to the present day; Reaching for the Stars, outlining the development of the Observatory since it opened just over a century ago; and Star Chamber, where displays explain the scientific advances that have made breakthroughs like radio astronomy and the Hubble Telescope possible.

After you leave the visitor centre, walk back down Observatory Road to the corner of Blackford Avenue to catch a 40 or a 41 bus back to the city centre.

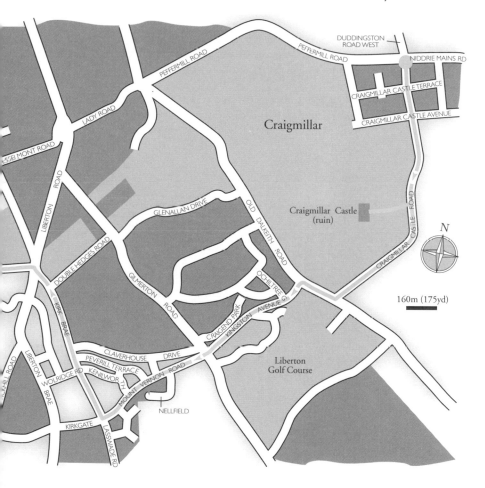

Around Stockbridge

Summary: This walk takes you from the elegant if austere terraces of the New Town through one of the most atmospheric village areas of the city, the eclectic district of Stockbridge, where a mixture of Victorian and Georgian buildings and streets is in pleasant contrast to the disciplined geometry of the New Town. Stockbridge owes much of its development to the painter Sir Henry Raeburn (1756–1823), who was born here, and has been home to a number of other painters and authors, among them the opium-taking writer Thomas de Quincey (1785–1859). It still retains a certain bohemian ambience.

Steep streets, some of them cobbled, lead downhill from the upper New Town to the lower streets and Stockbridge. Watch your step in icy winter weather, when the going on these steep pavements can be tricky.

Start:	Moray Place, just north of Queen Street.
Finish:	You have a choice of three options – Raeburn Place, the Royal Botanic Garden, or the Inverleith Row/Inverleith Terrace corner.
Length:	3.5km (2 miles).
Time:	2hr.
Refreshments:	Pâtisserie Florentin, North West Circus Place.
	Blue Parrot Cantina, St Stephen Street.
	Other cafés and restaurants in St Stephen Street.
Which day:	Not Saturday or Sunday.
To visit:	St Stephen's Church.
	Open Eye Gallery.
	Museum of Lighting.

This part of the city was until 1822 open country, the estate of the Earl of Moray. At that time, the current incumbent decided to cash in on the growth of the city by developing his land into an elegant residential area. The entire project was planned in elaborate detail, with Moray specifying not only the ground plan but the design of everything from stables to garden railings.

The centrepiece of the entire development, which was designed by the architect James Gillespie Graham (1777–1855), is Moray Place, where the walk starts: a grand twelve-sided circus with a circular central garden surrounded by almost overwhelmingly grand, four-storey houses. Each side is punctuated by a pedimented, four-columned centrepiece, and the arched ground-floor windows have decorative fanlights.

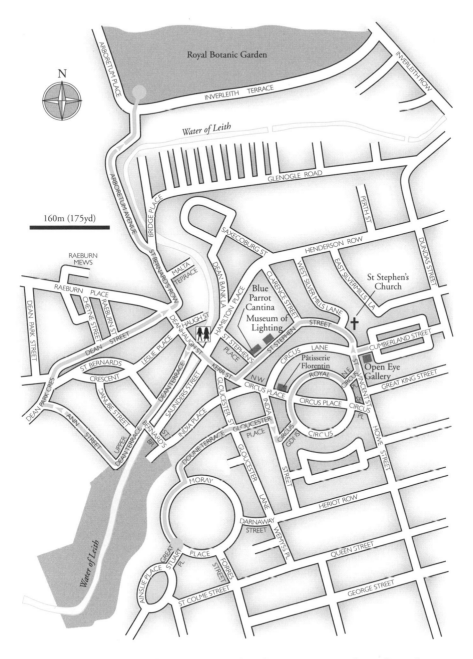

Among the leading lights of the Edinburgh aristocratic and intellectual scene who lived here during Moray Place's nineteenth-century heyday were the Earl of Moray himself, whose home was at No. 28; Baron Hume (1757-1838), judge, professor of law, nephew of the philosopher David Hume (1711–1776) and friend of Sir Walter Scott (1771–1832), at No. 34; and Francis Jeffrey (1773-1850), founder and editor of the controversial *Edinburgh Review* – controversial because Jeffrey, an ardent Whig, was strongly at odds with the prevalent Tory politics of his contemporary Edinburgh.

Though the grand façades have survived intact, most of these stately townhouses have long been subdivided into flats and offices, but it is not hard even today to imagine the grandees of Edinburgh arriving in carriages to dine elegantly at Moray Place.

A Vast Church

Leave Moray Place by Doune Terrace, which leads off its north side and curves steeply to your right. Cross Gloucester Street and walk along Gloucester Place to India Street. Turn right, then immediately left into Circus Gardens, and you come almost at once into Royal Circus. Turn left and walk around the northern crescent, which is lined with well proportioned three-storey buildings in typical New Town style; these are the work of William Playfair (1789–1857), architect of Old College (see page 77), the National Gallery of Scotland (see page 58) and much of the New Town (see pages 62–67).

Playfair also designed the gigantic church which greets you as you leave Royal Circus by North East Circus Place and turn left down St Vincent Street, named for a naval victory of the French Revolutionary War. Completed in 1828, St Stephen's Church combines the impact of Baroque with Classical discipline and, with its 50m (160ft) tower, is one of the most prominent landmarks of the northern New Town. Playfair designed it so that it could seat sixteen hundred; in the less devout twentieth century it became far too big for its dwindling congregation, and so was split in two horizontally, the lower part being turned into a separate hall.

Just before you reach this towering landmark, detour right into Cumberland Street to visit the Open Eye Gallery at Nos. 77-79. This gallery of fine and contemporary art hosts up to twenty exhibitions a year and is an excellent place to see the work of up-and-coming Scottish and international artists. It also specializes in prints from the early twentieth century.

Adventures in Bohemia

Returning to the west end of Cumberland Street, turn right into St Stephen Street. For anyone looking for something different to bring home from a visit to Edinburgh – rather than the tartan tat and Celtic kitsch which dominates so much of the city's tourist shopping – this street, which curves first northwest then back southwest, is a delight. It is packed with small antique and junk shops, selling everything from stamps and militaria to etchings, ceramics and the recycled fashions of bygone decades. Designed as a shopping street and market in the 1820s, its buildings have shops or cafés at street and basement level, with two storeys of flats above. In among the antique shops are scattered trendy clothing and crafts shops. All in all, this is the most attractively bohemian street in Edinburgh, if a little bit twee in places – vegetarian cafés, yoga, crystals and herbal healing seem to be very much in vogue here.

Midway along St Stephen Street, on the north side, the Museum of Lighting displays lights and lamps through the ages, from early tallow candles and rushlights to the whale-oil streetlamps that illuminated Edinburgh streets before the coming of gas in the nineteenth century and electricity in the twentieth. As recently as the 1970s, some streets in Stockbridge were still lit by gas lamps.

Raeburn Territory

At the end of St Stephen Street, turn right on Kerr Street, cross the Water of Leith as it flows through the heart of Stockbridge, and turn left on Dean Terrace. Follow this attractive street of two-storey, nineteenth-century houses, overlooking the Water of Leith, and at the end turn right into Ann Street, which is one of the prettiest streets in Edinburgh, with its beautifully detailed two- and three-storey townhouses set amid attractive gardens.

Among former residents was John Wilson (1785–1854), professor of moral philosophy at Edinburgh University and, under the pen-name Christopher North, an esteemed journalist and editor of the influential literary magazine *Blackwood's*. Wilson was elected to the chair of moral philosophy because of his strong Tory loyalties; surprising, then, to find that among his guests in 1829 was the notorious Thomas de Quincey, a fellow philosopher but also the author of *Confessions of an English Opium-eater* (1822) and a self-confessed laudanum addict. Perhaps the Tories had a softer line on drugs in those days.

At the end of Ann Street, turn right onto Dean Park Crescent and continue down Dean Street to its junction with Raeburn Place. This – like Raeburn Mews and Raeburn Street on either side – is named for Sir Henry Raeburn, the greatest of Scottish portraitists, the 'Scottish [Sir Joshua] Reynolds'. More than fifty of his portraits of Scottish notables can be seen in the Scottish National Portrait Gallery (see page 63) and the National Gallery of Scotland (see page 58), and many more hang in Scottish country houses. Raeburn is said to have painted every contemporary of note except Robert Burns (1759–1796). At the age of 22, he married a wealthy widow, Ann Leslie, and this allowed him the luxury of studying and perfecting his art in Rome before returning to Edinburgh in 1787. Here, as well as rapidly becoming Scotland's most fashionable society portraitist, he added to the property his wife had inherited in Scotland, and in 1813 he turned property developer. Ann Street is named after his wife.

Cross Raeburn Place and enter St Bernard's Row, then take the first left, Arboretum Avenue, to visit the Royal Botanic Garden (see page 96 for details of this park). Alternatively, end your walk here and catch a bus back to the city centre. As a third option, you could stroll along Arboretum Avenue and Inverleith Terrace to begin the Leith to Newhaven walk (see page 98).

Heriot's to the Zoo

Summary: This walk takes in two of Edinburgh's more esoteric museums as well as two attractions for animal lovers. It also offers you an opportunity to sample some of the ales of the city in the place where they are brewed.

Start:	Corner of Forrest Road and Lauriston Place.
Finish:	Edinburgh Zoo.
Length:	8km (5 miles) including Zoo visit; 5km (3 miles) if you decide to skip the Zoo (which you are strongly advised not to do).
Time:	All day, if you include the Zoo.
Refreshments:	Pubs and cafés en route.
	Café and restaurant at the Zoo.
Which day:	Any day.
To visit:	Museum of Fire.
	Scout Museum.
	King's Theatre.
	Fountain Brewery.
	Gorgie City Farm.
	Edinburgh Zoo.

Since this excursion starts at the corner of Forrest Road and Lauriston Place, you might like to connect it up with the Museums and University walk (see page 73) or with the Old Town walk (see page 68).

From the corner, walk west along Lauriston Place, keeping to the north pavement. On your right after about 100m (110yd) you will see the imposing buildings of George Heriot's School, founded with the legacy of 'Jinglin' Geordie' Heriot (1563–1624), court jeweller during the reign of James VI and I (1566–1625). One of Edinburgh's greatest benefactors, Heriot was one of the many Scottish carpet-baggers who followed James to London on his accession to the English throne, and prospered exceedingly. He left his fortune to be used for the schooling of orphaned sons of freemen of the city, and work was begun four years after his death on a building to house them. Heriot's Hospital, as it was initially called, was delayed by the troubles and civil wars of the first half of the seventeenth century. It was used as a barracks and a military hospital during the Cromwellian occupation of 1650–1658, and finally completed the following year, when thirty boys entered its gates. With its arcaded quadrangle and clocktower, it is one of the most imposing seventeenth-century buildings in the city and is considered one of Scotland's most respected schools.

Hospitals and Infernos

Continue along Lauriston Place, with the functional buildings of the Royal Infirmary and the Simpson Memorial Maternity Hospital on your left.

The Simpson is named after Sir James Young Simpson (1811–1870), professor of midwifery and pioneer of chloroform as an anaesthetic in childbirth. His success was assured when Queen Victoria (1819–1901) used it in 1853 during the birth of Prince Leopold (1853–1884), later Duke of Albany. Simpson would entertain friends by telling the story of how he and two colleagues first experimented with chloroform and of how, after inhaling the vapour, '. . . we were all under the table in a trice'.

Some 400m (440yd) after starting out, turn right into Lady Lawson Street and enter the Fire Brigade Headquarters and the Museum of Fire. Guided tours around the Museum and its collection of uniforms, equipment and engines, from horse-drawn wagons with man-powered pumps to more recent machines, should be arranged in advance (Tel: [0131] 228 2401).

Looking at Edinburgh today, a city of stone and concrete, it is hard to imagine how frequently and easily fire could sweep through the town. But tall buildings with wood-fitted interiors and cloth hangings for warmth, lit by candles and whale-oil or paraffin lamps and jammed closely together, could be a recipe for disaster. On the night of 15 November 1824, for example, fire broke out in a house just off the Royal Mile, and over the next forty-eight hours some four hundred homes and many public buildings between the High Street and the Cowgate were destroyed. Among the casualties was the Tron Kirk steeple (see page 33), though firemen managed to prevent the blaze spreading to the rest of the church. This absorbing museum is well worth the effort of making that telephone call!

Art of Camping

Leaving the Museum of Fire, return to Lauriston Place, cross it, and turn left onto Lauriston Gardens. Follow this for about 300m (330yd) and then turn right onto Lonsdale Terrace. Go along this to its west end, cross Brougham Street, and walk briefly along Leven Terrace, which curves to your left. Take the first on your right, Valleyfield Street, to the Scout Museum, where you will be treated to an exhibition of the history of the Scout movement in Edinburgh and around the world, including photographs, uniforms and badges. This is, admittedly, not a museum to suit all tastes, and you may choose to bypass it altogether – but it is actually more interesting than it sounds, so think twice before you do.

At the west end of Valleyfield Street, turn right onto Leven Street, past the King's Theatre at the junction of Leven Street and Home Street. Opened in 1906, the King's was restored inside and out in 1985, and is one of Edinburgh's premier venues for ballet, opera, drama, dance and comedy. If you are taking this walk during the Edinburgh Festival, you will probably find that the King's is hosting a variety of performances through the day and into the small hours. A substantial red sandstone exterior protects a cheerfully frivolous Edwardian baroque interior, with red velvet seats, a powder-blue dome and fancy plasterwork and gilt, that really begs for Can Can girls, saucy actresses and cads with side-whiskers and stovepipe hats.

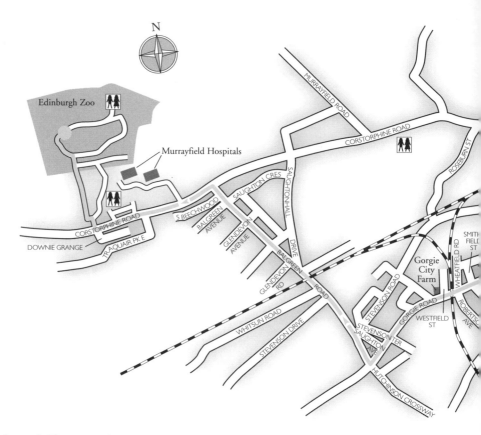

Art of Glass

Walk on along Home Street, over the unprepossessing junction of West Tollcross, and on down Earl Grey Street for 200m (220yd) to turn left into Fountainbridge. By now your nose, if the wind is in the right quarter (from the west), will have begun to detect one of the characteristic odours of western Edinburgh: the reek of roasting barley and hops that indicates the presence of brewing beer. Carry on along Fountainbridge for 600m (650yd) to discover the source: the Fountain Brewery, owned by Scottish & Newcastle Breweries.

This is no place for a real-ale purist: Scottish & Newcastle produces some of the least 'real' ale around, including Newcastle Brown Ale and Tartan Special. To its credit, the brewery, under pressure from enthusiasts, has also been persuaded that there is a market for tastier, more traditional ales as well as fizzy, pasteurised products that last almost indefinitely in a can or bottle.

Oddly enough, one of the Brewery's major export markets is Belgium, which has a national taste for sweet, powerfully alcoholic Scottish ales in tiny bottles. Known in Scotland as 'wee heavies', these find little favour these days in their native land, but the Belgians still have a taste for them, and if you ask for a 'Scotch' in a Brussels

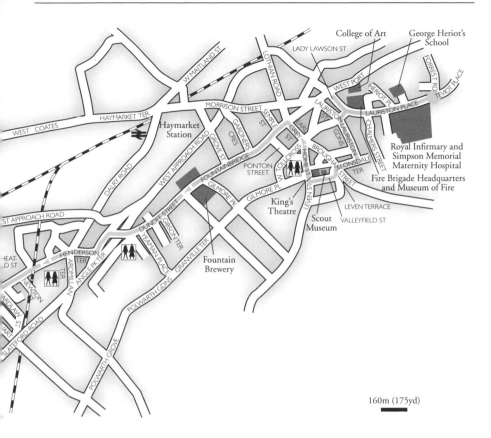

College of Art
George Heriot's School
LADY LAWSON ST
LOTHIAN ROAD
W. MAITLAND ST.
WEST PORT
HERIOT PL
FORREST RD
TEVIOT PLACE
MORRISON STREET
HAYMARKET TER.
WEST COATES
Haymarket Station
GROVE ST.
GARDNERS CRES.
SEMPLE ST.
EARL GREY ST.
LAURISTON ST.
LAURISTON GDNS.
LAURISTON PLACE
CHALMERS STREET
WEST APPROACH ROAD
FOUNTAINBRIDGE
PONTON STREET
W. TOLLCROSS
HOME ST.
BROUGHAM ST.
LONSDALE TER.
Royal Infirmary and Simpson Memorial Maternity Hospital
Fire Brigade Headquarters and Museum of Fire
DALRY ROAD
GILMORE PK.
GILMORE PL.
LEVEN ST.
King's Theatre
LEVEN TERRACE
ST APPROACH ROAD
DUNDEE STREET
GIBSON TER.
YEAMAN PLACE
GRANVILLE TER.
Scout Museum
VALLEYFIELD ST.
HEAT-D ST
HENDERSON TER.
ANGLE PK TER.
ARDMILLAN TER.
Fountain Brewery
NEWTON ST.
ARDLAW ST.
POLWARTH GDNS.
POLWARTH GROVE
SLATEFORD ROAD

160m (175yd)

bar you are more likely to get one of these than a glass of whisky.

There are brewery tours twice daily (10.15 and 14.15) that take you from beginning to end of the brewing process in what is claimed to be Britain's most highly automated brewery, with a canning line that fills fifteen hundred cans a minute. Some might argue that a bit less automation and a few more jobs might actually produce a better pint.

Animals, Domesticated and Otherwise

Leaving the brewery, walk westward for 500m (550yd) on Dundee Street, then turn right on Henderson Terrace. This leads you quickly to the junction of Gorgie Road with Ardmillan Terrace and Dalry Road, two main traffic arteries. Cross to the north side of Gorgie Road and continue west to No. 51 and the Gorgie City Farm.

Set up in 1982 on a one-hectare (2½-acre) patch of disused land, the farm is a favourite with kids: there are sheep, goats, pigs, ducks, hens and a Shetland pony, as well as the farm's own organic vegetable garden – though whether anything so close to the heavy traffic of Gorgie Road can really be 'organic' is open to question.

From the farm, walk on west along Gorgie Road, passing the Tynecastle ground

91

of Heart of Midlothian Football Club, one of Edinburgh's two major football teams. As in Glasgow (where Celtic traditionally commands the loyalties of Catholics and Rangers those of Protestants), support for the two teams is at least partly predicated on religious affiliation. In Edinburgh's case, it is the Hibernians (Hibs) that are traditionally identified with the city's Roman Catholic community and Hearts with the Protestants.

At Balgreen Road, turn right and walk north for some 600m (650yd) to Corstorphine Road. Cross the road and turn left, and after about 200m (220yd) more you will find yourself at the entrance to Edinburgh Zoo.

Founded in 1913, the Zoo occupies 32ha (80 acres) of steep hillside on the slope of the Corstorphine Hill and contains over fifteen hundred mammals, birds, reptiles and fishes, most of them in managed breeding programmes in cooperation with other zoos and conservation agencies. Key attractions within include the African Plains Experience, with zebra, ostrich and oryx viewed from a high walkway above their enclosure; a new Asiatic Lion Enclosure, giving the Zoo's endangered Asian lions a vast space in which to roam; and a herd of Przhevalski's (or Przewalski's, depending on the transliteration system used) horse, the last surviving subspecies of wild horses, a curious-looking creature that was saved from what seemed inevitable extinction, primarily by the efforts of Edinburgh Zoo.

The Zoo also has the world's largest penguin enclosure, with a deep-water pool in which you can view the birds beneath the surface through underwater viewing windows. For children of all ages the highlight of a visit to the Zoo is the Penguin Parade, held daily at 14.00 between April and September, in which the penguins are led among the visitors in a troupe on their way to be fed.

There is a very great deal to be seen at Edinburgh Zoo, far more than could be sensibly listed, let alone described, in this book, and you will probably want to spend the rest of the day here. One point that should be obvious but had better be mentioned anyway: if you have brought a picnic lunch with you, do not be tempted to feed any leftovers to the animals – your 'kindness' would in fact be a cruelty.

The Water of Leith: Dean Village, Stockbridge and the Botanic Garden

Summary: The Water of Leith is something between a small river and a large stream. At first sight its brownish waters look less than pristine, but nothing could be further from the truth; the colouring comes from the peat moors of the Pentland Hills, where it has its source. It is, in fact, clean enough to support healthy numbers of brown trout, which can be seen idling in pools and shadows beneath its bridges.

The designated Water of Leith Walkway is one of Edinburgh's most pleasant walks. Leading through patches of woodland and attractive village areas within the city, it is an ideal itinerary for a summer day.

Start:	Roseburn Park.
Finish:	Royal Botanic Garden/Inverleith Row.
Length:	8km (5 miles).
Time:	5hr.
Refreshments:	Numerous bars and restaurants in Dean Village and Stockbridge. Dill's Snack Bar and Terrace Café in the Royal Botanic Garden.
Which day:	Any day.
To visit:	Scottish National Gallery of Modern Art. Dean Gallery. Royal Botanic Garden. Inverleith House.

Reach Roseburn Park using any of buses 7A, 8, 23, 27 and 37 from the city centre. Enter the park, an area of urban greenery, off the south side of the busy Corstorphine Road and cross the Water of Leith by the footbridge to join the well signposted Walkway.

Just ahead of you are the high walls of Murrayfield Stadium, Scotland's national venue for rugby football. A certain class-consciousness prevails in Scottish rugby, and in Edinburgh it's widely seen as a middle-class sport, arousing nothing like the fanaticism that attends matches between the city's rival soccer teams, Hearts and Hibs.

The Water of Leith passes under Corstorphine Road, which you must cross to plunge into the increasingly steep-sided valley which the path now follows, winding along the south bank for about 750m (820yd) before detouring over a foot-

93

bridge to the Scottish National Gallery of Modern Art.

This is the Scottish nation's collection of twentieth-century painting, graphic art and sculpture, with work by heavy hitters including Pablo Picasso (1881–1973), Georges Braque (1882–1963) and Henri Matisse (1869–1954), as well as by artists of the Scottish School. Established in 1960, the Gallery was for many years housed in Inverleith House in the Royal Botanic Garden, moving to its current premises only in 1986. Outside the Gallery, a sculpture garden features the work of Jacob Epstein (1880–1959), Barbara Hepworth (1903–1975), Henry Moore (1898–1986) and the Edinburgh-born Eduardo Paolozzi (1924–). Within, paintings are grouped by theme. Works from the gallery's own collection are frequently rotated, but among those you can usually expect to see are Matisse's *The Painting Lesson*, Édouard Vuillard's *Two Seamstresses*, Joán Miró's *Composition*, Alberto Giacommeti's violently striking *Woman with her Throat Cut* and, from the frenetic arena of Pop Art, Roy Lichtenstein's *In the Car*.

Pride of place, however, goes, as it should, to the Scottish painters, notably those of the Colourist school, credited with bringing a new wave of vibrant light and colour to Scottish painting, which until the late nineteenth century had been dominated by somewhat gloomy representational landscapes and portraits. Among the leading Colourists shown here are S. J. Peploe (1871–1935), J. D. Fergusson (1874–1961), Francis Cadell (1883–1937) and George Leslie Hunter (1881–1943).

Leaving the gallery after as long a browse as you feel in the mood for, cross Belford Road. The imposing Victorian building in front of you, designed by the omnipresent William Playfair (1789–1857), was once the Dean Orphanage, then a nursing college and a local authority building, and in 1999 reopened as a spectacular new gallery, the Dean Gallery, featuring the Paolozzi Collection as well as the Penrose and Keiller collections, which were formerly housed in the Scottish National Gallery of Modern Art.

Light and Colour

Cross back over the footbridge to rejoin the Walkway along the right bank of the Water of Leith, passing beneath Belford Bridge, completed in 1887. The Coat of Arms of the City of Edinburgh and the Scottish Royal Coat of Arms are carved into the left pier of the bridge.

Just before you get to the bridge, the path crosses the stream by a footbridge to follow the left bank as far as a flight of steps that takes you back to street level, where you should cross Dean Path. Turn right to cross the water once again and walk on into the centre of Dean Village.

One of the oldest parts of the city, this settlement, dating from the twelfth century, was originally clustered around several watermills driven by the swift-flowing stream. There were as many as a dozen of these mills, none of which survive, though place names like Lindsay's Mill and Mar's Mill recall that era.

Turn left on Miller Row and rejoin the path as it runs along the right bank of the Water of Leith and under the Dean Bridge, which carries Queensferry Road, the main road out of the city centre to the Forth Bridge and the west, over the Water's deep gorge. Built in 1830–1831 by Thomas Telford (1757–1834), the bridge

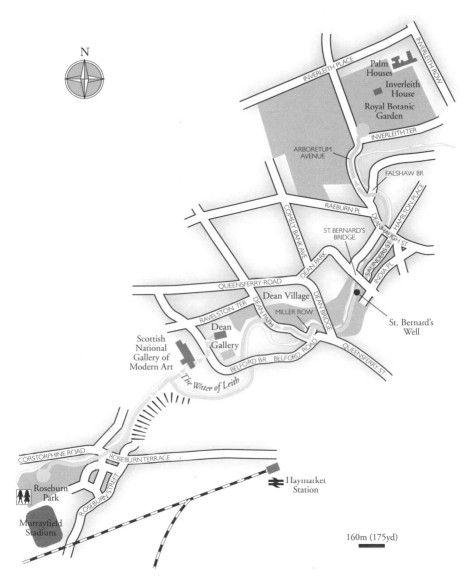

N

Palm
Houses

Inverleith
House

Royal Botanic
Garden

INVERLEITH PLACE

INVERLEITH ROW

INVERLEITH TER.

ARBORETUM
AVENUE

FALSHAW BR

RAEBURN PL.

COMELY BANK AVE

DEAN PARK

ST. BERNARD'S
BRIDGE

DEAN HAUGH ST

HAMILTON PLACE

SAUNDERS ST

INDIA PL.

QUEENSFERRY ROAD

Dean Village

DEAN BRIDGE

St. Bernard's
Well

RAVELSTON TER.

DEAN PATH

MILLER ROW

Dean
Gallery

QUEENSFERRY ST

Scottish
National
Gallery of
Modern Art

BELFORD BR.

BELFORD ROAD

The Water of Leith

CORSTORPHINE ROAD

ROSEBURN TERRACE

Haymarket
Station

Roseburn
Park

ROSEBURN STREET

Murrayfield
Stadium

160m (175yd)

is 32m (106ft) high. Telford was the greatest Scottish civil engineer of his time and indeed arguably of all time, supervising the building of about 1500km (almost 1000 miles) of roads and a hundred and twenty new bridges throughout Scotland, improving harbours and building the Caledonian Canal. His work was said at the time to have advanced the development of the country by at least a century. He is buried in Westminster Abbey.

This bridge was paid for by Lord Provost Learmouth, who wanted better access to land he had bought on the north side of the stream and intended to develop for housing. His project failed to catch on, however, and it was not until some decades later that Dean Village and the farmland and market gardens around it were swallowed up by genteel and elegant homes. By the 1860s, terraces and crescents of townhouses had usurped fields and pastures, and in 1876 another Lord Provost and landowner, Sir James Falshaw, bought the remaining open ground between Belgrave Crescent and Dean Village.

Healing Waters

Carry on down the stream – through the attractively landscaped gardens which rise steeply from either bank – to St Bernard's Well. In the early nineteenth century, the mineral spring here was thought to have health-giving properties, despite (or perhaps because of) its sulphurous taste and smell. The 'Greek Temple' built on the spot in 1789 was designed by the painter and architect Alexander Nasmyth (1758–1840), a close friend of Robert Burns (1759–1796). It was restored in 1888, when a statue of Hygeia, Greek goddess of health, was erected. The statue is the work of the Scottish sculptor David Watson Stevenson (1842–1904).

The path now passes under St Bernard's Bridge, which marks the end of the steep-sided Dean Gorge. After walking under the bridge, turn right and continue along Saunders Street to the traffic lights; next turn left onto Deanhaugh Street and into Stockbridge, and at the end of the bridge walk down the flight of steps to your right and follow the path along the left bank of the stream. Like Dean Village, Stockbridge was originally an outlying settlement of workmen and artisans involved in the making of paper, rope, textiles, leather, beer, spirits and snuff – all of which require a plentiful supply of water and water power.

The walkway ends at Falshaw Bridge (named after the same Sir James Falshaw we have just met). Returning to street level on the bridge, turn left and almost immediately right onto Arboretum Avenue. Walk along this street for 500m (550yd) or so until you reach the entrance to the Royal Botanic Garden (clearly signposted).

Just before you go in, notice on the opposite bank the harmonious houses of the Colonies, built by the Edinburgh Co-operative Building Company in 1861. The Colonies comprise eleven blocks of simple but attractive two-storey buildings, intended by the Company to provide homes for working-class owner–occupiers. This well-meaning project fell foul of market forces; originally sold for as little as £130 apiece, they were quickly snapped up by speculators and for more than a century have been highly desirable properties, commanding prices rather higher than most Edinburgh workers could (or can) afford.

Blaze of Colour

The Royal Botanic Garden boasts the world's largest collection of rhododendrons (best seen as a blaze of reds, pinks and purples when they flower in April and May) and a famous rock garden.

The Botanic Garden has a long pedigree. As early as 1667 the physician and botanist Sir Robert Sibbald (1641–1694) had founded a 'physic garden' for the cultivation and study of medicinal herbs. From these early beginnings, the Garden has grown to cover 28ha (70 acres) of magnificent greenery, ranging from herbaceous borders and splendid woodlands to azalea lawns and winter gardens.

The new Chinese Garden honours George Forrest, the Edinburgh botanist who brought many of the exotic flora of China back to the Garden in a series of expeditions between 1904 and 1932. It contains the largest collection of Chinese flora outside China itself.

At the highest point of the Garden stands Inverleith House, built in 1774. This is used for a changing schedule of exhibitions of painting and sculpture.

In fine weather the Royal Botanic Garden is an excellent place for a leisurely stroll, while on a wet day you can head for its huge climate-controlled glasshouses, where exotic plants are displayed in eleven different climate zones, from desert to rainforest. High points of the Glasshouse Experience include a two-hundred-year-old palm tree, housed in the striking Large Palm House, built in 1850. Adjoining it, the attractive Old Palm House, built in 1834, is the oldest of the glasshouses; next to it the more modern glasshouses, built in 1967, look like artificial habitats from a science-fiction movie – and in a sense, of course, that's what they are.

North of the glasshouses a statue of Karl von Linne (1707–1778) – usually better known under the latinized version of his name, Carolus Linnaeus – the Swedish botanist who singlehandedly devised the system of classifying plants and animals into species, genera, orders and kingdoms (the Linnaean system) that is still in use by botanists and zoologists. Designed by Robert Adam (1728–1792), the statue was commissioned by his contemporary, the Edinburgh University professor John Hope (1725–1786), who was among the first to adopt the Linnaean system of taxonomy.

How long you spend wandering around in the Royal Botanic Garden is obviously a matter for yourself to decide. When you have finished your exploration, catch a 7A, 8, 23, 27 or 37 bus back to the city centre. Alternatively, you could hook up with the start of the next walk and take yourself off to explore Leith.

Around Leith and Newhaven

Summary: If Edinburgh is the 'Athens of the North', then Leith must be its Piraeus. Leith is one of Edinburgh's remarkable success stories. The port of Edinburgh – north of the city centre, on the 10km (6 mile) wide Firth of Forth – was only gradually absorbed into the greater city, ceasing to be a separate municipality as recently as 1920. Leith's prosperity waned as road and rail gradually usurped the age-old role of sea transport. Moreover, it was hit hard by the worldwide economic Depression of the late 1920s and early 1930s, and again in the years following World War II by the steady decline of heavy industry, acquiring all the problems associated with run-down inner-city areas.

Since the mid-1980s, however, Leith – like other former dockland areas in Britain and worldwide – has been experiencing something of a renaissance. Nineteenth-century warehouses have been converted into loft apartments for the upwardly mobile, with sweeping views over the Firth of Forth. Rough and ready seamen's bars have given way to what is claimed to be the highest concentration of gourmet restaurants in Britain outside central London. And the £100 million Ocean Terminal complex of shops, restaurants and accommodation, designed by Sir Terence Conran (1931–) and scheduled to open in 2001, will set the seal on the renaissance of the community that the citizens of Edinburgh have nicknamed 'Leith-sur-Mer'.

Start:	At the corner of Inverleith Terrace and Inverleith Row, near the Royal Botanic Garden.
Finish:	Newhaven Harbour.
Length:	4km (2½ miles).
Time:	2hr.
Refreshments:	Port o' Leith, 58 Constitution Street – a great traditional Scottish bar.
	The Shore, 3 The Shore – a cosy bar with live jazz music on Wednesdays and Saturdays.
	The Malt & Hops, 45 The Shore – a small, friendly pub.
	The Waterfront, 1C Dock Place – a large, well-stocked wine bar that during summer has outside waterside tables.
	Harry Ramsden's restaurant, 5 Pier Place, Newhaven.
	The Peacock Inn, Newhaven.
Which day:	Any day.
To visit:	Andro Lamb's House.
	Ocean Terminal and the Royal Yacht *Britannia*.
	Newhaven Heritage Museum.

Start this walk at the corner of Inverleith Terrace and Inverleith Row, which you can reach by taking any one of the buses 7a, 8, 23, 27 and 37 from the city centre to the Royal Botanic Garden.

On your left, at the corner of Howard Place and Inverleith Row, is No. 8 Howard Place, birthplace in 1850 of Robert Louis Stevenson (1850–1894). Robert Louis Stevenson's father, Thomas Stevenson (1818–1887), was an engineer and meteorologist who made a number of innovations in the techniques of lighthouse illumination and harbour construction.

Cross the street and walk to the end of Warriston Crescent, where a sign marks the start of the footpath to Leith. This path will take you along the left bank of the Water of Leith for 2.5km (1½ miles). Although there are no specific sights to see, it is a lovely stroll, so feel free to take your time over it.

On reaching Leith, walk down to Quayside Street, Sandport Place and The Shore, where the Water of Leith flows into the inner harbour.

The Original Waterfront

This was Leith's original waterfront until the massive land reclamation and dock building of the nineteenth century created a huge harbour complex to the north of Commercial Street. Leith prospered as the port of Edinburgh from medieval times until the late nineteenth century. Its merchants traded with Hanseatic ports like Hamburg, Bergen and Danzig (modern Gdansk) for salt cod, timber and flax, and with Bordeaux for the claret that was the favoured tipple of the Edinburgh upper class. Indeed, until the Industrial Revolution, taking ships to or from Leith was the easiest way to leave or arrive in Edinburgh, and this was precisely what almost all of the Stuart monarchs did at some point in their reign. Mary Queen of Scots (1542–1587) landed here on her return to her native Scotland in 1561, and George IV (1762–1830) passed through on his triumphal royal visit to Edinburgh in 1822 – the first time in more than a century that a British king had set foot on Scottish soil.

Until the seventeenth century Leith was fortified, though all trace of its walls has long since vanished. It was occupied by the French garrison of Mary Queen of Scots's mother and regent, Mary of (Marie de) Guise (1515–1560), and besieged by Presbyterian troops during the struggle between Protestant and Catholic factions during the mid-sixteenth century. In 1650 Oliver Cromwell (1599–1658) landed his Roundheads here to subdue Scotland, and in 1779 the elderly cannons of the port were readied to repel an assault by the American privateer John Paul Jones (1747–1792). Born in Kirkcaldy, just across the Firth of Forth, Jones had already announced himself as 'local boy made good' by bombarding his native town. Happily, the wind turned against him and Leith escaped unscathed.

A Dockland Renaissance

New industries flourished with the coming of the Industrial Revolution, notably glass making and sugar refining, and new docks were built to handle the import of raw materials and the export of the finished product. The Victoria Dock was completed in 1851, the Albert Dock in 1869, the Edinburgh Dock in 1881 and the Imperial Dock in 1903. Times have changed yet again: The Shore is now the heart of the newly trendy Leith waterfront, with smart bars, gourmet restaurants, chic shops and desirable apartments overlooking the water.

Cross the Water of Leith by the Sandport Place Bridge, turn left, then take the first right on Burgess Street to the corner of Water Street and Andro (Andrew) Lamb's House. Andro Lamb was a wealthy Leith merchant of the early seventeenth century and his home, which now functions as an old people's day centre, is an excellent example of the domestic architecture of the time. Four storeys high, topped with an attic, it has the white, harled front and three crow-stepped gables typical of late-medieval Edinburgh buildings. Seven bays wide, its leaded and shuttered windows have been restored to their original proportions, and its round corbelled stair tower gives it a baronial air.

Turn left onto Bernard Street, where a statue of Robert Burns (1759–1796) in

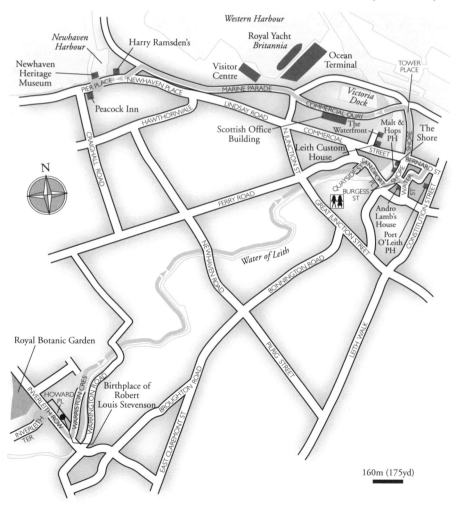

declamatory mode dates from 1898, and walk back to the Water of Leith. Facing you, across the Bernard Street Bridge, is a massive Georgian building, the Leith Custom House, designed in 1812 by Robert Reid (1776–1856) – who also designed the buildings of Parliament Square (see page 31) – with single-storey wings on either side of a square two-storey building. The Coat of Arms of King George III (1738–1820) embellishes the pediment, above a Doric portico.

Now go right and along The Shore to Tower Place, where the circular Signal Tower, built in 1686, has been a Leith waterfront landmark for centuries. Originally a windmill, it was converted into a watchtower during the Napoleonic War, when it gained its battlements and parapet. In those days, of course, it stood by the sea; the building of the nineteenth-century docks has left it far inland.

If your visit is in July or August, make this a Sunday walk, because on Sundays the stalls of Leith Market occupy the shore from Bernard Street to the dock gates at Malmaison, selling arts, crafts and fresh produce and featuring many local artists and designers.

A Yacht Fit for a Queen

At the north end of Tower Place, turn left and walk along Commercial Quay, past the gleaming new Scottish Office building looking out over Victoria Dock to Marine Parade. Cross over to the north side of the street, and enter Leith's showpiece for the twenty-first century, the £50 million Ocean Terminal, and the home of the former Royal Yacht *Britannia*.

Due to open in Spring, 2001, Ocean Terminal will set the capstone on the renaissance of Leith. The work of British design guru Sir Terence Conran, it will be a gleaming state-of-the-art leisure complex with shops, restaurants, hotels and exhibition and conference facilities that will make the Leith docklands a city within a city as far as tourism is concerned.

Enter the visitor centre, where the 12.5m (41ft) royal barge is the centrepiece of an exhibition which introduces you to the Terminal's showpiece, the Royal Yacht *Britannia*, telling her story from her launch in 1953, at the time of Queen Elizabeth II's Coronation, to her decommissioning in 1997.

Other features of the exhibition include an introductory video concerning the yacht's history; *Britannia*'s original wheelhouse and ratings' berths; and a technical area with CD-ROM and touchscreen facility and a video installation which lets you choose newsreel clips of some of *Britannia*'s most famous moments, such as the hand-over of Hong Kong from British to Chinese rule in 1997. Relics from *Britannia*'s wardroom are also displayed, including a gold button from the uniform of Admiral Horatio Nelson (1758–1805) and a fragment of the White Ensign flown by Captain Robert Falcon Scott (1868–1912), a Royal Navy officer, on his fatal journey to the South Pole, and recovered with his body.

Built on Glasgow's Clydeside, the 126m (412ft) yacht has been refurbished at a cost of £2.5 million. The vessel travelled more than 1.5 million km (one million miles) around the world in the course of its twenty-six-year career, serving as a mobile royal residence and setting for official engagements by the Queen and members of the royal family during state and private visits overseas and in Britain. Guests on board have included heads of state from all over the world, including South Africa's Nelson Mandela (1918–), the US President Bill Clinton (1946–) and British Prime Minister Tony Blair (1953–).

Britannia was the only ship in the world whose captain, by tradition, was always an admiral, and she was also the last ship in the Royal Navy in which sailors slept in hammocks. When she was refitted in 1970 and bunks were installed for her ratings, Leading Seaman Jamie Stewart insisted on keeping his hammock, thus ensuring himself a place in the history books as the last man in the Royal Navy to sleep that way.

Leaving Ocean Terminal, turn right onto Marine Parade. Continue westward with the Western Harbour on your right – for a little under a kilometre (½ mile) until you reach Newhaven, formerly a fishing village and now a desirable residential area.

A Fishing Community

Newhaven, west of Leith, was also a separate community until comparatively recently. Here, life centred around the village's fishing and oyster-catching activities. Newhaven's small harbour is dwarfed by the pier of Leith Docks, and there is little today of the atmosphere of the fishing village whose colourfully dressed fishwives hawked their wares around the streets of Edinburgh as recently as the 1920s.

In actual fact, Newhaven began life as a shipbuilding centre, when James IV (1473–1513) ordered the building of a mighty warship, the *Michael*. With a hundred and twenty guns and a crew of three hundred plus a complement of a thousand soldiers, the ship was intended to raise Scotland to naval-superpower status. The forests of Fife, across the Forth, were stripped of timber for the project. However, before the *Michael* could be launched, James was killed in the disastrous carnage of Flodden, and the ship never left Newhaven. It was eventually broken up and its timbers used for house building.

Turn right onto Pier Place, overlooking the harbour with its stone quay and lighthouse, and walk to the Newhaven Heritage Museum at No. 24. The Museum, staffed by local people, tells the story of Newhaven and its fisherfolk through displays of costumes, photographs and old-fashioned fishing equipment.

Leith to Prestonpans

Summary: This is a pleasant walk for a sunny day, following the coast eastward from the docks of Leith past the long and sandy beach at Portobello – once called 'Edinburgh's Brighton' and the birthplace of Sir Harry Lauder (1870–1950) – and the fishing settlement of Musselburgh to Prestonpans and the site of the Highland clans' last great victory over regular troops.

Start:	Corner of Leith Walk and Pilrig Street.
Finish:	Prestonpans Railway Station.
Length:	7km (4¼ miles).
Time:	3hr.
Refreshments:	See the heading for the previous walk (Around Leith and Newhaven, page 98) for bars and restaurants in Leith. Pubs and cafés along the way in Portobello and Musselburgh. The café in the Prestongrange Industrial Heritage Museum.
Which day:	Any day.
To visit:	James Pringle Weavers' Leith Mills and Clan Tartan Centre. Prestongrange Industrial Heritage Museum. Preston Tower and Garden.

You can reach the start of this agreeable excursion by taking any one of the buses 1, 7, 9, 10, 22 or 25 from the city centre to Leith Walk.

Turn north off Leith Walk and continue for about 200m (220yd) to Bonnington Road; next turn right and then left into Breadalbane Street. At the corner of Bangor Road you can visit James Pringle Weavers' Leith Mills and the Clan Tartan Centre, at Nos. 70–74. Pringle, one of Scotland's leading textile companies, makes fine wool and cashmere tartans and sportswear, and the Clan Tartan Centre here has a computerized research facility to help people trace their clan links. If you have even the faintest claim to Scottish ancestry (and tens of millions of people in the United States and Canada, Argentina and Chile, the Caribbean, Australia, New Zealand and South Africa do!) the assistants should be able to find a clan and a tartan for you.

The development of tartan into a fully fledged industry is a phenomenon born of the eighteenth and nineteenth centuries, as is the code of identifying each clan with its own unique tartan. In fact, in the heyday of the clan system, until the final defeat at Culloden (1746) and even after that, each clansman wore whatever pattern he liked. The kilt as worn today is likewise a recent invention; until the eighteenth century Highlanders wore the poncho-like plaid, into which they literally rolled themselves and which was held together with sword and pistol belts, and discarded

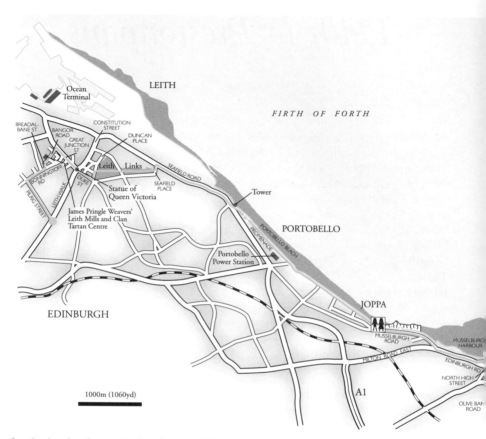

for the battle-charge. As for the age-old question of what is worn under the kilt, you may wear nothing or anything you please; I know of at least one proud member of the Clan Campbell who favours black silk bikini underwear.

It is ironic that, just as a tissue of tartan romance was being woven around the myth of the Highlands in the early nineteenth century, the infamous Clearances were seeing the real Highlanders being forcibly driven off the land (often by their own clan chiefs) to make way for more profitable sheep farming.

Drugs and Violence

Walk down Bangor Road to Great Junction Street, turn right onto it and continue along the south side of the street to the traffic roundabout where Great Junction Street meets Leith Walk and where a bronze statue of Queen Victoria (1819–1901) gazes dourly at Leith Central Station.

The long disused railway station – which has survived demolition because it is considered an interesting example of local industrial architecture – inspired the ironic title of Irvine Welsh's harsh novel *Trainspotting* (1991), filmed with Robert Carlyle and Ewan McGregor in 1996. Welsh's work, shot through with black

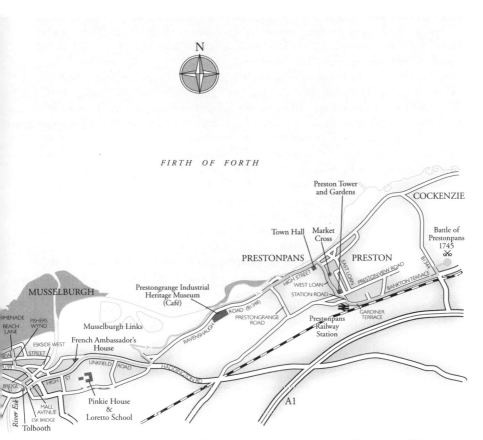

humour, paints a picture of violence, hard-drug use, alcoholism and disintegrating communities in Leith and in Edinburgh's grimmer housing estates. Edinburgh city fathers found it so hard to stomach that they blocked filming in Edinburgh – *Trainspotting* had instead to be shot in Glasgow. Inner-city dereliction still raises its head only a few blocks from the fashionable waterfront area.

Cross Constitution Street and take the second left off Duke Street onto Duncan Place, then turn right into Leith Links. The Links give Leith a strong claim to supplant St Andrews as the birthplace of golf in Scotland. 'Gowf' was played here as early as the fifteenth century, causing an irate James IV (1473–1513) to proscribe it in the belief that it distracted the young men of Edinburgh from the more practical, warlike and manly pursuit of archery. He tried to ban football, too, but sadly both his prohibitions failed to have much effect: the Scots are still obsessed with football, keen on golf, and produce no world-class archers.

Golf and Covenanters

Golf was probably brought to Leith either by young Scots who had studied in the Netherlands, where the game seems to have originated (historians are divided on the issue), or by Dutch merchants. Regardless of royal disapproval, the game flourished and by the late seventeenth century was popular with all classes. Both Charles I (1600–1649) and James (1633–1701), Duke of York – later King James VII and II – played at Leith during visits to Edinburgh.

The Links were also used as a mustering-place for troops. In June 1639, the Covenanter army gathered here under the generalship of Alexander Leslie (*c.* 1580–1661), later first Earl of Leven, the Scottish soldier of fortune who had learned the art of war in the campaigns of the Swedish King Gustavus Adolphus (1594–1632) during the Thirty Years' War (1618–48) and who had joined the Covenanters on his return to Scotland. Leslie had already succeeded in overcoming the King's garrison in Edinburgh Castle by stealth, and now he marched his men south to meet Charles I and his army on the border. In the event, this 'First Bishops' War' – so called because the Covenanters took arms to oppose Charles's efforts to impose his bishops on the Presbyterian Kirk – ended without bloodshed. The Royalist governor Sir Patrick Ruthven (1573–1651) was allowed to return to Edinburgh Castle, only to be forcibly ejected after a siege that September; he and the seventy survivors of his garrison were allowed to march to Leith, guarded from the furious inhabitants by a Covenanter escort, and take ship for England. Ruthven, who like Leslie had earned his spurs in Europe fighting in the Protestant armies of Gustavus Adolphus during the Thirty Years' War, went on to become the King's general in chief. In 1644 he was declared a traitor by the Scottish Parliament, and after the defeat of the Royalists he went into exile with Charles II.

Full-scale war between the Covenanters and Royalists erupted the following summer, when Leslie crossed into England, trounced the Royalist forces and occupied the northeast of England. This 'Second Bishops' War' ended with the victorious Scots being bought off for a hefty sum.

Seaside Attractions

Walk diagonally along the Links to come out on Seafield Road. Turn right here, and walk some 750m (820yd) to the beginning of Portobello beach and its seaside promenade. At low tide you can walk along the sand and shingle beach; otherwise walk along the promenade above it.

The island you can see from here, some 3km (2 miles) to the north, is Inchkeith. Now uninhabited, it still has the concrete bunkers and gun emplacements built during World War I and World War II to guard the approach to Leith.

Portobello is a relatively recent settlement. It grew up in the mid-nineteenth century on empty land between the town limits of Leith and the fishing village of Musselburgh, to the east, and was built as a residential suburb for the better-off and as a seaside resort. In the late nineteenth century it was by all accounts a lively place, with bathing machines, open-air concerts, amusements, food stalls and dining rooms. Like so many former British seaside resorts, however, it retains little of its appeal: its glory days are well and truly over.

The eccentric tower at the west end of the esplanade was built in 1785 and incorporates masonry recycled from demolished older buildings, including the Mercat ('Market') Cross and the old college buildings of Edinburgh University.

Midway along the beach, Portobello Power Station adds a jarringly industrial twentieth-century note.

Portobello beach ends at a rocky headland, around which is the nineteenth-century resort and fishing village of Joppa, now like Portobello a residential suburb of Edinburgh. The promenade rejoins the pavement of the coast road here; walk on through Joppa to Musselburgh, an attractive village with a small, working fishing fleet. At Musselburgh Harbour, turn left onto New Street and left again onto the Promenade to walk through Fisherrow, the oldest and most attractive part of the village, with its streets of low stone fishermen's cottages. At Beach Lane, turn right, cross New Street, and walk along Fishers Wynd to the junction of North High Street and Bridge Street. Here, turn left, and follow Bridge Street to the River Esk, which flows through the town centre. The main road crosses the river by a five-arched bridge designed by the civil engineer John Rennie (1761-1821) in 1806, but instead of walking across this, turn right, walk a short distance up Eskside West, and cross by the old, steeply arched Esk Bridge, a stone footbridge which dates from the early sixteenth century and is locally said to stand on the foundations of an earlier Roman structure.

A Frisson of the Past

In front of you at the junction of Mall Avenue and Olivebank Road is the Tolbooth, the earliest parts of which date from 1590, and the Mercat Cross.

The Tolbooth is Musselburgh's most prominent landmark, with a bell-tower that can be seen from all over the town. The tower is another early example of recycling. The Chapel of Our Lady of Loretto, on a site about 500m (550yd) east of the Tolbooth (where Pinkie House and Loretto School now stand), was torn down by Protestant zealots in the mid-1500s, and its masonry was later used to built the Tolbooth.

The Tolbooth is an architectural hotchpotch, with a Classical east wing, which was added in the 1730s, an early-twentieth-century hall bolted on at the back, and a modern outside stair. Opposite the front stands the Mercat Cross, marking the traditional site of Musselburgh's marketplace and topped by a much-eroded lion rampant.

Walk on east along the High Street. At its far end, immediately before it merges with Linkfield Road, is the early-seventeenth-century building with dormer windows known locally as the French Ambassador's House, having once reputedly housed the King of France's envoy to the Court of King James VI and I (1566–1625). The French *tricolor* is still flown from a flagstaff at roof level, courtesy of the Belgian Consul in Edinburgh.

A Frequent Battleground

Pinkie House, on the south side of the street, is now part of Loretto School, one of Scotland's most expensive private educational establishments, but its fourteenth-century tower and seventeenth-century turrets may be seen from the gateway. Its name commemorates the Battle of Pinkie in 1547 – actually fought at Barbachlaw, about a kilometre (½ mile)away to the southeast – where an English army, despatched by the Regent Somerset to aid Scotland's Protestant rebels, routed a Scots army.

Musselburgh was even then no stranger to invasion. Sited at a strategically important river crossing on the main road to Edinburgh, it was sacked and burned with monotonous frequency. Just three years before Pinkie, the Earl of Hertford's soldiery had burned the town during Henry VIII's so-called 'Rough Wooing' of Scotland; in 1549 an Anglo-French peace treaty, by which both sides withdrew their forces from Scotland, granted the town a respite.

Walk past Pinkie House and carry on east for 500m (550yd) to a crossroads and traffic roundabout on the outskirts of Musselburgh. Take the B1348 exit signposted to Prestonpans and walk along the footpath paralleling the road, on the south side of Musselburgh Links, for 700m (765yd).

Where the footpath meets the coast, cross the road to the Prestongrange Industrial Heritage Museum, located on the site of the Prestongrange coal mine, which closed in 1952. The most impressive exhibit here is probably the enormous, Cornish-built beam engine, erected in 1874 to pump water from the pit and still going strong at the time when the mine finally ceased working.

The Slow Death of a Vision

Prestonpans, as its name implies, originally made its living from the sea-salt trade, though the artificial salt pans that used to fringe the shore are no longer to be seen.

Carry on along the shore road for 750m (820 yd) or so, past the Town Hall, and then turn right on West Loan to walk into the centre of the village of Preston. After you've gone about 500m (550yd), note on your left the tall stone market cross, topped by a carved unicorn. Believed to be the only original market cross of that period still standing where it was built, it dates from about 1617. At the end of West Loan, follow Station Road, which curves to your left into Gardiner Terrace. Walk along this to the outskirts of the village and the site of the Battle of Prestonpans, the opening action of the Jacobite Rising of 1745. The battlefield is marked by a cairn.

Prestonpans was the last triumph of the Highland clans over conventional troops, and the ease with which the battle was won gave the fortunes of Prince Charles Edward Stuart (1720–1788), also known as 'Bonnie Prince Charlie', a huge boost.

Charles Edward, after landing in the northwest in early August 1745 and raising an army of some three thousand clansmen, marched briskly on Edinburgh, entering the city without meeting any effective resistance and at the Market Cross proclaiming his exiled father – the Old Pretender – to be King James VIII and III.

The English Commander in Chief, Sir John Cope (d. 1760), had avoided an encounter with the Jacobites at Inverness, fallen back on Aberdeen, and then evacuated his force by sea to land at Dunbar and march on Edinburgh. They camped overnight at Prestonpans, where shortly after dawn on 21 September, while half Cope's men were still in their tents, the Highlanders took them by surprise. The result was a rout, celebrated long after in one of the most rousing of pipe tunes, 'Hey Johnnie Cope are ye waukin' [waking] yet?', ironically now played as often as not by pipers of the British Army's Highland regiments.

After Prestonpans the Jacobites seemed unstoppable. With Scotland in his hands, Charles Edward marched rapidly south as far as Derby, only 250km (150 miles) from London, where there was panic – George II (1683–1760) himself was preparing to flee to his German principality of Hanover. But in December, Charles's supporters lost their nerve. They had hoped for a surge of popular support for Charles in England too – a hope that was in vain. Only a few hundred men from Manchester had joined them, and they had an army of only five thousand ill-disciplined Highland swordsmen to face thirty thousand Government regulars.

They turned back to Scotland, only to find that support for their cause was fading away, especially in the Lowlands. After an inconclusive engagement with Government troops at Falkirk, Charles Edward retreated to Inverness, the gateway to the Highlands, for the winter. During this time, the Government shipped regular troops to Aberdeen, and in April they marched west to meet the Highlanders at Culloden, outside Inverness.

The rest, as they say, is history: the Duke of Cumberland's regular troops, battle-hardened in the French wars, stood up to the formerly invincible Highland charge with volley-fire and bayonet; cannon and grapeshot mowed down the clans where they stood, and English cavalry butchered the wounded. It was the last battle fought on British soil.

Charles Edward fled back to France and died in exile in Rome many years later, and within less than a generation the Highland clans who for centuries had fought so often and so successfully against the Crown were mustering into the British Army's kilted regiments to become the most effective shock troops of the British Empire.

Your walk ends at the battleground of Prestonpans. From nearby Prestonpans Railway Station you can catch one of the frequent trains back to Edinburgh's Waverley Railway Station.

Lauriston Castle to Cramond

Summary: Cramond is an attractive eighteenth-century village on the mouth of the River Almond, which flows over a weir south of the centre of the village and into the Firth of Forth. Now a residential suburb on the western outskirts of the city, Cramond has been settled since at least Roman times. Pretty white houses rise in tiers above the harbour quay, which runs along the east bank of the Almond.

Start:	Davidson's Mains.
Finish:	Cramond Bridge.
Length:	3km (2 miles).
Time:	1½hr.
Refreshments:	Cramond Inn.
Which day:	Saturday or Sunday.
To visit:	Lauriston Castle.
	Cramond Roman Fort.
	Cramond Kirk.

A number 41 bus will take you from the city centre to Davidson's Mains; at the end of the walk it is again a number 41 that will take you back from Cramond Bridge to the city centre.

From the Davidson's Mains junction turn right off the A90 on to Quality Street and walk north over the junction of Barnton Avenue with Main Street onto Cramond Road South. Continue for 500m (550yd) on the right-hand side of the road, to the gates of Lauriston Castle (signposted) on your right.

A Distinguished Past

Lauriston Castle, a sixteenth-century tower house with extensive nineteenth-century additions in a pastiche of the seventeenth-century Jacobean style, stands in its own expanse of woods and lawns. It contains an outstanding collection of eighteenth-century Italian furniture, oriental rugs and Flemish tapestries, porcelain and silver. The original tower was the seat of the Napier family, having been built by Sir Archibald Napier (1534–1608), seventh laird of Merchiston and Master of the Scottish Mint. His son John (1550–1617), the eighth laird, invented logarithms and thus can be regarded as one of the fathers of modern mathematics; as a by-product of over twenty years' work constructing logarithmic tables, he devised the system of decimal fractions we still use.

By the seventeenth century, the tower had passed into the hands of the Law family, and in 1671 it was the birthplace of John Law (1671–1729), the adventurer and financier. Educated at Edinburgh University, Law moved to London where in 1694 he killed one Edward 'Beau' Wilson in a duel – over what, history is silent. Sentenced to death for murder, he fled to France where, after a chequered career, he established the Banque Générale, France's first bank, and set up the Western Company to encourage investment in the French territories in America. Such was the apparent success of this Mississippi Scheme that in 1720 the French Government appointed him controller general of finances, but in that same year the scheme crashed and Law prudently fled France. The economist Adam Smith (1723–1790), wise as ever after the event, described Law's pump-priming of the French economy by printing huge quantities of paper currency as 'the most extravagant project of banking and stock-jobbing that the world ever saw'. Law died in poverty in Venice nine years later.

The architect William Burn (1789–1870) was responsible for the extensive nineteenth-century additions to Lauriston Castle, which date from the 1820s. The Edwardian interior of the Castle, and most of the fine antiques within, are the legacy of its last private owner, W. R. Reid, owner of a prosperous Edinburgh furniture makers. The building became the property of the City of Edinburgh on his death in 1926.

The Romans Were Here

Leaving the Castle, turn right, follow Cramond Road South for about 500m (550yd) until it turns sharply left into Cramond Road North, and take the footpath which branches off to the north (your right) for another 500m (550yd) – passing Cramond House, a distinctive, H-planned house built in 1680 which is now the beadle's manse of Cramond Kirk – to the Firth of Forth, Cramond Tower and the site of a second century Roman fort.

Cramond Tower is a tall medieval keep. Four storeys high, it has an arched doorway and a turret stair running to its top. The land here belonged during the early Middle Ages to the bishops of Dunkeld, so the Tower may have been part of a palace or fortified mansion, but there are no definite records. Derelict for many years, it has now been converted into an enviable private home.

The Tower stands within the ancient perimeter of the Roman fort, close by the mouth of the river. The convenient anchorage and water supply of the Almond were what attracted the Romans, who built their fort here during the mid-second century AD. When built it was probably right on the bank of the River Almond, but this stream has shifted in its course over the last eighteen hundred years. Garrisoned by almost a thousand legionaries and auxiliaries, the Cramond fort was to be the eastern buttress of the Antonine Wall, designed during the reign of the Emperor Antoninus Pius (86–161) to separate Roman territory from the unconquered Pictish lands to the north.

Covering some 2.5ha (6 acres) – much of it now occupied by more recent buildings such as Cramond Kirk and its graveyard – the fortress was constructed to the standard plan used by the legions throughout the Roman Empire, with stone-clad earth ramparts, 8m (27ft) tall and up to 3m (10ft) thick. Gates pierced each of the four walls, and two main streets met at a crossroads in the centre of the fort. Like other Roman garrisons, this was a self-contained military town, with bathhouses, granaries and workshops in addition to the barracks, and the ground plan and foundations of many of these buildings may still be seen within the much-diminished turf walls in the grounds of Cramond Kirk.

By the time they began work here, the Romans were old hands at wall-building: Hadrian's Wall, some 180km (120 miles) to the south, had been begun more than twenty years previously. The Romans occupied the area between the two walls – known to them as Valentia – for about ninety years, but, unlike southern Britain, this region was never really Romanized: the occupation remained entirely military, administration of the area between the walls remained largely in the hands of local rulers, and, instead of extending their network of military roads through the border hills, the Romans seem to have supplied and reinforced the garrisons of Antonine's Wall mostly by sea.

In 208 the Emperor Severus (146–211) turned Cramond into a major naval base for an attempt to subdue Caledonia, but three years of campaigning achieved nothing; the Picts refused to stand and fight a setpiece battle, and the Romans were ill-equipped to conduct operations against such an elusive enemy. Severus died shortly after this, and Cramond and the Antonine Wall were abandoned, their garrisons being withdrawn to Hadrian's Wall, though there is some evidence that Cramond and other coastal forts were occasionally reoccupied for brief periods.

The village owes its name to the fort; after the fall of Roman Britain, the Britons of Rheged who settled here knew the place as *Caer Almond*, 'fort on the Almond'. The exact site of the fort was not discovered until the 1950s, though coins, potsherds and a supposed Roman carving of an eagle on a large rock on the foreshore provided clues to its presence. Further and more immediately striking evidence of Roman presence was discovered in 1996, when a statue of a lioness mauling her victim was found on the bed of the Almond during dredging of the harbour. It is on display in the new Museum of Scotland (see page 74).

Much of the evidence for the line of the Antonine Wall has been found only in the last decade or so, by the happy coincidence of a series of summer droughts which made the outline of Roman forts and camps (and other 'lost' archaeological structures) much more evident from the air – with increased funding for local archaeology.

Cramond Kirk

The present church dates from 1811, when an earlier building was restored and its distinctive castellations added, but there has been a church here since at least the sixteenth century – though that original is recorded as being in ruins by the mid-seventeenth century, no doubt as a result of the civil strife in which Scotland had been embroiled for almost a hundred years by that time. The interior is not exceptional, but it is worth a brief exploration. Turn left on leaving the kirk and enter the graveyard by the gate in the northeast wall.

Some of the tombstones here are as much as three hundred years old, and many, though eroded by time and weather, are carved with the medieval symbols of mortality – skull and crossbones, or hourglasses. The most distinctive, though, are of a later era; the grave markers of the Caddell family – late-eighteenth-century iron

Plate 19: The Royal Museum of Scotland, Chambers Street (see page 76).

Plate 20: The dome of the Old College is a University landmark (see page 77).

Plate 21: Doorway to ruined Craigmillar Castle (see page 80).

Plate 22: The elegant Georgian terraced houses of Moray Place, named for the Earl of Moray who lived at No. 28 (see page 84).

Plate 23: The mock baronial clock tower of Edinburgh Royal Infirmary (see page 89).

Plate 24: Floating restaurant at The Shore, on Leith's rejuvenated waterfront (see page 99).

Plate 25: Leith and the Firth of Forth from the top of Calton Hill (see page 98).

Plate 26: *Typical buildings on Musselburgh's old-fashioned High Street (see page 107).*

Plate 27: *The baronial splendour of Lauriston Castle's turrets and gables (see page 110).*

Plate 28: *Yachts at anchor at Cramond Harbour, a natural anchorage which has been in use at least since the time of the Romans (see page 114).*

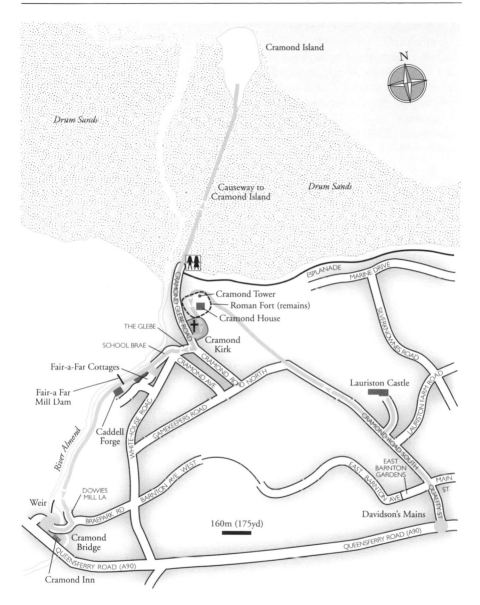

founders whose water-driven ironworks stood on the banks of the Almond – are made of cast iron. Leaving the kirkyard, turn right and walk down Cramond Glebe Road to Cramond Village and the mouth of the River Almond.

A Treasurable Island

From here you can sometimes walk (cautiously) across a slippery and dilapidated causeway to Cramond Island, some 750m (820yd) offshore. The causeway is covered at high tide, so it is important to check the times of low and high water before setting out; a tide table is no longer posted at the beginning of the causeway so check the tide table in the *Edinburgh Evening News*. At low water, especially in winter, the tidal Drum Sands which surround the island teem with waders and waterfowl, including Greenshank, Redshank, Lapwing, sandpipers, Dunlin, Dotterel, Whimbrel, Curlew, Oystercatcher and less common species.

Inhabited until 1947, the island was a favourite of the young Robert Louis Stevenson (1850–1894), and his childhood daydreams here inspired *Treasure Island* (1883), probably his best-known work.

Legacy of Iron

Now turn left and walk upstream, past the cluster of cottages which once housed the iron workers of the Caddell's mill, to the last relics of Cramond's iron-working days: the mill dam of Fair-a-Far Mill and, beside it, the overgrown ruins of the water-driven Caddell Forge, which turned out everything from nails and shovels to barrel hoops, anchors and gun barrels. At the height of Cramond's iron-working period, five mills, of which the Caddell works was the most important, stood here. All had ceased working by the 1820s, losing their trade to more conveniently located mills.

Until the nineteenth century, Cramond Harbour at the mouth of the River Almond was a thriving small port, importing iron from the Baltic for the ironworks and exporting finished iron goods all over Scotland. The arrival, first of the Forth and Clyde Canal and the Union Canal, then, in the 1840s construction of the railway, destroyed the trade of small harbours like Cramond, which is now used only by a few yachts.

Follow the path for 1km (½ mile) up the river, passing the weir, to the old Cramond Bridge. Overshadowed by the much newer bridge that carries the A90 across the Almond, this one is at least five centuries old, with records that show it was in use as early as 1500. Crossing the Almond on three pointed arches supported by massively buttressed piers, it bears its age well, and looks confident of being here five hundred years hence.

Next to the bridge stands the Cramond Inn, dating from the mid-seventeenth century (though with nineteenth- and twentieth-century additions). Like a good many other pubs, this was a favourite haunt of the young Robert Louis Stevenson and is a good place to round off your walk with a drink and a bite to eat.

After you've rested a while in the pub, you can take a number 41 bus back to the city centre or carry on to undertake the next walk.

Cramond to South Queensferry

Summary: This walk takes you from the outskirts of Edinburgh along one of the prettiest stretches of the Forth Coast, through woods and along seashore, to South Queensferry. The titanic outlines of the Forth rail and road bridges, each a remarkable piece of engineering for its time, are in sight almost all the way.

Start:	Cramond Bridge.
Finish:	South Queensferry.
Length:	7km (4 miles).
Time:	3hr.
Refreshments:	Cramond Inn.
Which day:	Sunday, Monday or Tuesday.
To visit:	Dalmeny House.
	Dalmeny Kirk (St Cuthbert's).
	Queensferry Museum.
	Inchcolm Abbey, Inchcolm Island.

Take a number 41 bus from the city centre to Cramond Bridge. On alighting, cross the bridge to the west bank of the River Almond and walk along the north pavement of the A90 main road for 150m (165yd). Here you should turn right to enter, by the Edinburgh Gate, the wooded grounds of Dalmeny House, the estate of the Earls of Rosebery. The path runs through a 2km (1¼ mile) strip of beeches to the foreshore, where it turns left to reach Dalmeny House after a further kilometre or so across lawns and woods. Before you take this left turn, however, walk onto the shore and detour briefly right for a 150m (165yd) to the rocky headland known as Eagle Rock; the faint outline of what is believed to be a Roman carving in the shape of an Imperial eagle, symbol of the legions, can still be seen.

An Ancestral Pile

Carry on through the grounds to Dalmeny House. This has been the seat of the Earls of Rosebery since the seventeenth century – the first earl, Archibald Primrose (1661–1723), was rewarded with his title on the succession of Queen Anne (1665–1714) for his support of King William III against James VII and II (1633–1701); he was later one of the architects of the Union with England. The fifth earl, Archibald Philip Primrose (1847–1929), was a leading Liberal Party statesman of the late nineteenth century, and was briefly Prime Minister, in 1894–1895.

Dalmeny House, designed in 1815 in the Gothic style by William Wilkins (1778–1839), houses a fine collection of eighteenth-century furniture and porcelain

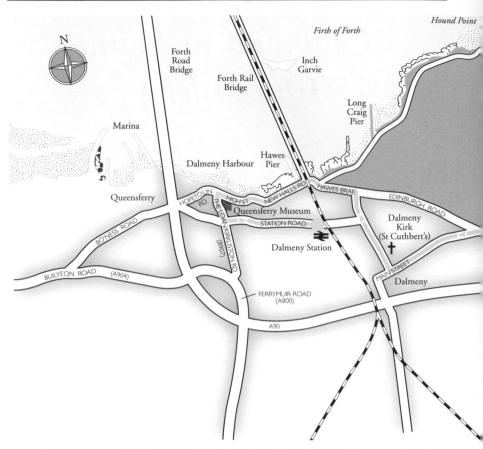

as well as portraits, including one of the fourth earl by the Scottish portrait painter Sir Henry Raeburn (1756–1823), and of the fifth earl by Sir John Millais (1829–1896).

Scottish Romanesque

From Dalmeny House, turn right and follow the path that takes you in a south-westerly direction through the woods and fields of the estate towards Edinburgh Road (B924). Cross the road, and walk for the best part of a kilometre (½ mile) into Dalmeny Village to visit its fine church.

This delightful, twelfth-century Romanesque kirk is one of the finest churches of its style and period in Scotland. Within, the small windows shed little light, but it is possible to see the fine carving on the arches and the typically grotesque and elaborate stonework on the arches and columns of the south doorway.

The small Norman-style tower at the west end is a later addition, designed by the Edinburgh architect Sir Robert Lorimer (1864–1929). Lorimer, knighted in 1911, was responsible for many of Scotland's late-nineteenth-century country mansions and city churches, and was the leading Scottish architect of his time; he also

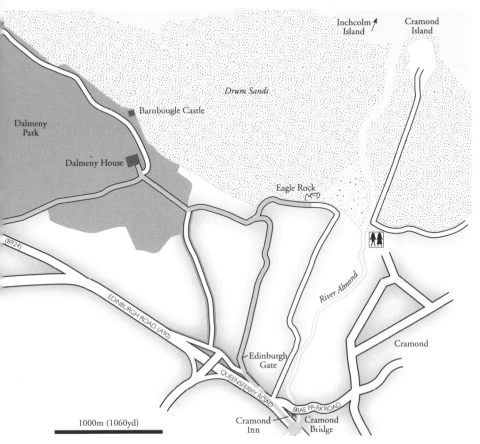

designed the Scottish National War Memorial (see page 27) at Edinburgh Castle. He is credited with rescuing the elements of Scottish architectural style from the overwhelming influence of Victorian Gothic, and with sponsoring the revival of the crafts in Scotland.

South Queensferry

Leaving the church, turn right and walk north to rejoin the B924, then turn left again and follow the road into South Queensferry and its harbour.

The Forth Rail Bridge, by far the dominant feature of South Queensferry, was completed in 1890 and carries twin railway tracks in a straight line for 3km (2 miles) across the Firth of Forth. Its three great cantilever spans reach 111m (360ft) above the high-water mark, and are mounted on gigantic caissons set into the bed of the Firth. At the height of the Victorian era, this massive structure of girders and of tubes 4m (12ft) thick was considered the Eighth Wonder of the World. Designed by Sir John Fowler (1817–1898) and Sir Benjamin Baker (1840–1907), the bridge was seven years in the building, used 54,000 tons of steel – and cost the lives of fifty-seven workers.

Just east of the bridge at its midpoint is the rocky island of Inch Garvie, now abandoned to seals and seabirds. This island was fortified during the Napoleonic Wars and later in World War I and II against the threat of invasion. Its gun positions can still be seen from the shore and from trains passing over the bridge.

Before the bridge was built, trains crossed the Firth of Forth on the world's first rail ferry, and in even earlier centuries the ferries between South and North Queensferry were the only way of crossing to Fife without taking the long inland route to Stirling, the lowest point at which the river could be bridged. As a result, Stirling became the strategic 'choke point' between southern and northern Scotland for any invading army, and was frequently fought over during successive wars (see the Stirling and Bannockburn walk, page 147).

The 'Queen's Ferry' got its name from the saintly Queen Margaret (*c.* 1046–1093), Saxon English queen of Malcolm III Canmore (*c.* 1031–1093); she frequently crossed the Forth here while travelling between the Royal Palace at Dunfermline (see page 140), in Fife, and Edinburgh. South Queensferry sits in the shadow of the colossal bridge, and the path along the Firth leads into the village High Street. At No. 53, visit the small Queensferry Museum, which contains odds and ends relating to local history and to the building of the two Forth bridges.

In summer, you can round off this walk with a boat trip from Dalmeny Harbour to the island of Inchcolm in the Firth of Forth and the ruins of its abbey. The Gaelic name *Inchcolm* ('Columba's Island') strongly suggests a – possibly illusory – link with the Irish missionary Saint Columba (521–597), who brought Christianity to Scotland by way of Iona, in the Hebrides, in the sixth century. There were certainly hermits here in the twelfth century; in 1123 one of them sheltered King Alexander I (*c.* 1077–1124) when he was stranded on the island by a gale. By way of thanks, Alexander founded an abbey on the island, and its ruins (the best preserved Scottish monastic buildings of their era) are the main reason for visiting the island – though the trip across the Forth, the multitudes of seabirds which nest on the island and the grey seals which colonize its seaweed-covered rocks offer a fairly convincing incentive in their own right.

Finish this excursion by walking up to Dalmeny Station to catch a bus to the city centre or for trains back to Edinburgh Haymarket or Edinburgh Waverley stations.

North Queensferry to Blackness Castle

Summary: This is a lengthy but rewarding walk, taking in an interesting visitor attraction, one of Scotland's man-made wonders (and a fine view of another), and the grandest stately home in Scotland.

Start:	North Queensferry Station.
Finish:	Blackness Castle.
Length:	10.5km (6½ miles).
Time:	3–5hr.
Refreshments:•	Deep Sea World café-restaurant.
	Stables Restaurant at Hopetoun House.
	Picnics possible in Hopetoun House grounds in summer.
	Blackness Inn, Blackness.
Which day:	Any day (but not recommended as a winter walk).
To visit:	Deep Sea World.
	Hopetoun House.
	Blackness Castle.

The train-ride from Edinburgh Waverley or Edinburgh Haymarket station to North Queensferry takes only about twenty minutes and gives you a trip across the Forth Rail Bridge, so it's almost certainly the preferable option for getting to the start of this walk even if you have a car. For the return journey you can either take a bus from Blackness to Edinburgh's St Andrews Square bus station or call a taxi from the Blackness Inn to Linlithgow Station and return from there to Edinburgh by train.

Leaving North Queensferry Station by the exit from the northbound platform (on the west side of the station), turn left and walk downhill on Station Road, then left again to pass under the bridge to Deep Sea World, which is clearly signposted.

Saving the Whales
Located in a flooded former stone quarry from which rock was cut for use in building the railway line, the lively, award-winning Deep Sea World features more than three thousand fish, from herring and seahorses to piranha and sand sharks, viewed from transparent underwater walkways whose length totals 112m (122yd). Sealife from Scottish waters is given pride of place, but there are plenty of exotic tropical species, and a touch pool lets you handle lobsters, starfish, crabs and even small sharks.

In 1997, Deep Sea World's team of divers and sea mammal experts hit the head-lines because of their efforts in the dramatic attempt to save a 13m (40ft) young

119

sperm whale which had become disoriented after swimming up the Firth of Forth. Sadly, attempts to steer the whale (inevitably nicknamed 'Moby' by the media) back into the open water of the North Sea failed, and it eventually became stranded and died. The event prompted the setting up of a 'Moby Fund', and Deep Sea World now has a team equipped with flotation equipment ready to help rescue whales and dolphins anywhere on Britain's coasts.

A Stroll Across the Forth

Leaving Deep Sea World, walk back under the railway bridge and around North Queensferry's small harbour, and then follow the footpath beside the B981 road that runs steeply up to the Forth Road Bridge approaches. Turn right and take the walkway across the bridge. The walk over the road bridge offers a fine view of the Firth of Forth, the Fife coast and the Forth Rail Bridge, with Arthur's Seat and Edinburgh Castle in the distance to the east.

Construction of the Forth Road Bridge began in 1958 and was completed six years later. When it opened in 1964, the bridge at 2km (1¼ miles), was the longest suspension bridge in the world, a record that has of course since been overtaken by several others. The main suspension towers reach a height of 157.5m (512ft) above the high-water mark, almost half as tall again as the towers of the railway bridge, and next to the railway bridge's massively over-engineered girders the road bridge looks almost flimsy. It does indeed sway (as it is designed to do) in high winds.

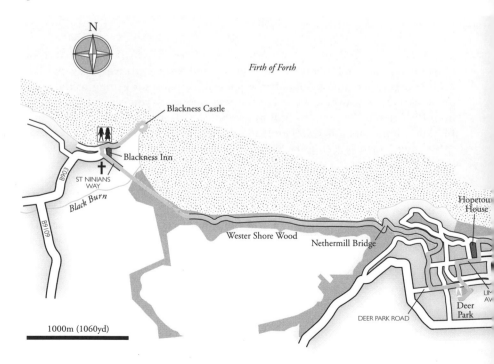

Hopetoun House

Leaving the road bridge at its southern end, turn right and walk downhill to Queensferry Marina, just west of the village, then turn left again and walk along the shore for about 3km (2 miles) to Hopetoun House, the grandest stately home in Scotland.

Set in 40ha (100 acres) of woodland, parkland and gardens, Hopetoun looks out over the Firth, and has been the seat of the Hope family – the Earls of Hopetoun and later the Marquesses of Linlithgow – since the first part of this magnificent mansion was built between 1699 and 1707. The architect was Sir William Bruce (1630–1710) who also designed the later parts of the Palace of Holyroodhouse (see page 39). The Hope family provided the Crown with a number of distinguished generals, admirals and statesmen.

The older part of the house displays fine examples of Scottish carving, wainscoting and ceiling paintings, and its giltwork and Classical motifs are among the finest examples of the grandeur of aristocratic interior design during the early eighteenth century. In 1721, the renowned architect William Adam (1689–1748) was commissioned to enlarge the house, and it was he who added the splendid façade, colonnades and state apartments which housed King George IV (1762–1830) on his visit to Scotland in 1822 and Queen Elizabeth II (1926–) when she came up here in 1988. On William Adam's death, his son Robert Adam (1728–1792), architect to King George III (1738–1820), completed the work. The house is now preserved by a charitable trust, and the magnificent Adam

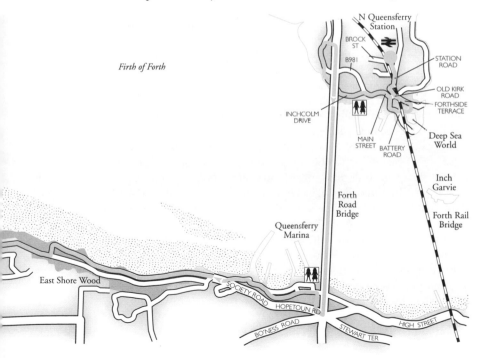

121

Ballroom is used for banquets and corporate events.

The central section of the house is three storeys high, capped by an attic storey and eighteen massive urns. Below, a rank of fourteen Corinthian false pillars ornament the façade. Single-storey wings, the work of Robert Adam, stand on either side and are connected to the centre by Corinthian colonnades. The entire frontage spans some 170m (185yd).

From the entrance hall, with its semicircular stone stairs enclosed by an eight-sided wooden stairwell beautifully decorated with mural paintings and carvings of flowers and fruit, pass through a series of relatively small, interconnecting rooms hung with fine Dutch tapestries into the much larger State Apartments, each with its own colour theme. First on the route is the Yellow Drawing Room, with silk damask walls and a fine marble chimneypiece; then comes the Red Drawing Room, again with damask walls, this time matched by eighteenth-century red damask chairs and set off by an elaborately Rococo ceiling and fine period paintings, including a gorgeous waterscape of Venice by Canaletto (1697–1768); and finally the State Dining Room, a later addition by James Gillespie Graham (1777–1855), furnished and decorated throughout in the style of the 1820s. Portraits by Sir Henry Raeburn (1756–1823) and Thomas Gainsborough (1727–1788) look down on the fine mahogany dining table and chairs.

Returning to the outside of the building, walk up ninety steps to the roof terrace, from which there are lovely views of the park and the Firth of Forth.

A Grim Little Stronghold

Back at ground level, turn to follow the signposted path due south, then turn right into Lime Avenue and then left (due south) into the deer park, where roams a flock of red deer – a species otherwise rarely seen outside the Highlands. Exiting the deer park, turn left along Deer Park Road and then right (north), and follow the path along the right bank of a small stream for about 400m (440yd) to the shore. Turn left and walk 3km (2 miles) along the shore, through Wester Shore Wood and, shortly after crossing the Black Burn stream, to the village and castle of Blackness (the stress is on the second syllable).

This castle is the very opposite of Hopetoun House. While its grand neighbour in a sense celebrates and symbolizes a Scotland no longer at war with itself or with England, this grim little fifteenth-century stronghold is a memento of a Scotland that was torn by internal struggle and threatened by invasion. Guarding a strategic landing place, it was felt to be important enough that even under the terms of the Treaty of Union it was one of the four Scottish castles to continue to be left fortified in Government hands – the others were Edinburgh, Stirling and Inverness.

Blackness Castle has seen more than its fair share of history. Burned twice by the English during the fifteenth century, it was rebuilt each time. Covenanter prisoners were imprisoned here during the 'Killing Time' in the second half of the seventeenth century. During the French and Napoleonic Wars it was used as an ammunition depot.

After pottering around the Castle, stroll through the village to the pleasant Blackness Inn for a rest and maybe a wee dram while waiting for your bus or taxi.

Linlithgow to Bo'ness

Summary: Linlithgow was a royal seat from the time of David I (*c.* 1080–1153), who built a fortified manor here in the twelfth century, until the Union of the Crowns when King James VI and I (1566–1625) decamped to London, taking his court with him. After a spell in the doldrums – during which it lost much of its trade to the new Forth ports of Bo'ness and Queensferry – Linlithgow was revitalized by the building of the Union Canal, connecting it with Edinburgh and, via the Forth and Clyde Canal, with Glasgow.

Part of this walk is along farm tracks which can be muddy; stout footwear is required.

Start:	Linlithgow Station.
Finish:	Bo'ness town centre.
Length:	5km (3 miles).
Refreshments:	There are plenty of pubs, cafés and restaurants in Linlithgow and Bo'ness town centres.
Which day:	Saturday or Sunday.
To visit:	Linlithgow Union Canal Society Museum.
	Linlithgow Heritage Trust Museum.
	St Michael's Church.
	Linlithgow Palace.
	Kinneil House and Bo'ness Museum.
	Bo'ness and Kinneil Railway.
	Birkhill Fireclay Mine.

There are half-hourly trains from Edinburgh's Haymarket Station to Linlithgow, with a journey time of about twenty minutes, and it is assumed that this is the means of transport that you've used to reach the start of this charming excursion. At the other end of the walk your best bet – unless it's a nice day and you're feeling energetic and want to retrace your steps – is to catch a bus back from Bo'ness town centre to Linlithgow, then a local train to Edinburgh.

Linlithgow is built in a crescent around the south shore of Linlithgow Loch. The Union Canal runs just south of the town, with the railway running parallel to it, and the M9 Edinburgh–Glasgow motorway runs along the north side of the loch.

Transport by Water
Arriving on the westbound platform, leave Linlithgow Station by the south exit, turn right on Back Station Road and then almost immediately left, across the Union

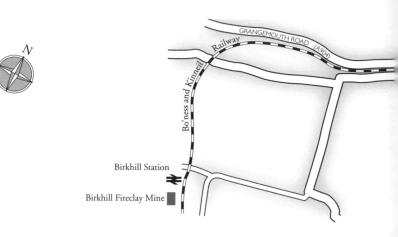

Canal. Next turn right onto Manse Road and pause to take a look at the canal.

The Union Canal was begun in 1817, when an Act of Parliament authorized formation of a joint stock company to finance the building of a canal to join Edinburgh with the Forth and Clyde Canal, which had been completed in 1790 and terminated on the River Carron, just north of the important iron and coal town of Falkirk (the small ship's cannon known as 'carronades' took their name from the Carron ironworks nearby). Finished in 1822, the Union Canal joined the Forth and Clyde Canal just west of Falkirk and had its Edinburgh terminus near Fountainbridge, west of the city centre. Since it was now possible to haul heavy goods and raw materials to inland towns along its route, the canal ushered in a new era of industrial growth for Edinburgh and the surrounding region. The two canals flourished until 1842, when the railway came to Linlithgow, providing a much faster alternative form of transport.

The Linlithgow Union Canal Society Museum, at Manse Road Basin on the canal, is housed in stables built in the early 1820s to house the heavy draught horses that towed the canal barges. The Museum features an audiovisual display, documents, photographs and historical relics. The society runs half-hour cruises along the canal aboard the canal boat *Victoria* to the remarkable twelve-arched aqueduct, a feat of nineteenth-century engineering that carries the canal over the River Avon, 4km (2½ miles) west of Linlithgow.

Murder and Mayhem

Walk back across the canal, cross the railway by the station footbridge, and turn left along the High Street.

On the north side of the street, the nineteenth-century Cross Well marks the spot where the medieval Market Cross stood in front of the grand Town Hall, which was rebuilt in the 1660s after being destroyed during the Cromwellian invasion of 1650. The Town Hall now houses the Linlithgow Tourist Information Office.

Some 20m (20yd) further on, on the south side of the street, a plaque on the wall of the Sheriff Court indicates the spot at which an assassin shot the Regent, James

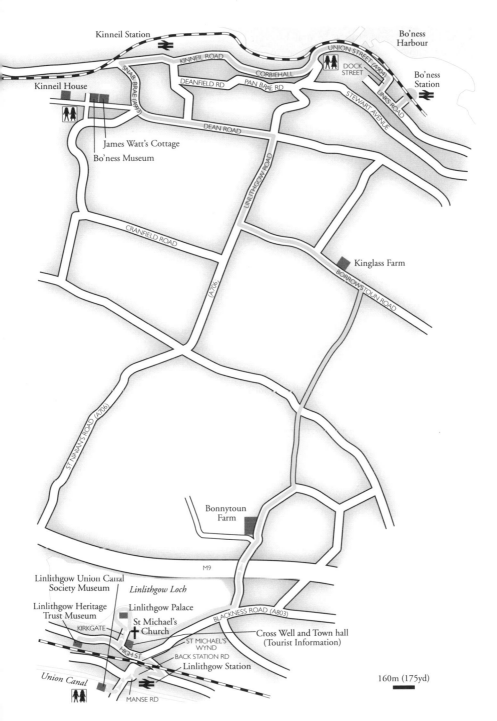

Kinneil Station

Bo'ness
Harbour

KINNEIL ROAD

UNION STREET (A904)

Bo'ness
Station

SNAB BRAE (A993)

CORBIEHALL

DOCK
STREET

Kinneil House

DEANFIELD RD

PAN BRAE RD

LINKS ROAD

STEWART AVENUE

James Watt's Cottage

DEAN ROAD

Bo'ness Museum

LINLITHGOW ROAD

CRANFIELD ROAD

Kinglass Farm

(A706)

BORROWSTOUN ROAD

ST NINIAN'S ROAD (A706)

Bonnytoun
Farm

M9

Linlithgow Union Canal
Society Museum

Linlithgow Loch

Linlithgow Palace

BLACKNESS ROAD (A803)

Linlithgow Heritage
Trust Museum

St Michael's
Church

KIRKGATE

Cross Well and Town hall
(Tourist Information)

ST MICHAEL'S
WYND

HIGH ST

Union Canal

BACK STATION RD

Linlithgow Station

MANSE RD

160m (175yd)

125

Stewart (1531–1570), Earl of Moray, in January 1570. Moray, a bastard son of James V (1512–1542) and therefore half-brother of Mary Queen of Scots (1542–1587), was the leader of the Protestant faction in Scotland, and it was he who schemed with Elizabeth I (1533–1603) of England to imprison Mary at Loch Lomond in 1569. His assassin was James Hamilton (*c.* 1540–*c.* 1580) of Bothwellhaugh, a somewhat shady figure in the pay of the French faction; after the deed, Hamilton fled to France, where he became an agent for Philip II (1527–1598) of Spain in two attempts on the life of the rebel Dutch Prince William the Silent (1533–1584), in 1573 and 1575. Hamilton fired the shot that killed Moray from the house of Archbishop John Hamilton (1511–1571), who was a natural son of James Hamilton (*c.* 1477–1529), first Earl of Arran, a leading figure in the pro-French faction. The archbishop was hanged as an accomplice in the murder.

Walk on, and on the south side of the street, at No. 139, you will find the Linlithgow Heritage Trust Museum. Here, displays tell the story of Linlithgow, with exhibits on the ground floor stressing the town's royal past and on the upper floor outlining the development of Linlithgow's trade and industry.

St Michael's Church

Now cross the High Street and walk back toward the site of the Market Cross, turning left immediately before the Town Hall to walk up to the fine Gothic St Michael's Church, which stands on the right-hand side of the street.

One of Scotland's largest pre-Reformation churches, St Michael's took over a hundred and thirty years from start to finish. It is known that it was built on the site of an earlier church which burned down. The nave and choir were begun in 1497, and the tower and apse were finally completed in 1531. The plain interior (swept clear of its saints, Virgin and crucifix by the fundamentalist Protestant Lords of the Congregation in 1559) is notable for the three apse windows filled with striking Perpendicular tracery, and for the stained glass.

The high point is the so-called Flamboyant window, lighting a chapel where James IV (1473–1513) is said to have been told by a ghost of his forthcoming doom at the Battle of Flodden. James went anyway, and was slaughtered along with his men; in relation to the population of Scotland at the time, the toll of Flodden was ten times that of the whole of Britain in World War I. It was said – and with only a little by way of hyperbole – that there was not a household in the entire Border region that did not lose a man at Flodden.

Outside, the church's most striking – and controversial – feature is the gleaming, jarringly modernistic aluminium-clad spire. This was erected in 1964 to replace an earlier spire.

Linlithgow Palace

Linlithgow Palace, an imposing ruined shell on a grassy knoll overlooking Linlithgow Loch, stands just across the road from the church.

Originally, the royal residence was no more than a manor used by the early Scottish kings when travelling to worship at St Michael's Church. Appropriated as a base by Edward I (1239–1307) – 'The Hammer of the Scots' to his English admirers, 'Langshanks' ('Longlegs') to the Scots – who had a defensive wooden stockade built around it, it was destroyed in due course by the soldiers of Robert the Bruce (1274–1329). A new manor was built by David II (1324–1371), but it did not survive long before being destroyed by fire along with the rest of Linlithgow. The town was mostly, in those days, built of wood – the church and the royal manor were exceptions.

James I (1394–1437), perhaps influenced by the eighteen years he spent in his youth as a royal hostage at the English court, set out in 1435 to create a residence more fit for a king, and over the next century or more he and his heirs turned Linlithgow into the finest royal palace Scotland had yet seen, and they often spent more time here than in Edinburgh Castle or Holyroodhouse. James IV added to and altered the original fabric, and it became the favourite residence of his English queen, Margaret Tudor (1489–1541), until James's death at Flodden, when she and the infant James V (1512–1542) left for the more defensible Stirling Castle. During James IV's reign, and again under James V, Linlithgow became a kind of Scottish Camelot, with minstrels, jugglers, tournaments, archery, falconry and the hunt. James V's French queen, Mary of (Marie de) Guise (1515–1560), may have been flattering her husband when she said she had never seen such a princely palace; nevertheless, Linlithgow was for a while the cradle of a Scottish Golden Age.

That age ended with the death of James V and the years of civil strife and English invasion that followed. As regent, Mary of Guise moved to Edinburgh, and as Queen of Scots, her daughter Mary (1542–1587) was rarely able to go where she chose. When the latter's son and heir, James VI (1566–1625), became James I of England and Scotland, Linlithgow Palace was deserted, and it gradually fell into disrepair. Cromwell's soldiers occupied it between 1650 and 1659. Much later, in 1746, while it was being used as a barracks by the Duke of Cumberland's Hanoverian troops after the defeat of the Jacobites at Culloden (1746), a fire broke out that reduced the Palace of Linlithgow to a roofless shell. Today, with its empty windows gazing out over the loch, this is one of Scotland's most haunting and melancholy royal palaces.

The House of Hamilton

From the north side of Linlithgow Palace, turn right and follow the footpath along the south shore of the loch. As this footpath leaves the loch at its east end, turn left onto the first narrow side road running north off the A803, which is the eastward continuation of the High Street, and pass under the M9 motorway. Immediately north of the motorway, take the right fork at Bonnytoun Farm, then after walking about 300m (330yd), take the second farm track on the left. This cuts across the shoulder of a low hill then runs due north for a little under 2km (1¼ mile) to Kinglass Farm. Turn left here on the narrow tarred road, follow this for half a kilometre (¼ mile) or so to the A706, and turn right to walk along the pavement of Linlithgow Road towards Bo'ness town centre. After 350m (380yd) turn left at the crossroads – follow the signs marked 'Hospital' – to Kinneil House and Bo'ness Museum.

The Museum is housed in the seventeenth-century stables of Kinneil House, and contains displays of the cast-iron work and the pottery for which Bo'ness was noted during the nineteenth century and which was still being made as recently as the 1950s. Next to the Museum stands 'James Watt's cottage', the outbuilding used by the inventor as a workshop while he was conducting his experiments in steam power (see below).

After you have spent as long as you want to exploring the Museum, leave it and walk 75–80m (80yd) down the signposted footpath to Kinneil House, now a picturesque semi-ruin. In its sixteenth-century heyday it was the home of one of the mightiest men in Scotland, James Hamilton (1516–1575), second Earl of Arran, Governor of Scotland during the minority of Mary Queen of Scots.

The Hamiltons were among the most powerful noble families of central Scotland, but had a record of shifting loyalties that was remarkable even for the time. The second earl himself was originally one of the leaders of the anti-French Protestant faction. Later he changed sides – John Hamilton, the archbishop hanged for his part in the assassination of the Earl of Moray in Linlithgow, was Arran's bastard son, and it is hard to believe that Arran knew nothing of this anti-Protestant plot. Arran also planned to marry his heir James Hamilton (1530–1609) to Mary Queen of Scots, but James had other ideas and wooed his father back to the Protestant cause, as well as unsuccessfully wooing Queen Elizabeth I (1533–1603) of England. It is perhaps hardly surprising, with hindsight, that young James lost his mind, being judged insane at the age of 32.

The house was built between 1546 and 1553, and takes the form of a fortified tower and an adjoining mansion, grandly called the Palace, connected to the tower by end pavilions. The painted ceiling of the barrel-vaulted Arbour Room and the Hamilton arms on one of the window vaults survived demolition of derelict parts of the building in 1936.

All Steamed Up

Return to the Museum, turn left and then right at the next intersection and walk around to the harbour, which once handled cargoes as diverse as leather, iron, coal and fireclay, and even had its own whaling fleet, supplying whale oil to light the lamps of Edinburgh and lubricate the machinery of the Falkirk mills.

Just east of the harbour, follow the road round to join Links Road and then turn first left to enter the nostalgic world of the Bo'ness and Kinneil Railway, where the Scottish Railway Preservation Society has collected rolling stock, steam locomotives and railway paraphernalia from the great days of steam. The station, with its old-fashioned booking office, waiting rooms, platform signs and signal box, is a throwback to the heyday of steam, as is the engine shed, which used to stand at Edinburgh Haymarket Station.

The steam train is, of course, one of the many inventions the world owes to Scotland – along with the waterproof overcoat, the rubber motor tyre, tarmac, the telephone, penicillin, whisky and the bolt-action rifle (in short, all the essentials of civilization!). The work of the Scottish engineer James Watt (1736–1819) made it possible for the first time to build engines small enough to drive a locomotive (the earliest static engines were used only to drive pumps), though it was not until 1814 that the Englishman George Stephenson (1781–1848) successfully tested his first locomotive. The railways reached Scotland in the 1840s, and for much of the second half of the nineteenth century, the *Flying Scotsman*, running between Edinburgh and London, was the fastest train in the world, with an average speed of nearly 80km/hr (50mph) over the 630km (390-mile) journey, taking just under eight hours. Today, the fastest trains cover the same distance in just about four hours, at an average speed of just under 160km/hr (100mph).

The Bo'ness and Kinneil Railway, however, attains nothing like this speed, as it potters along under steam power over its 6km (3½ miles) of track by the shore and then turns inland to terminate at the Birkhill Fireclay Mine. Fireclay, so called because it withstands extreme heat, was essential to the iron-working industries of the surrounding area, where it was used to line furnaces. The mine reopened during the 1990s as a visitor attraction, and features a display of 300-million-year-old fossils found in the underground clay beds.

After you have enjoyed pottering among the fossils, catch a bus to Linlithgow, from whose railway station there are frequent trains (every half hour) back to Edinburgh Haymarket Station.

Around Edinburgh

It would be a shame to leave Edinburgh without seeing at least some of the historic towns and attractive, sometimes dramatic coastline scenery around the city. Many of the events that shaped Scotland from the earliest times have taken place within an hour's travel of the capital.

Stirling, with one of Scotland's most dramatic castles and the battlefields where William Wallace (1270–1305) and Robert the Bruce (1274–1329) won victories against England; St Andrews, a delightful cathedral and university city and the home of golf; and Dunfermline, capital of Scotland more than a thousand years ago – all three are close enough to the capital for a half-day expedition at any time of year.

The often windswept shores of the Firth of Forth, which have seen Roman, Saxon, Viking, French and English fleets – and even one enterprising American revolutionary privateer! – can make a welcome change from city streets. The south shore of the Forth offers dramatic, ruined clifftop castles, sandy beaches and great views out to sea, while the Fife coast is dotted with postcard-pretty fishing harbours.

Adroit use of public transport will allow you to combine some of these walks to make a full day trip from Edinburgh. Pick any two out of the three Fife walks (or even all three if you start early on a summer's day and are feeling energetic), or combine Dunfermline (page 137) with North Queensferry to Blackness Castle (page 119), or Tantallon to Dirleton (page 142) with Leith to Prestonpans (page 103).

St Andrews

Summary: The home of golf and of Scotland's oldest university, St Andrews is rich in history. As late as the sixteenth century it was one of the most important towns in Scotland and the seat of its most powerful prelates, the Archbishops of St Andrews, whose dramatic ruined castle and cathedral are the high points of this walk.

Transport to and from Edinburgh: Take a bus from Edinburgh's St Andrews Square Bus Station, or catch one of the hourly trains from Edinburgh Waverley to Leuchars and then take a connecting bus. Both journeys last about an hour and a half.

Start/finish:	St Andrews Bus Station, City Road.
Length:	2.5km (1½ miles).
Time:	3hr.
Refreshments:	Numerous pubs, cafés and restaurants in St Andrews town centre.
Which day:	Any day.
To visit:	British Golf Museum.
	St Andrews Sea Life Centre.
	St Andrews Preservation Trust Museum.
	St Andrews Castle.
	St Andrews Cathedral and Priory, and Museum.
	St Andrews University.
	Holy Trinity Church.

Start this walk by turning left out of the bus station on City Road and walking along 200m (220yd) or so to North Street. Cross North Street, turn right and then, after only about 20m (20yd), turn left onto the appropriately named Golf Place to walk up to what is internationally recognized as the home of golf.

The Royal and Ancient Golf Club, whose headquarters you can see on your left, is the body that sets the standards for golf all over the world, and rolling off to the west is the world's most revered golfing turf. If you are a golfer, you will already have booked to play here – which is something you will have to have done well in advance. If you are a 'golf widow' or 'widower', deposit your spouse here, having made arrangements to meet later, and proceed.

The 'Metropolis of Golf'

Immediately past the Royal and Ancient's pompous clubhouse, built in 1854 in Victorian Gothic, turn right into the British Golf Museum, where exhibits reveal 'the glorious history of golf'. (For more about the history of golf see the appropriate part of the Leith to Prestonpans walk, page 103.) The first surviving reference to golf in St Andrews dates from Archbishop Hamilton's edict of 1552, which reserves the right of the townsfolk to use the links for 'golff, futball, schuteing and all gamis'. Today, of course, golf has eclipsed these other pastimes at St Andrews. As early as 1691, the city was being called the 'metropolis of golf' and in 1754 the Society of St Andrews Golfers was created.

This became the Royal and Ancient Golf Club eighty years later, the 'Royal' part of the title being bestowed by William IV (1765–1837), but it was not until the growing craze for the game in the late nineteenth century that the world came to look to St Andrews as the home of golf. As any fanatical golfer knows, the waiting list to play the world-famous Old Course is months if not years long – though the recent collapse of the so-called Asian Tiger economies may have done something to reduce the number of golf-mad Japanese *sararimen* waiting to tee off. The museum also contains utterly fascinating displays of old golf balls, old golf clubs, new golf clubs, new golf balls, and even – one's excitement knows no bounds – pictures of people playing golf.

Protecting the Seal

Leaving the Museum, turn right and walk along the sea front to the St Andrews Sea Life Centre.

Until the 1980s, this was the site of the public Step Rock swimming pool, filled by the tide twice daily with natural, unheated North Sea water. (I can vividly remember swimming in this frigid pond as a small boy.) With the appearance of modern, indoor heated pools, the Step Rock facility became less popular, and it is now used as a convalescent home for sick or injured grey seals which are brought here to the Sea Life Centre to recover – there are large seal colonies not far away, near the mouth of the River Eden and in the Firth of Tay. The Sea Life Centre also features examples of North Sea marine life – sharks, rays, conger eels, cuttlefish and many others.

Clerics and Academics

Coming out of the Sea Life Centre, walk south and then left onto The Scores, right down Murray Park and left onto North Street. Proceed 100m (110yd) or so before turning left into the fifteenth-century precincts of St Andrews University.

The oldest university in Scotland – and, with Oxford and Cambridge, one of the three oldest in Britain – St Andrews was founded in 1411 by the then Bishop and tutor to James I (1394–1437), Henry Wardlaw (d. 1440) and got its first buildings forty years later, when St Salvator's College was created by Bishop James Kennedy (*c.* 1408–1465). The chapel and the tower which surmounts the North Street archway are fine examples of Scottish fifteenth-century Gothic architecture.

Bishop Kennedy was a power in the land during the troubled fifteenth century and was one of the regents of Scotland during the minority of James III (1451–1488). His tomb, inside the collegiate church of St Salvator's, is a superb

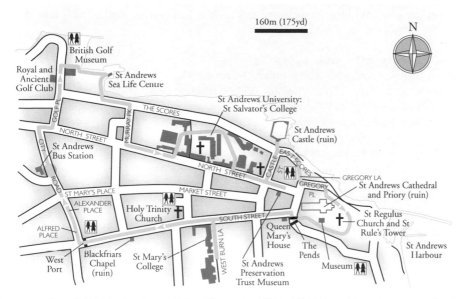

160m (175yd)

N

British Golf Museum

Royal and Ancient Golf Club

St Andrews Sea Life Centre

GOLF PL

THE SCORES

MURRAY PK

NORTH STREET

St Andrews Bus Station

CITY ROAD

St Andrews University: St Salvator's College

St Andrews Castle (ruin)

EAST SCORES

NORTH STREET

CASTLE ST

GREGORY LA

GREGORY PL

St Andrews Cathedral and Priory (ruin)

ST MARY'S PLACE

MARKET STREET

ALEXANDER PLACE

Holy Trinity Church

SOUTH STREET

St Regulus Church and St Rule's Tower

ALFRED PLACE

Queen Mary's House

The Pends

St Andrews Harbour

West Port

Blackfriars Chapel (ruin)

St Mary's College

WEST BURN LA

St Andrews Preservation Trust Museum

Museum

example of Gothic intricacy. John Knox (*c.* 1513–1572) is said to have preached from the pulpit opposite.

Just outside the church, the initials PH inlaid in the pavement are where Knox's mentor, the Protestant reformer Patrick Hamilton (1504–1528), was burned at the stake. Hamilton was a wealthy student, a scion of one of the most powerful Lowland families and a direct descendant via the wrong side of the blanket of James II (1430–1460). Graduating from St Andrews in 1524, he went on to study in Germany, where he met the great German reformers Martin Luther (1483–1546) and Philip Melancthon (1497–1560) and was strongly influenced by their doctrines, which he brought back to Scotland. Archbishop James Beaton (1470–1539) had him charged with heresy, tortured and burned when he refused to recant his reformist beliefs and in so doing, Beaton gave an enormous boost to the fortunes of the Reformation in Scotland.

The Reformation came late to Scotland, but when it came it was quickly fuelled by popular dislike of one of the most blatantly corrupt and worldly clergy in Europe. Scottish bishops, most of them the legitimate sons or by-blows of the Lowland nobles or even of the king – like Alexander Stewart (1493–1513), a bastard son of James IV (1473–1513) who was made Archbishop of St Andrews at the age of 11 – had no qualms about meddling in politics. The princes of the Church controlled immense resources – half the national wealth of Scotland. Meanwhile, parish priests lived close to destitution, and everywhere attendance at Mass dwindled as the people became disgusted by the behaviour of their supposed spiritual leaders. So when the ideas of the Reformers finally crossed the border, contained in English translations of the Bible, they were sparks to a brimful keg of powder. 'My Lord,' one of Beaton's associates said, 'if you burn any more, let them be burned in cellars, for the reek [smoke] of Patrick Hamilton has infected as many as it blew upon.' Beaton paid little attention to this advice, hammering further nails into the coffin of his own cause by burning three more reformers.

An Ecclesiastical Castle

Now turn left and walk along North Street to No. 12, where you'll find the St Andrews Preservation Trust Museum, housed in a row of fishermen's cottages. Inside are recreations of an old-fashioned grocers and a chemist's shop, fishing equipment and photographs from the now defunct local fishing fleet, and displays on the work of the trust in conserving the old town.

Once you've looked around the Museum, walk back a few paces along North Street and turn right into Castle Street, which, unsurprisingly – given its name – leads you straight to the ruined shell of St Andrews Castle.

This was the seat of the bishops and archbishops of St Andrews, which was made Scotland's ecclesiastical capital in 1472. The Castle predates this, however, by almost three centuries. Founded around 1200, it was, like most Scottish castles, badly knocked about during the Wars of Independence in the thirteenth and fourteenth centuries, when both Scots and English armies were in the habit of destroying castles to prevent the enemy using them.

During the troubled times of Mary Queen of Scots (1542–1587) the Castle was the seat of the Cardinal and Archbishop David Beaton (1494–1546). Nephew of the archbishop who had burned Patrick Hamilton, and a close ally of the French and of Mary of (Marie de) Guise (1515–1560), Beaton was for a while the most powerful man in Scotland and, like his uncle, an enthusiastic burner of heretics, among them the Protestant leader George Wishart (c. 1513–1546), who was executed on charges of plotting to murder Beaton.

Wishart may well have been innocent, but his followers were most certainly not. Two months after Wishart's death, a group of Protestant nobles sneaked into the Castle disguised as stonemasons, stabbed Beaton to death and hung his body from his own window. Besieged by Mary of Guise's Catholic faction, the assassins and their supporters, including the young John Knox, held out for more than a year in hopes of help from England, but were finally captured with the help of a French fleet and taken to France. Some, like Knox, were sent as slaves to the galley fleet. (Knox was freed in 1549, after France and England agreed to withdraw their troops from Scotland.)

Cross East Scores to enter the Castle through a gateway which originally had two round towers, neither of which survives, though the Fore Tower, in the middle of the front wall, still stands. The Castle was built around a central court. Walk clockwise around this from the entrance to the Sea Tower, in the northwest corner, and its grim Bottle Dungeon, cut 8m (26ft) deep into the living rock. This dungeon got its name because of its internal shape, which resembles that of a round-bottomed flask. The especial cruelty of this construction was that those thrown into its pitch darkness – and thrown was what they generally were – were, because of the curved floor, unable to lie flat for sleep and soon developed agonizing spinal problems.

Relics of a Mighty Edifice

Leaving the Castle, walk along East Scores, turn right on Gregory Lane and left through Gregory Place to reach St Andrews Cathedral. This too is in ruins; sacked by Protestant zealots during the Reformation, it was used in the seventeenth century as a handy source of ready-cut masonry for other buildings, and it requires some imagination to picture it as one of the most magnificent monastic complexes in Scotland.

The cathedral precincts are enclosed by a sixteenth-century wall. In the centre stands St Regulus Church, built between 1127 and 1144; climb the hundred and fifty-one steps to the top of its tower for a fine view of St Andrews and the coast of Fife in either direction. Following the building of this church, which was probably erected to hold relics of the apostle Saint Andrew himself, a priory was built in 1159, and the Cathedral was consecrated in 1318.

What remains of the Cathedral is still impressive: the twelfth-century east walls, the thirteenth-century gables, and the south wall of the ten-bayed nave give some indication of the building's imposing size and, surrounded by the one- and two-storey buildings of medieval St Andrews, it must have seemed even more enormous.

Walk south from the cathedral ruins to the Museum, which contains some fine early Christian stone carvings as well as slabs from eighth- and ninth-century Celtic crosses.

A City of Many Churches

Leave the cathedral precincts by The Pends, the fourteenth-century arched gateway to the priory, and walk along the left-hand side of South Street, passing on your left Queen Mary's House, a pretty pantiled house with rubble-built walls, whose only real claim to a connection with Mary Tudor (1516–1558) is that, erected in 1523, it was still standing during her reign.

After a further 250m (270yd), turn left to visit St Mary's College, founded by Archbishop James Beaton in 1537. In College Hall, one of the original student rooms, with its box beds, is preserved. Also worth a visit is the Upper Hall, with an elegant, galleried and paneled room which was the workplace of James Gregory (1638–1675), the mathematician and inventor, whose work in telescopy was developed in 1668 by Sir Isaac Newton (1642–1727) in devising the reflecting telescope. Mathematical professor at St Andrews from 1668, Gregory went on in 1674 to be the first professor of mathematics at Edinburgh University, a career shift he made because he felt that at St Andrews he was being offered too little respect. Edinburgh gave him the desired respect in the very tangible form of a one hundred per cent pay rise.

On the ground floor of the Upper Hall, in the chamber now called Parliament Hall, the Scottish Parliament sat in 1645–1646.

Carry on along South Street for about 100m (110yd) and then cross the street to enter Holy Trinity Church. This twelfth-century church has been extensively rebuilt, first in 1410, again in the late eighteenth century and most recently in the early twentieth century – the only original fifteenth-century part is the steeple. Inside is a memorial to Archbishop James Sharp (1613–1679), ambushed and murdered at Magus Muir, near Ceres in Fife, during the 'Killing Time' of the late seventeenth century.

Passing the sixteenth-century Blackfriars Chapel on the south side of the street, continue westward along South Street to the West Port, the sixteenth-century gateway through the walls into the old town.

Turn right here to stroll back up City Road to the bus terminus and the conclusion of your walk around this ancient university city.

Alternatively, if it's a pleasant spring, or summer day and you are in an energetic mood, walk back to the Sea Life Centre and turn left for a long walk along the sands, with views out to the North Sea. The sandy beach extends for almost 8.5km (5 miles) to the north of the River Eden.

Dunfermline

Summary: Nicknamed 'the old grey town' – a nickname it most assuredly deserves – Dunfermline was one of the earliest capitals of Scotland. It was a thriving place from medieval times onwards – even after the Scottish monarchs relocated to Edinburgh – thanks to its linen-weaving industry and the prolific coal fields around it. Today, although it is increasingly a dormitory suburb of Edinburgh, there are still some interesting relics of its royal past, notably the Romanesque Dunfermline Abbey, the ruins of Dunfermline Palace, the birthplace of a great Scots-American industrialist and philanthropist and the tomb of one of the greatest of Scottish kings, Robert the Bruce (1274–1329). Although Dunfermline first flourished during the reign of Malcolm III Canmore (*c.* 1031–1093) and his queen, Margaret (*c.* 1046–1093) – later Saint Margaret – its most significant buildings date from the reign of their youngest son, David I (*c.* 1080–1153).

Transport to and from Edinburgh: There are hourly trains to and from Edinburgh Haymarket, Edinburgh Waverley, North Queensferry and Dalmeny. The journey lasts about half an hour.

Start/finish:	Dunfermline Station.
Length:	3km (2 miles).
Time:	2hr.
Refreshments:	Pubs and cafés on the way.
Which day:	Any day.
To visit:	Andrew Carnegie Birthplace Museum.
	Abbot House and Heritage Centre.
	Dunfermline Abbey.
	Royal Palace.
	Pittencrief Park and Pittencrief House.
	Dunfermline District Museum and Small Gallery.

Leaving the station, turn left and then, after maybe 100m (110yd), turn right at the traffic roundabout onto Nethertown Broad Street. Walk west to the corner of Moodie Street. Turn right here and walk up the west side of the street, then turn left into Moodie Street to visit the Andrew Carnegie Birthplace Museum.

A Great Benefactor
Andrew Carnegie (1835–1919) was in many ways the epitome of the self-made man. His father, a Dunfermline handloom weaver, emigrated to Pennsylvania when

Andrew was a boy. Starting work as a telegraph boy in 1850, he eventually became America's iron and steel king – and the richest man in the world. But instead of clinging to his fortune, Carnegie, worth US$400 million (about £80 million at the time and a truly colossal fortune in today's terms), retired from business in 1901 to devote himself to distributing his wealth by founding libraries, parks and meeting halls throughout the world.

The world's first Carnegie Library is in Dunfermline, which is the headquarters of four charitable trusts set up by him. At the time of his death in 1919, he had managed to give away more than US$350 million of his fortune to schools, colleges, churches and libraries, but there still seems to be plenty left – the British trusts alone distribute an average of more than US$150 a minute. Exhibits within the museum include a working Jacquard handloom similar to that used by Carnegie's father. Also on display are gifts and awards presented to Carnegie by communities which had benefited from his largesse.

A Literary Heritage

Leaving the museum, turn right and then left into Margaret Street. Follow this (passing on your left the original Carnegie Library) to the junction of Abbot Street,

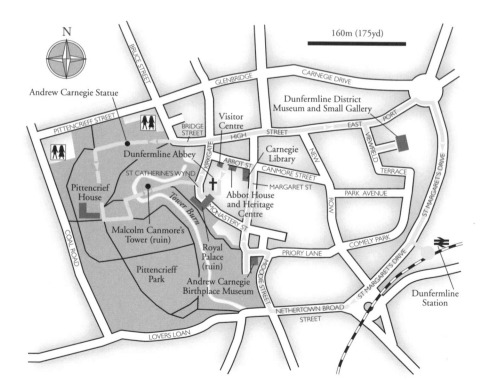

where you will see the Dunfermline Abbey and its cemetery on your left.

Before visiting the Abbey Church, however, turn left onto Abbot Street to enter the Abbot House and Heritage Centre. This building – the oldest in Dunfermline – is a pleasing jumble of dormers, tall stone chimneys, conical turrets and typical medieval crow-step gables, and it is a mine of information on the Abbey and its role in Dunfermline's history. There is also a display on the poet Robert Henryson (*c.* 1425–*c.* 1508), who was a schoolmaster in Dunfermline and is regarded as the Scottish Chaucer; indeed, his best-known work, *The Testament of Cresseid*, is a sequel to Chaucer's *Troilus and Criseyde*. He also reset the fables of Aesop into a Scottish setting, perhaps as moral tales for the edification of his Dunfermline pupils.

Above the main door of the building are carved two lines by another famous Scots poet, this time a royal one: King James I (1394–1437), who wrote the lengthy *Kingis Quair* ('King's Book') during his eighteen-year captivity in England. Ironically, he was taken prisoner while on his way to France, where he was being sent at the age of 12 for safety. The lines read:

> *Sen Vord is Thrall and Thocht is Free*
> *Keip Veill Thy Tonuge I Coinsell Thee*

('When word is thrall [enslaved] and thought is free,
Keep well thy tongue, I counsel thee.')

James was eventually freed to return to Scotland in 1424, but he reigned for only thirteen years before being murdered by several of his own barons, who had rather enjoyed running the country during his long absence and resented his efforts to bring them to heel. His uncle, the Duke of Atholl, and his cousin, Sir Robert Stewart, were among the assassins; James's widow, Queen Joan (d. 1445) had them tortured to death.

Abbot House was the residence during 1670–99 of Lady Anna Halkett (1622–1699), a woman who was remarkable in her time for her skills in medicine and surgery. A firm royalist, she helped James (1633–1701), Duke of York (later King James VII and II) to flee to France after the defeat of the Royalists in 1647, and she assisted the wounded after the Battle of Dunbar in 1650.

Righteous Monarchs and Otherwise

From Abbot House, walk south to the Abbey Church, built on the site of an earlier Celtic church during the reign of Malcolm Canmore in 1072 by his saintly queen, Margaret, and dedicated to the Holy Trinity.

It was their youngest son, David I, who in 1128 rebuilt the church once again and founded the Abbey. David, who succeeded his brother, Alexander I (*c.* 1077–1124), had been raised at the Norman English court and was Prince of Cumbria and, by marriage, Earl of Northampton and Huntingdon in England as well as King of Scots; this dual inheritance was to cause trouble for Scotland in later years, when Edward I (1239–1307) of England used it as a basis for his claim that the Scots kings were his vassals. David brought many Anglo-Norman nobles into southern Scotland, granting estates to families whose names would become part of Scottish history: de Brus (Bruce), de Bailleul (Balliol), de Comines (Comyn) and Fitzalan. William Fitzalan (*c.* 1105–1160) became High Steward of Scotland and thus forefather of the Stewart (or Stuart) dynasty.

With the end of David's line in 1129, when his infant great-great-granddaughter Margaret (1283–1290) died in childhood shortly after the death of her father, Alexander III (1241–1286), dynastic chaos, war and invasion followed. Edward I of England had intended to marry the Maid of Norway, as Margaret was known, to his son; when she died, with no clear heir to the throne, Edward sponsored the claim of John de Balliol (*c.* 1250–1315) to the throne, intending to make Balliol his puppet, and eventually invaded Scotland. In 1303, Edward sacked Dunfermline and burned the Abbey on the grounds that it was a meeting place for the rebel Scots Parliament. After the War of Independence, it was restored by Robert the Bruce (1274–1329), but the centre of power was shifting towards Edinburgh, and Dunfermline never regained its former glory.

Enter the church through the west door. The fine Norman nave is the most striking part of the Abbey architecturally. Five pairs of massive columns support semicircular arches and divide the nave from the aisles. Immediately to your left as you enter stands a monument to William Schaw (1550–1602), Royal Chamberlain and Master of Works to Anne of Denmark (1574–1619), queen to King James VI and I (1566–1625); he restored the Abbey's nave at the turn of the sixteenth/seventeenth century. At the other end of the nave there is a monument to Robert Pitcairn (1520–1584), commendator of Dunfermline and Scottish secretary of state during the reign of Mary Queen of Scots (1542–1587). Following the Reformation, the abbots of Dunfermline were replaced by Protestant commendators as leaders of the religious community, and Dunfermline Abbey fell into decline.

Continue through the church to the east end of the building. Rebuilt in 1821 and now the Dunfermline Parish Church, this is most interesting for its historic associations. Robert the Bruce's remains were discovered here, beneath the floor of the original Abbey choir, when the site was dug up to lay the foundations of a new church in 1818. A cast was made of his skull (it can be seen in the Museum of Scotland in Edinburgh – see page 74) and his bones were reinterred here; a brass plaque in the floor marks his tomb.

On his death (possibly of leprosy) in 1329, the Bruce ordered that his heart should be removed and taken to Jerusalem, the next best thing to joining the Crusades in the Holy Land in person. It never got there, however. Sir James Douglas (1286–1330), known as the Black Douglas, chosen by the Bruce to carry his heart to Jerusalem, was killed *en route* in battle with the Moors of Andalucia.

Leaving the church by the Norman east door, pass the modern royal pew placed here to mark the nine-hundredth anniversary of the Abbey in 1972. Look up to see the words 'King Robert the Bruce' carved into the stonework of the church tower. He is one of no fewer than twenty-two Scottish royals buried at Dunfermline.

Walk straight ahead to the complex of monastic buildings which date from the Abbey's heyday. A gatehouse connects the four walls that are all that remains of the refectory with the ruins of the Royal Palace, of which a single wall still stands. This was the birthplace of King Charles I (1600–1649). Systematically destroyed during the Cromwellian occupation of Scotland in the early 1650s, the palace was never rebuilt; it takes a powerful imagination to recreate in the mind's eye anything of its Stewart grandeur.

The Macbeth Connection

Leaving the stark ruins of the palace, turn right and walk up Kirkgate, past the ornate mock-Gothic town hall, then left onto the Bridge Street, and walk 100m (100yd) to the entrance of Pittencrief Park, another of Carnegie's legacies. A statue of the great man, bearded and frock-coated, faces you as you enter, where you will hear the screeching of a flock of peacocks which have the run of the park. On the banks of the Tower Burn, which flows through the park, once stood Malcolm Canmore's Tower, built in the 11th century as Malcolm's stronghold and his seat of government, but unfortunately virtually nothing of it remains.

Malcolm, great grandson of the first great King of Scots, the ninth-century Kenneth Mac Alpin, came to the throne as the result of the series of events on which William Shakespeare (1564–1616) based his play *Macbeth* (1623). The real Macbeth (or Maelbeatha; c. 1005–1057) was Mormaer (sub-king) of Moray, in what had been the Pictish heartland of northeast Scotland, and he may have been of Pictish descent. He did not, as Shakespeare has it, murder his cousin, King Duncan I (reigned 1034–40), in his sleep but killed him in battle; and the real Macbeth was not a bloody-handed tyrant but a wise and successful king who ruled over a prosperous Scotland for seventeen years. He even went on pilgrimage to Rome, in 1050, where it is recorded that his generosity to the poor was open-handed.

In 1057, however, Duncan's son Malcolm returned from exile in England, defeated and killed Macbeth and made himself Malcolm III. In 1069 he married the English Princess Margaret; she was the daughter of King Harold II (c. 1022–1066) of England, who died in battle against the Normans at Hastings. Malcolm himself was killed in battle against the English in 1093, and Margaret, who died only three days later, was eventually canonized as Saint Margaret.

Continue westward through the park, following the path downhill to Pittencrief House, a seventeenth-century manor which houses a collection of contemporary costumes and is also worth looking at for its fine plasterwork ceilings, added during restoration in the early 1900s. From here, walk eastwards through the park and exit left just north of the Royal Palace onto St Catherine's Wynd. Now walk up the Kirkgate and turn right onto the High Street. Proceed to Viewfield Terrace and the Dunfermline District Museum and Small Gallery. The gallery has monthly exhibitions of paintings, prints and photography, but more interesting from the visitor's point of view is the permanent exhibition telling the story of Dunfermline and its weaving industry, with displays of damask, the fine linen for which the Dunfermline weavers were famous. Handloom weaving survived here longer than elsewhere in Britain because the early power looms could not handle such delicate material; it was not until the 1870s that the fine table linen that was Dunfermline's hallmark could be machine-woven.

From here, follow the High Street to its east end, turn right and walk back to the railway station.

Forth Coast Castles: Tantallon to Dirleton

Summary: This is a long, exhilarating walk along the south coast of the Firth of Forth where it opens into the North Sea, with sweeping views from cliffs out to sea. Its start and finish are each marked by a dramatic medieval stronghold, and you have the option of breaking the journey with a boat trip.

Transport to and from Edinburgh: The fastest way to get to Tantallon Castle by public transport is to take a train from Edinburgh Waverley to North Berwick Station, and then catch a bus or a taxi for the last 4km (2½ miles) to the castle. For the return journey simply take a train back from North Berwick Station to Edinburgh Waverley.

Start:	Tantallon Castle.
Finish:	North Berwick Railway Station.
Length:	8km (5 miles).
Time:	4hr – but all day if you go on the Bass Rock boat excursion.
Refreshments:	Quadrant Café Bar, 7–9 Quality Street.
	Mariners Coffee Shop, 81 High Street.
	Other pubs and cafés in North Berwick.
	The Open Arms pub in Dirleton.
Which day:	Any day, but best in summer because of the exposed nature of the walk.
To visit:	Tantallon Castle.
	Scottish Seabird Centre.
	North Berwick Auld Kirk.
	North Berwick Museum.
	Dirleton Castle.
	Bass Rock (optional excursion by boat from North Berwick Harbour)

'Bold, massive, high and stretching far', as Sir Walter Scott (1771–1832) described it in his ballad *Marmion* (1808), Tantallon Castle, a colossal wreck on its beetling sea cliff, could hardly be a more romantic ruin.

A Mighty Stronghold

Surrounded on three sides by sea cliffs, defended on its landward side by deep ditches, and ringed by a 16m (50ft) curtain wall up to 4m (12ft) thick, it had a better record of resisting siege than most Scottish strongholds. It was built by William

(1327–1384), first Earl of Douglas, and from within its metres-thick walls several Douglas earls defied the Stewart kings in the centuries-long struggle for power between the two houses. The House of Douglas led several rebellions, and one reason the Stewart kings were so keen on artillery was to reduce otherwise impregnable castles like Tantallon.

The untimely deaths of so many of the Stewarts, from Robert III (*c.* 1340–1406) to Mary Queen of Scots (1542–1587), meant that more often than not the heir to the throne was a minor, even an infant, with noble factions fighting to control the young monarch and the country. James I (1394–1437) returned from years of captivity in England to find the Douglases, led by the Duke of Albany (*c.* 1340–1420), running the country. He promptly executed Albany, Albany's father-in-law and two of his sons, seized their lands, and imprisoned the surviving son, the Earl of Buchan. When James was assassinated in 1437, an infant son, James II (1430–1460), once again inherited, and once again a Douglas – Archibald (*c.* 1391–1439), fifth Earl of Douglas – became regent. Archibald died just two years later, and the regency passed into the hands of the Keeper of Edinburgh Castle, Sir William Crichton (d. 1454), who had William (*c.* 1426–1440), the 14-year-old heir to the Douglas title, murdered, with his younger brother David, in Edinburgh Castle.

This kept the Douglases quiet for a while, but after James II took control of his own realm at the age of 19, in 1449, he felt obliged to murder yet another rebellious Douglas, William (*c.* 1425–1452), the eighth earl, after the latter had made an alliance with England and with the clans of the Western Isles to overthrow the king. William's younger brother and heir, James (1426–1488), the ninth and last earl, fled to England and was killed with his three brothers at the Battle of Arkinholm in the Borders after raising a force to invade Scotland. The king's commander at Arkinholm was a Douglas too – George (*c.* 1412–1462), fourth Earl of Angus, of the line of the family known as the 'Red' Douglases; the Douglases of the south and the Borders were known as the 'Black' Douglases. George was rewarded with the rebels' lands.

James II was killed in 1460 by the explosion of one of his own cannon at the siege of Roxburgh, and once again a minor was left as heir to the throne. By the time James III (1451–1488) came into his own, the Douglases were at it again, led by the fifth earl, Archibald (*c.* 1449–1514), known as 'Bell-the-Cat' because of his firm determination to curtail the power of the monarchy. This he did, virtually kidnapping the young James and later laying hold of his son and proclaiming him the true king. On 11 June 1488, the king's troops met with the rebels at Sauchieburn and, in a battle for which neither side showed much enthusiasm, James was thrown from his horse and murdered by an enterprising passer-by after he had called for a priest.

James IV (1473–1513) was 15 when he succeeded to the throne, and for a while 'Bell-the-Cat' Douglas was the power behind the throne. To his credit, he tried to persuade James against fighting a losing battle at Flodden (1513). Archibald died the following year.

His successor, the sixth earl, also called Archibald (*c.* 1489–1557), was no less of an intriguer and by the time James V (1512–1542) was declared fit to govern in 1526 at the age of 14, the Douglases were firmly in the saddle, having slaughtered their main rivals, the Hamiltons, in a pitched battle in the streets of Edinburgh. But James

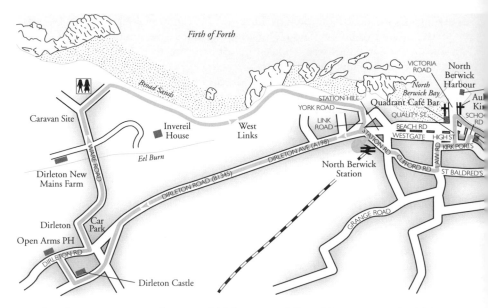

proved to be no puppet; at the age of 16 he escaped from his captors and within a few years, after laying siege to Tantallon, had driven the Douglases and their followers out of the country, where they took to plotting ineffectually with Henry VIII (1491–1547) and never regained their former power.

Looking at the awe-inspiring natural and man-made defences of Tantallon, it is easy to imagine the Douglas earls feeling they could defy the king's authority. You enter the inner castle by passing over a system of ditches and earth barriers and through the ruinous outer gate to reach an inner fortress dominated by three towers: the four-storey Mid Tower, built in the late fourteenth century, the five-storey East Tower and the six-storey Douglas Tower, which has a dungeon hewn out of the rock of its floor.

Tantallon's final downfall came with the Cromwellian invasion of Scotland in 1651; even then, it took twelve days of bombardment before the Roundheads could achieve their goal of taking the Castle.

Bird Life

Leaving Tantallon Castle by the outer gate, turn right and follow the signposted cliff path to North Berwick. The huge boulder on the horizon, 1km (1100yd) offshore, is Bass Rock, a 108m (350ft) volcanic plug which dominates the entry to the Firth of Forth. The island is uninhabited except for huge numbers of seabirds, including Guillemots, Fulmars, Razorbills, Puffins, gulls and especially Gannets. It hosts one of only thirteen nesting Gannet colonies in Britain, and these huge and elegant birds may be seen diving after fish, arrowing into the water in a gust of spray.

You can take a boat trip from North Berwick Harbour (see below) to Bass Rock to see the birds for yourself; as an alternative, you can follow the signs to North Berwick's pocket-sized harbour and the Scottish Seabird Centre. This fascinating

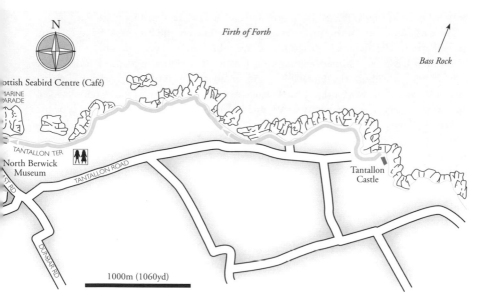

new £2.9 million visitor centre, opened in the year 2000, features screens showing live footage from spy cameras on Bass Rock; sophisticated computer systems also link the centre to bird centres in France and Ireland.

North Berwick and the Auld Kirk

As the footpath enters North Berwick, follow the shore road and signposts to the harbour until you reach the Auld Kirk, which stands on a rocky promontory at the west end of Marine Parade. Little remains of this twelfth-century church except the foundations. It fell into disuse in 1682, when the Parish Church immediately opposite, was built. This too is now a ruin, but in the churchyard is the grave of John Blackadder (1615–1686), the covenanting preacher who was outlawed and in 1681 imprisoned on the Bass Rock, where he died five years later. His fifth son, also called John Blackadder (1664–1729), went on to command the Cameronian regiment, raised by Covenanters to fight for William of Orange (1650–1702) against James VII and II (1633–1701), and became deputy governor of Stirling Castle.

From the Parish Church graveyard, walk south along Quality Street and turn left at the end of the street to School Road and the North Berwick Museum. Here, an exhibition tells the story of the Bass Rock, its lighthouse and its castle, which in 1691 was the last Stewart garrison to surrender to the forces of William of Orange. There are also displays of medieval finds from Tantallon and North Berwick Priory and of household implements and tools from the eighteenth and nineteenth centuries.

Dirleton

At the foot of School Road, turn right onto Kirk Ports and left onto Law Street. At the crossroads turn right onto Clifford Road and walk for 400m (440yd), past the station. Turn left on Dirleton Avenue (A198) and follow the footpath beside it for about a kilometre (½ mile) to the pretty village of Dirleton and its castle.

The earliest owners of this now ruined stronghold were the Norman-Scots de Vaux family. Parts of the original thirteenth-century building survive, notably the Lord's Hall, which has a fine domed ceiling. The Castle then passed into the hands of the Hallyburtons, who built the Great Hall, and finally to the Ruthven Earls of Gowrie, who added the Ruthven Lodging, a Renaissance mansion next to the original tower. The Castle was confiscated by James VI and I (1566–1625) in 1600 when two of the Gowrie sons were accused of plotting to kill him (their father, the earl, had been executed fifteen years previously after a similar plot). Like Tantallon, it was besieged, bombarded and destroyed by Oliver Cromwell's invading Roundheads in 1650.

From the Castle, walk on to Dirleton's main street and through this pretty village, with its white stone cottages and their red pantiled roofs. Turn left just before the car park and walk northwards for some 800m (875yd), crossing the Eel Burn stream. Ignore the first crossroads, where tracks lead to Dirleton New Mains Farm on your left and Invereil House on your right, and walk on past the caravan site to the point where the path branches left and right.

Take the right fork and walk back along the head of Broad Sands Beach and West Links; from here a footpath, signposted, leads you to North Berwick Station, which is where you started and which is also the end-point of your day's excursion – unless, that is, you choose to round things off by returning to North Berwick Harbour to take a boat trip out to Bass Rock.

Stirling and Bannockburn

Summary: Commanding the first point at which the Forth could be bridged, and the natural route between central and northern Scotland, Stirling was a natural place for opposing armies to meet. So it is hardly unexpected that it has been the scene of more than one major, history-changing battle, from William Wallace's victory at Stirling Brig in 1297 to the defeat of the Jacobites in 1715. Most famously of all, it was the site of Robert the Bruce's decisive victory in 1314 over Edward II (1284–1327). Stirling's strong castle, built like Edinburgh's on a high crag, was often a place of refuge for Scottish monarchs when Edinburgh fell into enemy hands.

Transport to and from Edinburgh: There are half-hourly trains between Stirling Station and Haymarket. The journey time is about 35 minutes.

Start/finish:	Stirling Station.
Length:	5km (3 miles).
Time:	3hr.
Refreshments:	Pubs, cafés and restaurants along the way.
Which day:	Any day.
To visit:	Old Town Jail.
	Argyll's Lodging.
	Stirling Castle.
	Argyll and Sutherland Highlanders' Regimental Museum.
	Church of the Holy Rude.
	Bannockburn Heritage Centre.

Leaving the station, cross Murray Place and follow the signs to the Castle, which will take you up Spittal Street and into St John Street. On the left, opposite Jail Wynd, you can experience nineteenth-century penal reform in the Old Town Jail, where cells, manacles and displays indicate just how harsh prison life could be in the Victorian era.

Leaving the jail, cross St John Street and go along Jail Wynd to the corner of Broad Street, and then walk past the fine Tolbooth with its six-storey tower, designed by Sir William Bruce (1630–1710), who also designed the Palace of Holyroodhouse (see page 39) and several other Scottish stately homes. Opposite is the Mercat ('Market') Cross, the landmark of Stirling's medieval marketplace.

Mar's Wark and Argyll's Lodging

Turn left on Broad Street. At the top of Broad Street, on the left, is the ruined front of Mar's Wark, the uncompleted sixteenth-century palace of John Erskine

(1510–1572), sixth Earl of Mar, hereditary Keeper of Stirling Castle and guardian of the young James VI (1566–1625). Mar was briefly Regent of Scotland, from 1571 until his death, but was little more than a puppet of James Douglas (*c.* 1516–1581), fourth Earl of Morton, who succeeded him as Regent. Mar's Wark was begun in 1570 but, after Mar's death two years later, remained uncompleted. The façade is decorated with carved stone panels bearing coats of arms and heraldic emblems.

Walk some 20m (20yd) up Castle Wynd to Argyll's Lodging, on your right. The town house of Sir William Alexander (*c.* 1567–1640), Earl of Stirling, it was built in 1632 around a courtyard which is entered from the street by a graceful Renaissance gateway and which is itself ornamented in Renaissance style. Sir William Alexander was a close associate of James VI and I and tutor to the Princes Henry and Charles. He was Secretary of State for Scotland from 1826 until his death, and was made Earl of Stirling in 1633. He was granted jurisdiction over the fledgling colonies of Nova Scotia and Canada in 1631, but these royal favours died insolvent in London and the property passed to the Campbells of Argyll, who by the mid-seventeenth century were becoming a great power in Scotland.

The main rooms, including the hall, dining room, drawing room and bedroom, have been immaculately restored and are furnished with fine carved and inlaid tables and splendid tapestries, as they would have been in the 1680s, when the house was the residence of the ninth Earl of Argyll, Archibald Campbell (d. 1685). Campbell had been captain of Charles II's Scottish Lifeguards during the civil wars, and after the Restoration was one of Scotland's few moderates, urging the Government to deal less savagely with the Covenanters during the 'Killing Time' of the later seventeenth century. In May 1685, he declared for the pretender to the throne, James (1649–1685), Duke of Monmouth, but failed to win the support of his clan, and was captured and executed. His son, another Archibald Campbell (d. 1705), supported William of Orange (1650–1702) against James VII and II (1633–1701) in the 'Glorious Revolution' of 1689–91, for which he was restored to his father's estates. He was created Duke of Argyll in 1701.

A Grand Scottish Castle

From Argyll's Lodging, continue to Stirling Castle by Castlehill and the visitor centre, entering what is claimed to be the grandest of all Scotland's castles via the Castle Esplanade. A statue of Robert the Bruce (1274–1329) stands guard over the approach.

Cross over the outer defensive ditch and through an outer gateway, then turn right through an inner gateway and pass through the fifteenth-century Portcullis House, built in the reign of James IV (1473–1513), into the Lower Square. Turn left here to enter the Royal Apartments of the Palace, built between 1496 and 1540 by James IV and James V (1512–1542). Like Linlithgow, James IV's other favourite palace (see page 126), Stirling shows strong European Renaissance influences, and this sets it apart from the mainstream of Scottish royal and aristocratic architecture. It is simply planned around a central courtyard, the Upper Square. Within, the Queen's Outer Hall and the Queen's Own Hall have been finely restored, and are adorned by unique Renaissance carvings known as the Stirling Heads, some fifty oak cameos which depict kings, queens, saints and nobles; they

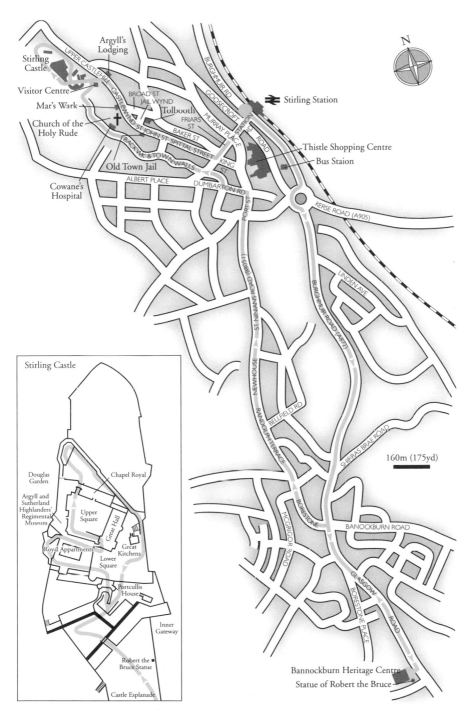

N

Argyll's Lodging

Stirling Castle

UPPER CASTLEHILL

Visitor Centre

Mar's Wark

Church of the Holy Rude

Cowane's Hospital

Old Town Jail

CASTLEWYND

BROAD ST
JAIL WYND

Tolbooth

FRIARS ST

ST JOHN ST SPITTAL STREET

BAKER ST

BACK WK & TOWN WALLS

ALBERT PLACE

BURGHMUIR RD

GOOSECROFT

MURRAY PLACE

STATION ROAD

KING ST

PORT ST

DUMBARTON RD

Stirling Station

Thistle Shopping Centre

Bus Staion

KERSE ROAD (A905)

ST NINIANS ROAD (B8051)

BURGHMUIR ROAD (A872)

LINDEN AVE

NEWHOUSE

RANDOLPH TERRACE

BELLFIELD RD

SHIRRAS BRAE ROAD

160m (175yd)

BORESTONE

McGRIGOR ROAD

BANOCKBURN ROAD

GLASGOW ROAD

BORESTONE PLACE

Bannockburn Heritage Centre

Statue of Robert the Bruce

Stirling Castle

Douglas Garden

Argyll and Sutherland Highlanders' Regimental Museum

Royal Appartments

Chapel Royal

Upper Square

Great Hall

Great Kitchens

Lower Square

Portcullis House

Inner Gateway

Robert the Bruce Statue

Castle Esplanade

were originally part of the ceiling of the King's Own Chamber.

From the apartments, enter the Great Hall, which occupies the east side of the Upper Square. This is a splendid Gothic chamber with fine oriole windows, a minstrel gallery and a hammer-beam roof, all of which have been recently restored; much of the hall's original grandeur was lost during its use as a military barracks from the eighteenth century onwards.

Exit the Great Hall and walk clockwise around the Upper Square, from which you have a good perspective of the plain exterior of the Great Hall and the much more ornate Palace, decorated by carved figures of James V and of allegorical male and female figures.

On the west side of the square, detour into the Argyll and Sutherland Highlanders' Regimental Museum. Originally raised by the Campbell Dukes of Argyll – the first of the Highland magnates to recognize the advisability of allying with the government in Edinburgh instead of resisting it – the regiment went on to serve the British Empire for two centuries, and this museum houses their colours, battle honours, medals and ephemera, as well as a fine collection of silver.

From here walk through to the Douglas Garden, where William (*c.* 1425–1452), eighth Earl of Douglas, was murdered and his body flung from the ramparts under the orders of the young James II (1430–1460). As Douglas had been invited under promise of safe conduct to dine with the king, this was considered not quite the done thing, even by the relaxed standards of the time.

Now walk clockwise around the battlements. To the southeast you should be able to make out the rotunda and the Scottish flag that mark the battlefield of Bannockburn, 3km (2 miles) away. To the northwest, the Wallace Monument overlooks the site of another Scottish victory, at Stirling Brig ('Bridge'), where in 1297 William Wallace's Scots wiped out a large English army under Edward I's viceroy, John de Warenne, Earl of Surrey. Wallace's victory was short-lived. The following year he was defeated at Falkirk, and he lived on the run for the next seven years before being captured and taken to London, where he was hanged, cut down while still living, and disembowelled. A martyr and hero to contemporary Scots, William Wallace (1270–1305) was turned into a legend for posterity one hundred and seventy years after his death by the poet Blind Harry (1450–1493), whose *Actes and Deidis of the Illustre and Valliant Campioun Schir William Wallace* ('Acts and Deeds of the Illustrious and Valiant Champion Sir William Wallace') recounts, in often gorily realistic detail, Wallace's battles.

On your way out of the castle, pass through the Great Kitchens, where displays recreate the busy preparation of a feast for the king and his nobles – though the real thing, like much else in Scottish history, was certainly a good deal noisier, smellier and messier than the re-creation.

Stany Breeks

Leaving the Castle, take the first right off the Esplanade and walk down a flight of steps and then on a footpath for less than 100m (110yd) to the Back Walk. Follow this past a sturdy seventeenth-century building, Cowane's Hospital, built as an almshouse by John Cowane (*c.* 1570–1633), whose statue is above the doorway.

Nicknamed by Stirling folk 'Stany Breeks' ('Stone Breeches'), Cowane, according to local legend, comes to life at the stroke of midnight on every Hogmanay to take a turn around the hospital.

Turn left here to enter the Church of the Holy Rude. The fifteenth-century nave, the oldest part of the church, still has its original oak roof. The infant James VI was crowned here in 1567.

Bannockburn

Leaving the church, continue down Back Walk and cross over Corn Exchange Road, turn left on Dumbarton Road and then right onto Port Street. This becomes St Ninians Road (the B8051; signposted 'Hospital'); follow this for some 750m (820yd) to the traffic roundabout where it joins Burghmuir Road (A872), and then carry on for a further three or 400m (440yd) to the Bannockburn Heritage Centre, on your right.

The Heritage Centre is actually about a kilometre (½ mile) to the southwest of the centre of the battlefield where on 24 June 1314 Robert the Bruce's Scots drubbed a much larger army of English knights led by Edward II (1284–1327), who were on their way to relieve Stirling Castle, which by that time was the last Scottish stronghold still in English hands. Next to the Heritage Centre, however, a rotunda with a mounted statue of Robert the Bruce (1274–1329) marks the vantage point from which Bruce is said to have commanded his troops. The audiovisual presentation shows how Bruce, outnumbered three to one and with no archers or heavy cavalry, astutely used the marshy, treacherous land around the Bannock Burn ('stream') to neutralize Edward's heavily armoured knights, who were easy meat for the Scots as they floundered.

Interestingly enough, identical tactics had been used less than two years previously by the infantry of the Catalan Company of Lepanto against the armoured knights of Othon de la Roche, King of Athens, at Plateia in central Greece. The Catalans were mercenaries; could some wandering soldier of fortune have brought the news to Scotland?

From the visitor centre, walk back about a kilometre (1 mile) and a half up Glasgow Road and then Burghmuir Road to Stirling Station, or take a local bus.

The East Neuk

Summary: The Scots word 'neuk' means 'corner', and the East Neuk of Fife is indeed a corner, where the peninsula that is the Kingdom of Fife juts eastward into the North Sea, being separated from Edinburgh and Lothian by the Firth of Forth.

This is a coastal walk, along beaches and clifftop paths and through a string of attractive fishing villages, each built around its own small stone harbour. On the way, several small museums provide insight into the life and history of these fishing and trading communities. These villages retain much of their old-fashioned charm, with old cottages crammed together around the harbour, and modern building generally only outside the village centre.

Fife has been known as the 'Kingdom' for centuries, for reasons that are long forgotten, and it has fought tenaciously to retain the title through successive reorganizations of regional government. James VI and I (1566–1625) famously described Fife as a 'beggar's mantle fringed with gold', and as early as the eleventh and twelfth centuries, these little ports were among Scotland's wealthiest burghs, sustaining a thriving trade with mainland Europe. As the balance of economic power and trade shifted south, to Edinburgh and its port of Leith, that trade dwindled, but the Fife towns continued to make a living from the sea by fishing.

Transport to and from Edinburgh: Buses link Edinburgh, Dunfermline and St Andrews with both St Monance and Crail.

Start:	St Monance.
Finish:	Crail.
Length:	6.5km (4 miles).
Time:	3–4hr – but all day if you go on the Isle of May boat trip.
Which day:	Not Sunday.
Refreshments:	Tearoom at Scottish Fisheries Centre.
	Pubs and cafés in each of the villages through which you pass.
To visit:	St Monan's Church.
	St Fillan's Cave and Priory.
	Scottish Fisheries Museum.
	North Carr Lightship.
	Isle of May (boat trip).
	Crail Museum and Heritage Centre.

St Monance is one of those compact fishing villages typical of the Fife coast which have their stone cottages huddled in a labyrinth of narrow closes around a tiny harbour.

Plate 29: A splendidly decorated bedroom at Hopetoun House (see page 121).

Plate 30: Linlithgow Palace, once the home of Scottish kings and queens (see page 126).

Plate 31: The Forth Rail Bridge, one of the great engineering achievements of the Victorian age of steam, crosses the Firth of Forth between North and South Queensferry (see page 120).

Plate 32: St Salvator's quadrangle, the heart of St Andrews
University (see page 132).

Plate 33: St Andrews with the
ruined walls of its Cathedral,
destroyed during the
Reformation (see page 135).

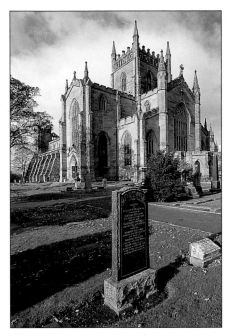

Plate 34: *Dunfermline Abbey in Scotland's first capital (see page 139).*

Plate 35: *The Abbot House at Dunfermline Abbey (see page 139).*

Plate 36: *Tantallon Castle, ruined stronghold of the once-mighty Douglas earls (see page 142).*

Plate 37: *Statue of Robert the Bruce near the battlefield of Bannockburn (see page 151).*

Plate 38: *Stirling Castle, in time of war the key to central Scotland (see page 148).*

Plate 39: *Fishing boats at anchor at the pretty Fife village of Crail (see page 154).*

A Royal Church

On alighting from your bus, follow signs first to Kirk Wynd and then to St Monan's Church, which is built on what may be one of the oldest Christian sites in Scotland, founded by followers of Saint Ninian as early as 400AD. Ninian, a Briton of Strathclyde, was the first of the great Christian missionaries to Scotland, sending his followers into the pagan north from his monastery at Whithorn in southwest Scotland. Queen (and Saint) Margaret (*c.* 1046–1093), in the eleventh century, and several later Scottish monarchs contributed to the building of what is now the village's parish church. David I (*c.* 1080–1153) was miraculously cured of an arrow wound here, and made it into a royal chapel. Further additions were made by Alexander III (1241–1286) in the mid-thirteenth century, and in 1362 David II (1324–1371) built a new choir in thanksgiving after surviving a storm at sea. A hanging model ship inside the church commemorates the event, and there are royal coats of arms on the walls. Worth noting, too, is the church's groined stone roof.

Pittenweem

Leaving the church, walk down to St Monance's small harbour and set out eastward along the footpath to Pittenweem which follows the line of the rocky foreshore for a kilometre (½ mile), with the sea on your right and farmland on your left. The footpath joins a narrow street: follow this for 200m (220yd) to Cove Wynd and St Fillan's Cave, just after the crossroads in the centre of the village and clearly signposted.

Saint Fillan (d. 777) was another early missionary, and it is said that he made his hermitage in this cave, which is now in the garden of a priory built by Augustinian monks in the twelfth century and restored in 1935. Despite the saint having given his seal of approval to the cave, and the consequent Christian reverence thereafter accorded to it, the cave and its Holy Well were almost certainly a pagan religious site before the arrival of Christianity – wells and springs were often associated with pre-Christian Celtic deities, whose shrines were taken over and rededicated by the Christian Church. The very name of the village, Pittenweem, is said to mean 'Place of the Cave' in Pictish, which seems to indicate that the shrine was in use before Fillan arrived.

The story of the cave may be more interesting than the site itself, which is reached through a drably functional stone shed and has little to offer by way of spectacle other than its crude stone altar.

From here walk down to the harbour, which is the base for most of the remaining East Neuk fishing boats, though Pittenweem's fleet too is now dwindling, along with the North Sea's fish stocks, due to the joint impact of European Union quotas and past overfishing.

Anstruther

From the harbour, walk straight on through the village to once more pick up the coastal footpath on the outskirts of Pittenweem. Continue along it for something under 2km (1¼ mile) to Anstruther, the largest of the East Neuk fishing villages, with a population of almost three thousand and, to judge by the number of tearooms, fish and chip ships and souvenir stores it supports, a thriving tourist industry.

Standing beside the harbour, and housed in a collection of sixteenth- to nineteenth-century cottages and boatsheds, is the village's main attraction, the Scottish Fisheries Museum. This is one of the best small museums in Scotland, with exhibits both inside and outside the harbour, with traditional nineteenth-century fishing boats and an aquarium full of North Sea marine life complementing the collection of boats, models, fishing gear and the recreated interior of a typical nineteenth-century fisher-family's home. Anstruther, like the other East Neuk harbours, enjoyed a spell of prosperity towards the end of the nineteenth century, thanks to a boom in the herring fishery. Such was the demand, however, that the herring fleets eventually wiped out the great shoals, and the fishing industry has been in decline almost ever since.

The Museum's 'Whaling Corridor' sheds light on what was once a major industry on the east coast of Scotland. Whalers from Scottish ports first depleted the Arctic whale fishery and, when that was no longer profitable, followed their prey south to the Antarctic. Whale oil was a vital industrial resource until the development of paraffin (kerosene) lighting and then gas lighting, and was essential for streetlights and domestic lamps, as well as for lubricating machinery.

Another room highlights the fastest-ever commercial sailing ships, the China tea clippers, many of which were designed, built and skippered by Scots – among them Captain John Keay, master of the *Ariel*, which in 1879 set a record time of eighty-three days for the passage from Gravesend in Kent to Hong Kong.

After you come out of the Museum, walk around the harbour to the North Carr Lightship, which was stationed off Fife Ness (the eastern tip of Fife) between 1933 and 1975, in which latter year it was retired to Anstruther. It is now a floating museum, the only one of its kind in the world. The ship is fitted out as if it were still crewed and in use, and a permanent exhibition, Lightships of the World, illustrates the history and work of these floating beacons.

The Isle of May
Between May and September, boats sail from Anstruther harbour to the Isle of May, an uninhabited island nature reserve some 8km (5 miles) offshore. The trip takes about three-quarters of an hour each way. Nesting on the island are raucous rookeries of Puffins, Razorbills, Eider Ducks, Guillemots, Kittiwakes and terns, not to mention Cormorants, and birdwatchers visiting in May always look forward to seeing the first Shag of the summer. Also on the island are the ruins of Scotland's first lighthouse, put up in the 1630s, and those of a much earlier chapel, built in the twelfth century, when a community of Augustinian monks lived here.

Crail
After walking around the harbour, take the Shore Road eastward and rejoin the coastal footpath as it leaves Anstruther. After 2km (1¼ mile) or so, close to the shore, you pass yet another cave with a trickling stream – this one is known as the Hermit's Well – and a further kilometre (½ mile) after that you reach Crail, the most prettily picturesque of the East Neuk fishing villages, a clutter of red-tiled low houses with typical crow-step gables, built around a circular harbour. Off to the south you have

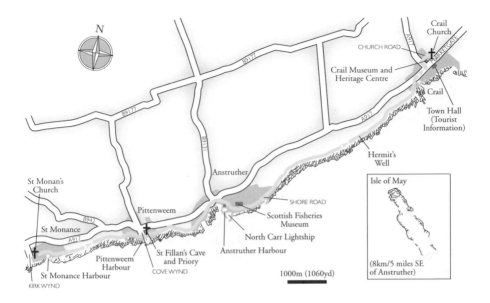

fine views of Bass Rock and the other shore of the Firth of Forth. It is hard to believe, looking at sleepy little Crail today, that its ships once traded as far afield as Stockholm and Danzig (modern Gdansk), where they sold their catches of herring and brought back cargoes of Swedish iron.

Follow the footpath inland to your left to join the main road (the A917) as it passes through the centre of the village, and at the crossroads there walk straight ahead to the Marketgate. A prominent landmark is the Tolbooth – now the Town Hall, library and tourist information office. It has an impressive Dutch Tower crowned by a distinctive weather vane in the shape of a fish. Built in the early six- teenth century, the tower displays the burgh's Coat of Arms, dated 1602; its bell, imported from Holland, dates back even further, to 1520.

Outside the Town Hall is Crail's Mercat ('Market') Cross, crowned by a carved unicorn, and opposite the Town Hall at 62-64 Marketgate is the Crail Museum and Heritage Centre, a small museum dedicated to the history of the burgh, its harbour and its fishing fleet, not to mention its venerable golf club, founded in the late eigh- teenth century.

Before you end this walk by catching your bus back to Edinburgh, make one final, small detour. Cross the Marketgate and walk about 50m (55yd) north on the main road to turn right on Church Road, next to the modern church building. Go on a further 20m (20yd) or so to the thirteenth-century Collegiate Church, where an early Pictish cross slab proves the community's antiquity.

Further Information

Glossary of Scots Terms

Though Scots no longer qualifies as a language in its own right – as distinct from a collection of variants on standard English – Edinburgh street and other names offer evidence of a separate identity, revealing different influences and origins for many Scots terms. Some words you are likely to encounter on your walks, especially in the older part of town, are included in the list below.

brae: hill
brig: bridge
burn: stream
byre: cowshed
ceilidh (Gaelic): evening of music and dancing
close: a narrow alley, usually covered over by the storey above
craig: crag
dike/dyke: wall or ditch
dram: glass of whisky
gallus: Scottish equivalent of *macho* (perhaps derived from 'gallows meat' – i.e., fit to be hanged)
-gate (as suffix): street or way
hauf: a large whisky ('half')
hauf and hauf: a large whisky and a half pint of beer
heavy: dark ale, similar to English bitter
haugh: area of flatland, usually beside the sea or a river
Hibie: supporter of Hibernian Football Club

howff: meeting-place, public house
kirk: church
land: tenement with several floors of flats
law: hill
lea: hill
muir: moor
nether- (as prefix): lower
over- (as prefix): upper
pend: alley or lane
port: gateway
sassenach (n. or adj., Gaelic): English (pejorative, derived from 'Saxon')
scheme: postwar housing project
schemie: resident of above (pejorative)
sette: cobblestone
teuchter: Highlander, Gaelic-speaker (pejorative, has connotation similar to English 'yokel')
wynd: alley or lane

Although it is by no means an essential part of your packing, you might like to have with you for general interest a copy of *The Pocket Scots Dictionary* (1988), published by the Aberdeen University Press and full of fascinating Scottish terms and usages.

Practical Hints

Airport
Edinburgh International Airport,Tel: (0131) 333 1000, is 11km (7 miles) west of the city centre; access by bus from Waverley Station. A rapid-transit bus service is scheduled to start in 2001 with a 25 minute journey time; the current journey time is between 35 minutes to 1 hour.

Art Galleries
Edinburgh's Fine Art collections are listed at the beginnings of the relevant walks. In addition, there are many private galleries, especially in the New Town area. See also the listing on pages 161–163 under 'Museums and Art Galleries'. A more comprehensive and regularly updated list is available from tourist information offices (see page 160).

Churches
Admission is free (though many welcome donations for upkeep and restoration programmes). Scottish churches are generally open 10.00–12.00 and 13.00–16.00 or 17.00. Obviously you should be quiet and respectful should you happen accidentally to enter while a service is in progress.

Cinemas
Edinburgh has an excellent choice of cinemas showing mainstream and arthouse movies. Main cinemas include:
* ABC Film Centre, 120 Lothian Road. Tel: (0131) 229 3030.
* Cameo, 38 Home Street. Tel. (0131) 228 2800.
* Dominion, 18 Newbattle Terrace. Tel: (0131) 447 2660.
* Filmhouse, 88 Lothian Road. Tel: (0131) 228 2688.
* Lumière, Royal Museum, Chambers Street. Tel: (0131) 247 4219.

Consulates
* *Australia:* 25 Bernard Street. Tel: 0131 467 8333.
* *Canada:* 3 George's Street. Tel: (01141) 204 1373.
* *USA:* 3 Regent Terrace. Tel: (0131) 556 8315.

Eating and Drinking
Edinburgh has a very large choice of restaurants offering every cuisine under the sun. Indian curry houses and Chinese restaurants abound and are among the cheapest. Vegetarians are well catered for by a number of herbivore restaurants in the city centre. For a wide choice of affordable places to eat and drink in a small area, the Grassmarket, below the Castle, is a good bet.

Edinburgh also has enough bars to have the puritanical John Knox spinning in his grave, from old-fashioned vaults to bright new cocktail bars. Licensing hours – which until the 1980s were among the most restrictive in Europe – are very relaxed, and pubs, bars and restaurants are open until the early hours (03.00–04.00). Rose Street is legendary for its high concentration of bars, but best avoided when a major football or rugby event is taking place in Edinburgh.

For food on the move, there are lots of cheap takeaway kebab and burger joints throughout town, as well as shops selling the fish and chips that have been the traditional fast food of the urban Scots for generations. Scottish fast food in general is almost by definition deep-fried: not only fish (usually cod or haddock) in batter, but meat or chicken pies, pizza, black pudding, white or mealie pudding, haggis and various types of sausage may be deep-fried and served with chips, usually flavoured with a squirt of brown sauce, ketchup or, for the more adventurous, curry sauce. A recent innovation is the deep-fried Mars bar, perhaps unique to Scotland, although there are rumours that the craze has now spread to some establishments in northern England.

An exception to the deep-fried rule is Spudulike, a chain of fast-food emporia which started with a single branch in Edinburgh and can now be found all over the United Kingdom: here you can buy baked jacket potatoes with a choice of fillings.

The ideal accompaniment to your fast-food repast, greasy or otherwise, is generally agreed to be Irn Bru (pronounced 'iron brew'), a rust-coloured, carbonated, caffeinated drink advertised variously as 'your other national drink' and 'made in Scotland – frae girders'. Irn Bru is also valued as a hangover remedy and as a mixer with vodka.

Festivals and Events
The Edinburgh Festival is one of the world's greatest cultural events. Festival season, lasting for three to four weeks in August and September, really features three events in one.

The core Edinburgh International Festival is very much a feast of high culture, featuring the world's leading musicians, orchestras and ballet and theatre companies; the Edinburgh International Film Festival, the longest-running film festival in the world, features personal appearances and debates with directors, producers and actors; and the Festival Fringe does for the absurd, bohemian and irreverent end of the cultural spectrum what the main Festival does for the highbrow. Meanwhile, a book festival, TV festival and jazz festival have all sprung up to complement the core events.

If you intend to visit Edinburgh at Festival time, make sure you book accommodation well in advance. The programme for each year's Festival is available from April onwards from: Edinburgh International Festival, 21 Market Street, Edinburgh EH1 1BW. Tel: (0131) 473 2000.

The Edinburgh Military Tattoo, held each year during the Edinburgh Festival on Castle Esplanade, is a stirring show of bellicosity, with pipes, drums, drill and gymnastic displays by the massed tartan ranks of the Highland regiments. For information and tickets: Tattoo Office, 22 Market Street, Edinburgh EH1 1QB. Tel: (0131) 225 1188.

Hogmanay (New Year's Eve) has evolved from a free-for-all impromptu gathering of thousands of people to hear the midnight bells of the Tron Kirk ring in the New Year into a full-scale performance event with bands and funfair rides. The Royal Mile and streets to either side, where the crowds congregate, are sealed off, and admission to this part of town is by ticket only to prevent overcrowding; the tickets are free. For information: Tel: (0131) 557 3990.

There is more tartan in evidence at the Edinburgh International Highland Games, held on three separate occasion in July and August, with pipe bands, Highland dancing, tossing the caber and throwing the hammer, and an international strongman competition.

Contact details, in addition to those given above, for further information and festival programmes are:

- Edinburgh Film Festival, Filmhouse, 88 Lothian Road, Edinburgh EH3 9BZ. Tel: (0131) 228 4051.
- Edinburgh Festival Fringe Office, 180 High Street, Edinburgh EH1 1QS. Tel: (0131) 226 5257.
- Edinburgh Jazz Festival, 116 Canongate, Edinburgh EH8 8DD. Tel: (0131) 557 1642.
- Edinburgh Book Festival, Scottish Book Centre, 137 Dundee Street, Edinburgh EH11 1BG. Tel: (0131) 228 5444.

Health

For an ambulance, telephone 999. For accidents and emergencies (24 hours) go to: Royal Infirmary, 1 Lauriston Place. Tel: (0131) 536 4000.

Pharmacy:

Boots, 48 Shandwick Place, open Monday–Saturday 08.00–21.00 and Sunday 10.00–17.00. Tel: (0131) 225 6757.

Loos

Good, clean facilities at museums and art galleries and in restaurants. Bars and cafés, conveniently located at frequent intervals on most streets, provide another alternative.

Money

Edinburgh is a major tourist destination and changing foreign currency or travellers' cheques in US, Canadian, New Zealand and Australian dollars, South African rand and most European currencies at banks and *bureaux de change* should not be a problem. Most banks also have Automatic Teller Machines which will advance you money in local currency via your bank guarantee or credit card.

Note that Scotland uses the same currency, the pound sterling, as the rest of the UK, and English banknotes are perfectly legal tender and are in common use. However, several Scottish banks (the Clydesdale Bank, Royal Bank of Scotland and Bank of Scotland) also issue their own sterling banknotes in denominations of £1, £5, £10, £20, £50 and £100. These are technically legal tender throughout the United Kingdom, but are sometimes not accepted in less sophisticated and more parochial parts of the country (for example London,) or by banks and exchange offices outside the UK. It is therefore advisable to spend all your Scottish notes before leaving Edinburgh, or to change them for Bank of England notes at any bank before departure.

Telephone
You can buy phonecards from the tourist office, most newsagents and hotels. Most payphone booths in bars and hotels and on the street also accept credit cards.

Telephone Dialling Codes
The dialling code for all Edinburgh telephone numbers from within the United Kingdom is 0131. For calls from outside the United Kingdom the prefix is 00 44 131.

Tourist Offices
- Edinburgh Tourist Office, 3 Princes Street (above Waverley Market shopping mall). Tel: (0131) 557 1700 *or* Edinburgh International Airport. Tel: (0131) 333 2167.
- Crail Tourist Information Office, Museum and Heritage Centre, Town Hall, Marketgate, Crail. Tel: (01333) 450 869.
- Dunfermline Tourist Information Office, 13/15 Maygate, Dunfermline. Tel: (01383) 720 999.
- St Andrews Tourist Office, 70 Market Street, St Andrews. Tel: (01334) 472 021.
- Scottish Tourist Board, 23 Ravelston Terrace, Edinburgh EH4 3EU. Tel: (0131) 332 2433.
- Stirling Tourist Information Office, 41 Dumbarton Road, Stirling. Tel: (01786) 475 019 or Stirling Castle Esplanade. Tel: (01786) 479 901.

OUTSIDE SCOTLAND

- *Australia:* British Tourist Authority, Midland House, 171 Clarence Street, Sydney, NSW 2000.
- *Canada:* British Tourist Authority, Suite 450, 111 Avenue Road, Toronto, Ontario, M5R 3J8.
- *England:* Scottish Tourist Board, British Travel Centre, Lower Regent Street, London SW1Y 4NS.
- *New Zealand:* Suite 305, 3rd Floor, Dilworth Building, Auckland.
- *USA:*
  625 North Michigan Avenue, Suite 1510, Chicago, Illinois 60611. Tel: (312) 787 0490.
  Cedar Maple Plaza, Suite 210, 2305 Cedar Springs Road, Dallas TX 75201 1814. Tel: (214) 720 4040.
  World Trade Centre, 350 Figueroa Street, Suite 450, Los Angeles, CA 90071. Tel: (213) 628 3525.
  551 5th Avenue, Suite 701, New York, NY 10176. Tel: (212) 986 2266.

What's On
The List, a fortnightly magazine published in Edinburgh and sold at newsagents throughout Scotland, offers a comprehensive listing of every imaginable event, activity and venue in Edinburgh and Glasgow and is essential reading for any visitor, especially at Festival time.

The *Edinburgh Evening News* newspaper offers a good guide to what's happening in the city.

Where to Stay

The Scottish Tourist Board publishes an annual guide to accommodation in Edinburgh and throughout Scotland. Available from British Tourist Authority offices worldwide, this provides contact addresses and phone numbers for all sorts of accommodation, from youth hostels and backpackers' hostels to bed and breakfast, guesthouses and hotels from one- to five-star standard. Booking well ahead is very strongly advised for June to mid-September and for the Hogmanay period, when accommodation is hard to find at short notice. If you do arrive at this time and find no room at the inn, try the Edinburgh Tourist Office's roomfinder service, which will probably be able to locate you a bed for the night, though not necessarily in the city centre.

Museums and Art Galleries

The major museums and art galleries are listed with other attractions at the beginning of each walk; see also the Opening Times section on pages 163–169. As a general rule of thumb, most museums are open daily, with shorter opening hours on Sundays. Many museums and other attractions have restricted opening times in winter, reflecting the drop in visitor numbers in the out-of-peak season and the shorter hours of daylight. Attractions Frequently have extended hours during the Edinburgh Festival season (August/early September).

Main museums, art galleries and visitor attractions are:

EDINBURGH
- Brass Rubbing Centre, Trinity Apse, Chalmers Close (off the Royal Mile). Tel: (0131) 556 4364.
- Camera Obscura, Castlehill, Royal Mile. Tel: (0131) 226 3709.
- City Art Centre, 2 Market Street. Tel: (0131) 529 3993.
- Clan Tartan Centre, Leith Mills, 70/74 Bangor Road, Leith. Tel: (0131) 553 5161.
- Craigmillar Castle, Craigmillar Castle Road. Tel: (0131) 661 4445.
- Dalmeny House, South Queensferry. Tel: (0131) 331 1888.
- Edinburgh Castle, Castlehill. Tel: (0131) 225 1012.
- Edinburgh Experience, City Observatory, Calton Hill. Tel: (0131) 556 4365.
- Edinburgh New Town Conservation Committee, 13A Dundas Street. Tel: (0131) 557 5222.
- Edinburgh University Collection of Historic Musical Instruments, Reid Concert Hall, Bristo Square. Tel: (0131) 650 2423.
- Edinburgh Zoo, Corstorphine Road. Tel: (0131) 334 9171.
- Fruitmarket Gallery, 45 Market Street. Tel: (0131) 225 2383.
- Georgian House, The National Trust for Scotland, 7 Charlotte Square. Tel: (0131) 225 2160.
- Gladstone's Land, 47B Lawnmarket. Tel: (0131) 226 5856.

- Hopetoun House, South Queensferry. Tel: (0131) 331 2451.
- Huntly House Museum, 142 Canongate, Royal Mile. Tel: (0131) 529 4143.
- John Knox House, 43/45 High Street. Tel: (0131) 556 9579.
- Lauriston Castle, Cramond Road South. Tel: (0131) 336 2060.
- Museum of Childhood, 42 High Street. Tel: (0131) 529 4142.
- Museum of Scotland *see* Royal Museum of Scotland.
- National Gallery of Scotland, The Mound. Tel: (0131) 624 6200.
- Nelson Monument, Calton Hill. Tel: (0131) 556 2716.
- Newhaven Heritage Museum, 24 Pier Place, Newhaven. Tel: (0131) 551 4165.
- Palace of Holyroodhouse, Canongate, Royal Mile. Tel: (0131) 556 1096.
- People's Story Museum, Canongate Tolbooth, Royal Mile. Tel: (0131) 529 4057.
- Prestongrange Industrial Heritage Museum, Morison Haven, Prestonpans, East Lothian. Tel: (0131) 653 2904.
- Queensferry Museum, High Street, South Queensferry. Tel: (0131) 331 5545.
- Royal Botanic Garden, 20A Inverleith Row. Tel: (0131) 552 7171.
- Royal Museum of Scotland/Museum of Scotland, Chambers Street. Tel: (0131) 225 7534.
- Royal Observatory Visitor Centre, Blackford Hill. Tel: (0131) 668 8405.
- Scotch Whisky Heritage Centre, 354 Castlehill, Royal Mile. Tel: (0131) 220 0441.
- Scottish Genealogy Society Library & Family History Centre, 15 Victoria Terrace. Tel: (0131) 220 3677.
- Scottish National Gallery of Modern Art, Belford Road. Tel: (0131) 624 6200.
- Scottish National Portrait Gallery, 1 Queen Street. Tel: (0131) 624 6200.
- Talbot Rice Gallery, Old College, South Bridge. Tel: (0131) 650 2210.
- Writers' Museum, Lady Stair's Close, Lawnmarket. Tel: (0131) 225 2424.

AROUND EDINBURGH
- Abbey Church, Dunfermline. Tel: (01383) 724 586.
- Abbot House, Dunfermline. Tel: (01383) 733 286.
- Andrew Carnegie Birthplace, Dunfermline. Tel: (01383) 724 303.
- Bo'ness and Kinneil Railway, Bo'ness Station, Union Street, Bo'ness. Tel: (01505) 822 298.
- Deep Sea World, North Queensferry, Fife. Tel: (01383) 411 411.
- Dirleton Castle and Gardens, Dirleton, near North Berwick. Tel: (01620) 850 330.
- Linlithgow Palace, Linlithgow. Tel: (01506) 842 896.
- The Linlithgow Story, Annet House, 143 High Street, Linlithgow. Tel: (01506) 670 677.
- Linlithgow Union Canal Society, Manse Road Basin, Linlithgow. Tel: (01506) 671 215.
- St Andrews Cathedral and Castle and St Rule's Tower, St Andrews. Tel: (01334) 472 536.
- St Andrews University. Tel: (01334) 462 102.
- St Michael's Parish Church, Linlithgow. Tel: (01506) 842 188.
- Stirling Castle and Argyll's Lodging, Castlehill, Stirling. Tel: (01786) 475 165.
- Stirling Visitor Centre, Castlehill, Stirling. Tel: (01786) 451 881.

Parks

Edinburgh is well supplied with city-centre green spaces, including its own pocket-sized mountain wilderness around Arthur's Seat. Right in the city centre, the Princes Street Gardens offer an escape from the crowds, shoppers and traffic of Edinburgh's main thoroughfare, while Calton Hill affords panoramic views. In the northern part of the city, the Royal Botanic Garden has gorgeous floral displays and rare plants; in the south, Meadow Park is a broad expanse of grass, trees and playing fields just south of the University campus at George Square, while the Braid Hills and Blackford Hill offer more energetic walkers a chance to stretch their legs. The even more energetic should take a number 37 bus to the end of the line, at Fairmilehead, and set off into the open highlands of the Pentland Hills.

Opening Times

EDINBURGH

Battlements and Banners: Edinburgh Castle (pages 23–27)

EDINBURGH CASTLE
Daily April–September 09.30–18.00, October–March 09.30–17.00. Last tickets sold 45 minutes before closing.
    Your ticket gives you admission also to attractions within the castle:
• St Margaret's Chapel
• King's Lodging
• Crown Room
• Great Hall
• Scottish United Services Museum

EDINBURGH TATTOO
Performances nightly during the last three weeks in August. For details of precise dates and times, and for tickets, contact:

Edinburgh Tattoo Ticket Sales Office
33–34 Waverley Bridge
Edinburgh
Tel: (0131) 225 1188

The Royal Mile (1): from the Castle to the Tron (pages 28–33)

SCOTCH WHISKY HERITAGE CENTRE
Daily 10.00–17.30.

OUTLOOK TOWER AND CAMERA OBSCURA
April–October daily 09.30–18.00.
November–March 10.00–17.00.

GLADSTONE'S LAND
1 April–31 October, Monday–Saturday 10.00–17.00, Sunday 14.00–17.00.

LADY STAIR'S HOUSE (WRITERS' MUSEUM)
Monday–Saturday 10.00–17.00.
Additionally Sunday 14.00–17.00 during Edinburgh Festival.

ST GILES CATHEDRAL (HIGH KIRK)
Open daily, usual church hours.

The Royal Mile (2): the Canongate from the Tron Kirk to Holyrood Palace (pages 34–40)

MUSEUM OF CHILDHOOD
June–September weekdays 10.00–18.00.
October–May weekdays 10.00–17.00.
Sundays during Festival 14.00–17.00.

BRASS RUBBING CENTRE
June–September weekdays 10.00–18.00.
October–May weekdays 10.00–17.00.
Sundays during Festival 14.00–17.00.

JOHN KNOX HOUSE
Monday–Saturday 10.00–17.00, last admission 16.30.

NETHERBOW ARTS CENTRE
Monday–Saturday 10.00–17.00, last admission 16.30.
Also open at other times for performances.

PEOPLE'S STORY MUSEUM (TOLBOOTH)
Monday–Saturday 10.00–17.00.
Sunday 14.00–17.00 during Edinburgh Festival.

CANONGATE KIRK
Open daily, usual church hours.

HUNTLY HOUSE MUSEUM
Monday–Saturday 10.00–17.00.
Sunday 14.00–17.00 during Edinburgh Festival.

PALACE OF HOLYROODHOUSE
1 April–31 October daily 09.30–17.15.
1 November–31 March daily 09.30–15.45.
Occasionally closed for special occasions.

HOLYROOD ABBEY
1 April–31 October daily 09.30–17.15.
1 November–31 March daily 09.30–15.45.
Occasionally closed for special occasions.

Wilderness in the City: Around Arthur's Seat (pages 41–45)

DYNAMIC EARTH
April–October 10.00–18.00 daily.
November–March 10.00–17.00 Wednesday to Saturday.
Closed Christmas Eve and Christmas Day.

HOLYROOD PARK VISITOR CENTRE
Daily 09.30–17.30, Sunday 13.30–16.30.

BAWSINCH AND DUDDINGSTON LOCH BIRD SANCTUARY
For access contact Scottish Wildlife Trust. Tel: (0131) 312 7765.

DUDDINGSTON KIRK
Open daily, usual church hours.

Monuments and Follies: Calton Hill (pages 46–49)

NELSON MONUMENT
April–September: Monday 13.00–18.00, Tuesday–Saturday 10.00–18.00.
October–March: Monday–Saturday 10.00–15.00.

EDINBURGH EXPERIENCE
July and August daily 10.30–17.00.
Other months Monday–Friday 14.00–17.00, weekends 10.30–17.00.

GENERAL REGISTER HOUSE
Monday–Friday 09.00–16.45.

Ghosts and Galleries: Waverley Station to the Tron (pages 50–54)

MARY KING'S CLOSE
Tours daily 10.30, 11.30, 14.30, 15.30, 16.30, 20.30 and 21.30, except Sunday morning and Tuesday evening.

CITY ART CENTRE
June–September Monday–Saturday 10.00–18.00.
October–May Monday–Saturday 10.00–17.00.

FRUITMARKET GALLERY
Year round Tuesday–Saturday 11.00–18.00.
During Festival also Sunday 12.00–18.00.

RUSSELL COLLECTION OF EARLY KEYBOARD INSTRUMENTS
Wednesday and Saturday 14.00–17.00.
During Festival Monday–Saturday 10.30–12.30.

369 GALLERY
Tuesday–Saturday 12.00–18.00.

The Heart of the City: Along Princes Street (pages 55–61)

SCOTT MONUMENT
October–March, Monday–Saturday 10.00–15.00.
April–September 10.00–18.00.

ROYAL SCOTTISH ACADEMY
Monday–Saturday 10.00–17.00, Sunday 14.00–17.00.

NATIONAL GALLERY OF SCOTLAND
Monday–Saturday 10.00–17.00,
Sunday 14.00–17.00.

ST JOHN'S CHURCH
Open daily, usual church hours.

ST CUTHBERT'S CHURCH
Open daily, usual church hours.

**The New Town Stride: Georgian
Edinburgh** (pages 62–67)

SCOTTISH NATIONAL PORTRAIT GALLERY
Monday–Saturday 10.00–17.00, Sunday
14.00–17.00, extended hours during Festival.

ST ANDREW'S AND ST GEORGE'S CHURCH
Open daily, usual church hours.

NEW TOWN CONSERVATION CENTRE
Monday–Friday 09.00–13.00, 14.00–17.00.

GEORGIAN HOUSE
April–October Monday–Saturday
10.00–17.00, Sunday 14.00–17.00.

WEST REGISTER HOUSE
Exhibitions open 10.00–16.00. Search
Room open 09.00–16.45.

**The Auld Toun Shuffle: Around the
Old Town** (pages 68–72)

USHER HALL
Open for performances.

TRAVERSE THEATRE
Open for performances.

LYCEUM THEATRE
Open for performances.

GREYFRIARS KIRK AND KIRKYARD
Easter–September Monday–Friday
10.00–16.00, Saturday 10.00–14.00.
Kirkyard 09.00–16.00.

Museums and the University
(pages 73–79)

NATIONAL LIBRARY OF SCOTLAND
Monday–Friday 10.00–17.00, Saturday
10.00–17.00, Sunday 14.00–17.00.

SCOTTISH GENEALOGY SOCIETY LIBRARY
AND FAMILY HISTORY CENTRE
Tuesday 10.30–17.30, Wednesday
10.30–20.30, Saturday 10.00–17.00.

ROYAL COLLEGE OF SURGEONS
Monday-Friday 14.00–16.00.
Closed on public holidays.

MUSEUM OF SCOTLAND AND
ROYAL MUSEUM
(same ticket and opening hours)
Monday–Saturday 10.00–17.00
(late opening until 20.00 Tuesday),
Sunday 12.00–17.00.
Closed Christmas Day.

TALBOT RICE ART GALLERY
Tuesday–Saturday 10.00–17.00.

SIR JULES THORNE HISTORICAL MUSEUM
Monday-Friday 14.00–16.00.
Closed on public holidays.

EDINBURGH UNIVERSITY COLLECTION OF
HISTORIC MUSICAL INSTRUMENTS
Wednesday 15.00–17.00, Saturday 10.00–
13.00.

Blackford Hill and the Braid Hills
(pages 80–83)

CRAIGMILLAR CASTLE
April–September Sunday–Wednesday
09.30–18.30, Thursday 09.30–12.30.
October–March Sunday–Wednesday
09.30–16.30, Thursday 09.30–12.30.

ROYAL OBSERVATORY VISITOR CENTRE
Monday–Saturday 10.00–17.00,
Sunday 12.00–17.00.

Around Stockbridge (pages 84–87)

ST STEPHEN'S CHURCH
Open daily, usual church hours.

OPEN EYE GALLERY
Monday–Friday 10.00–18.00,
Saturday 10.00–16.00.

MUSEUM OF LIGHTING
June–September weekdays 10.00–18.00.
October–May weekdays 10.00–17.00.

Heriot's to the Zoo (pages 88–92)

MUSEUM OF FIRE
Guided tours by arrangement.
Tel: (0131) 228 2401.

SCOUT MUSEUM
Monday–Friday (except public holidays)
09.30–16.30.

KING'S THEATRE
Open for performances. Foyer open daily
09.00 until the end of the day's performance.

FOUNTAIN BREWERY
Tours Monday–Friday at 10.15 and 14.15.

GORGIE CITY FARM
Open daily 09.30–16.30 except Christmas
and New Year.

EDINBURGH ZOO
April–September 09.00–18.00.
October–March 09.00–16.30.
Penguin Parade daily 14.00
April–September.

**The Water of Leith: Dean Village,
Stockbridge and the Botanic Gardens**
(pages 93–97)

SCOTTISH NATIONAL GALLERY OF
MODERN ART
Monday–Saturday 10.00–17.00,
Sunday 14.00–17.00.

DEAN GALLERY
Monday–Saturday 10.00–17.00,
Sunday 14.00–17.00.

ROYAL BOTANIC GARDEN
September–October 10.00–18.00 daily.
November–February 10.00–16.00 daily
except Christmas and New Year.

Plant houses:
Summer Monday–Saturday 10.00–17.00,
Sunday 11.00–17.00.
Winter Monday–Saturday 10.00 until 30
minutes before sunset, Sunday 11.00 until
30 minutes before sunset.

INVERLEITH HOUSE
September–October 10.00–18.00 daily.
November–February 10.00–16.00 daily
except Christmas and New Year.

Around Leith and Newhaven
(pages 98–102)

ANDRO LAMB'S HOUSE
Monday–Friday 10.00–12.30 and
13.30–16.30.

ROYAL YACHT *Britannia*
Daily 09.30–17.30, but *prebooked tickets
essential.* Tel: (0131) 555 5566.

NEWHAVEN HERITAGE MUSEUM
Open daily 12.00–17.00.

Leith to Prestonpans (pages 103–109)

CLAN TARTAN CENTRE
November–March Monday–Saturday
09.00–17.00, Sunday 10.00–17.00.
April–November Monday–Saturday
09.00–17.30, Sunday 10.00–17.00.

PRESTONGRANGE INDUSTRIAL HERITAGE
MUSEUM
April–October Monday–Sunday
11.00–16.00.

PRESTON TOWER AND GARDEN
Gardens daily dawn–dusk.
Access to tower by prior arrangement.
Tel: (01875) 810 232.

Lauriston Castle to Cramond
(pages 110–114)

LAURISTON CASTLE
Mid-June to mid-September
Saturday–Thursday 11.00–17.00.
April to mid-June and mid-September to
October Saturday–Thursday 11.00–13.00

and 14.00–17.00.
November–March weekends 14.00–16.00.
Grounds open daily year round from 09.00
to dusk.

CRAMOND ROMAN FORT
Daily from 09.30 until sunset.

CRAMOND KIRK
Open daily, usual church hours.

Cramond to South Queensferry
(pages 115–118)

DALMENY HOUSE
July and August, Monday–Tuesday
12.00–17.30, Sunday 13.00–17.00.

DALMENY KIRK (ST CUTHBERT'S)
Same hours as house.

QUEENSFERRY MUSEUM
Monday and Thursday–Saturday 10.00–13.00
and 14.15–17.00, Sunday 14.00–17.00.

INCHCOLM ABBEY
April–September Monday–Saturday
09.30–18.30, Sunday 14.00–18.30.
Boat times according to tide.
Tel: (0131) 4857 for sailings.

North Queensferry to Blackness Castle
(pages 119–122)

DEEP SEA WORLD
March–November daily 10.00–18.00.
July–August daily 10.00–18.30.
November–March Monday–Friday
11.00–17.00, weekends and public holidays
10.00–18.00.

HOPETOUN HOUSE
10 April–27 September daily 10.00–17.30,
last entry 16.30.

BLACKNESS CASTLE
April–September daily 10.00–17.00.
October–March as above but closed
Thursday afternoon and Friday.

Linlithgow to Bo'ness (pages 123–129)

LINLITHGOW UNION CANAL SOCIETY
MUSEUM
Easter–September Saturday and
Sunday 14.00–17.00.

LINLITHGOW HERITAGE TRUST MUSEUM
Monday–Saturday 10.00–16.00,
Sunday 13.00–16.00.

ST MICHAEL'S CHURCH
Open daily, usual church hours.

LINLITHGOW PALACE
April–September Monday–Saturday
09.30–18.30, Sunday 14.00–18.30.
October–March Monday–Saturday
09.30–16.30, Sunday 14.00–16.30.

KINNEIL HOUSE AND BO'NESS MUSEUM
April–September Monday–Saturday
10.00–17.00, Sunday (June–August only)
10.00–17.00.
October–April Saturday only 10.00–17.00.

BO'NESS AND KINNEIL RAILWAY
Weekends April–December, June
Wednesday–Friday, July–August.
Tel: (01506) 822 298 for timetable details.

BIRKHILL FIRECLAY MINE
April to mid-July and September–October,
weekends only, 11.00–16.00.
Daily mid-July to August 11.00–16.00.

AROUND EDINBURGH

St Andrews (pages 131–136)

BRITISH GOLF MUSEUM
Mid-April to mid-October
09.30–17.30 daily.
Mid-October to Mid-April 11.00–15.00,
closed Tuesday and Wednesday.

ST ANDREWS SEA LIFE CENTRE
September–June 10.00–18.00 daily.
July–August 10.00–21.00 daily.

St Andrews Preservation Trust Museum
Mid-June to mid-September 14.00–16.30 daily.

St Andrews Castle
April–September Monday–Saturday 09.30–18.00, Sunday 14.00–18.00. October–March Monday–Saturday 09.30–1600, Sunday 14.00–16.00.

St Andrews Cathedral and Museum
April–September Monday–Saturday 09.30–18.00, Sunday 14.00–18.00. October–March Monday–Saturday 09.30–16.00, Sunday 14.00–16.00.

St Andrews University
Guided tours July–August Monday–Saturday, 10.30 and 14.30.

Holy Trinity Church
Open daily, usual church hours.

Dunfermline (pages 137–141)

Andrew Carnegie Birthplace Museum
April–May Monday–Saturday 11.00–17.00. June–August Monday–Saturday 10.00–17.00. September–October Monday–Saturday 11.00–17.00. April–October also open Sunday 14.00–19.00. November–March 14.00–16.00 daily.

Abbot House and Heritage Centre
Open daily 10.00–17.00.

Dunfermline Abbey and Palace
April–September Monday–Saturday 09.30–18.00, Sunday 14.00–18.00. October–March Monday–Saturday 09.30–16.00, Sunday 14.00–16.00.

Pittencrief Park and Pittencrief House
Open year round from 08.00 until dusk.

Dunfermline District Museum and Small Gallery
Open year round (except public holidays) Monday–Saturday 11.00–17.00.

Forth Coast Castles: Tantallon to Dirleton (pages 142–146)

Tantallon Castle
April–September Monday–Saturday 09.30–18.00, Sunday 14.00–18.00. October–March Monday–Saturday 09.30–16.00, Sunday 14.00–16.00.

Scottish Seabird Centre
Opening hours not announced at time of writing. Tel: (0131) 313 4000 for information.

North Berwick Auld Kirk
Open daily, usual church hours.

North Berwick Museum
Easter to end May Saturday and Monday 10.00–13.00 and 14.00–17.00, Friday and Sunday 14.00–17.00. June to mid-September Monday–Saturday 10.00–13.00 and 14.00–17.00, Sunday 14.00–17.00. Mid-September to late October Saturday and Monday 10.00–13.00 and 14.00–17.00, Friday and Sunday 14.00–17.00.

Dirleton Castle
April–September Monday–Saturday 09.30–18.00, Sunday 14.00–18.00. October–March Monday–Saturday 09.30–16.00, Sunday 14.00–16.00.

Bass Rock boat excursion
North Berwick Harbour. Tel: (01620) 89 3863/2838 for schedules.

Stirling and Bannockburn (pages 147–151)

Old Town Jail
April–September 09.30–17.15. October–March 09.30–16.15.

Argyll's Lodging
April–September 09.30–17.15. October–March 09.30–16.15.

Stirling Castle
April–September 09.30–17.15. October–March 09.30–16.15.

ARGYLL AND SUTHERLAND HIGHLANDERS'
REGIMENTAL MUSEUM
April–September 09.30–17.15.
October–March 09.30–16.15.

BANNOCKBURN HERITAGE CENTRE
Open daily 10.00–18.00.

CHURCH OF THE HOLY RUDE
Open daily, usual church hours.

The East Neuk (pages 152–155)
ST MONAN'S CHURCH
Open daily, usual church hours.

ST FILLAN'S CAVE
Open daily 10.00–17.00.

SCOTTISH FISHERIES MUSEUM
April–October Monday–Saturday
10.00–17.30, Sunday 11.00–17.00.
November–March, Monday–Saturday
10.00–16.30, Sunday 14.00–16.30.

NORTH CARR LIGHTSHIP
Easter–October 11.00–17.00.

ISLE OF MAY BOAT EXCURSION
May–September daily departures from
Anstruther. Tel: (01333) 310 013
for schedules.

CRAIL MUSEUM AND HERITAGE CENTRE
Easter and June through to mid-September,
Monday–Saturday 10.00–12.30 and
14.30–17.00.
Rest of year open only Sundays and public
holidays, 14.30–17.00.

The Cinéaste's Edinburgh

Not surprisingly, a city as rich in stories and storytellers as Edinburgh has been the backdrop and the inspiration for more than its fair share of movies, from the sugary-sweet tale of Greyfriars Bobby, the Skye terrier who refused to leave his master's grave, to the grisly tales of Jekyll and Hyde and Burke and Hare.

Robert Louis Stevenson's stories have been filmed again and again – Jekyll and Hyde alone has inspired about two dozen film versions, from the high-camp *Dr Jekyll and Sister Hyde* (Hammer, 1971) to the dire playing-it-for-laughs *Abbott and Costello Meet Dr Jekyll and Mr Hyde* (Universal, 1953). The best of them all is undoubtedly *Doctor Jekyll and Mister Hyde* (Paramount, 1931) starring Fredric March in an astonishing performance in the dual role; the director, Rouben Mamoulian, also deserves special mention. *The Nutty Professor* (Paramount, 1963), starring Jerry Lewis, is an entertaining update transposing the tale to a US campus; it was recently revamped with Eddie Murphy in the starring role. A much funnier and far from tasteful update is *Jekyll and Hyde … Together Again* (Paramount/Titan, 1982). *Mary Reilly* (TriStar, 1996), starring John Malkovich as Jekyll/Hyde and Julia Roberts as the eponymous maidservant who falls in love with Jekyll, was panned by the critics but is very much worth watching; the novel upon which it was based, Valerie Martin's retelling of the story from the maid's point of view, *Mary Reilly* (1990), is highly recommended.

Treasure Island, too, practically created the pirate-movie genre, from the original 1934 MGM version through the 1950 Disney version with Robert Newton in the Long John Silver role. For a completely different take on the story there's *Muppet Treasure Island* (Buena Vista, 1996), an uproarious and often very funny version with Kermit as Captain Smollett and Miss Piggy as Benjamina Gunn, plus, among the live actors, Tim Curry as Long John Silver.

Sir Walter Scott's tales of derring-do have also been frequently filmed, *Quentin Durward* in 1955 and *Ivanhoe* in at least three versions: in 1952 by MGM, starring Robert Taylor and most recently in 1996 in the form of *Young Ivanhoe*, starring Tracy Keach and Margot Kidder. The 1970 BBC TV serialization starring Eric Flynn is also worthy of attention. A close analysis will reveal *Ivanhoe* as the basic plot inspiration behind *Robin Hood: Prince of Thieves* (Warner, 1991) starring Kevin Costner.

Classics filmed in Edinburgh include *The Prime of Miss Jean Brodie* (Twentieth Century-Fox, 1969), the story of a sharp-minded Edinburgh headmistress, which won an Oscar for Maggie Smith; *Shallow Grave* (Rank, 1994), in which three young flat-sharers dispose of a body and fall out over a fortune; and *Trainspotting* (Polygram, 1996), the in-yer-face, blackly and surreally comic film of Irvine Welsh's classic story of low-life in Leith and elsewhere.

Bibliography

Touring Guide to Scotland (Scottish Tourist Board, published annually).
Comprehensive listings guide to visitor attractions, historic sights, monuments, museums, art galleries and craft centres throughout Edinburgh and Scotland. Comes with map locating all top attractions.

Edinburgh, by David Daiches (Hamish Hamilton, 1978).
Sympathetic history of the city and its people, shedding light on the murkier corners of Edinburgh's past as well as recounting the backgrounds to the best-known historical figures and events.

The Literature of Scotland, by Roderick Watson (Macmillan, 1984).
Comprehensive account of Scottish language and literature from Barbour and Blind Harry, the fourteenth- and fifteenth-century chroniclers of Robert the Bruce and William Wallace respectively, to the 1970s.

Scotland: A Concise History, by Fitzroy Maclean (Thames & Hudson, revised edition 1993).
Superbly readable account of Scotland's history from Roman times to the present day.

A History of the Scottish People 1560-1830, by T.C. Smout (Fontana, 1987).
More scholarly and detailed account of the making of modern Scotland from the Reformation up to the time of the Industrial Revolution.

The Jacobite Cause, by Bruce Lenman (Richard Drew, in association with the National Trust for Scotland).
Entertaining and objective rendering of the struggle between the Houses of Hanover and Stuart for the crowns of Scotland, England and Ireland.

The Master of Ballantrae (1889), *Kidnapped* (1886) and *Catriona* (1893), by Robert Louis Stevenson (all republished in many editions since).
Historical romances that vividly evoke Scotland around the time of the '45 Rebellion.

Dr Jekyll and Mr Hyde (1886), by Robert Louis Stevenson (republished in many editions since).
Inspired by the double life of Deacon Brodie (see page 31), respectable merchant by day, burglar by night.

The Prime of Miss Jean Brodie (1961), by Muriel Spark (republished in many editions since).
Arguably the epitome of the twentieth-century Edinburgh novel, filmed in 1969 with Maggie Smith (who won an Oscar for her performance) in the title role as a quasi-fascistic schoolmistress during World War II whose public image belies her private life. Much of the movie was actually shot on location in Edinburgh and Cramond, so if some building or street seems oddly familiar to you it may well be because you've seen it in the movie. Spark was born and bred in Edinburgh but eventually went to live in Italy.

Complicity, by Iain Banks (Little, Brown, 1994).
Extremely violent and sex-filled novel – definitely not for the squeamish – set largely in and around Edinburgh.

Index